Warriors and Wilderness
in Medieval Britain

D0584119

Warriors and Wilderness in Medieval Britain

*From Arthur and Beowulf
to Sir Gawain and Robin Hood*

ROBIN MELROSE

McFarland & Company, Inc., Publishers

Jefferson, North Carolina

ISBN (print) 978-1-4766-6826-0
ISBN (ebook) 978-1-4766-2758-8

LIBRARY OF CONGRESS CATALOGUING DATA ARE AVAILABLE

BRITISH LIBRARY CATALOGUING DATA ARE AVAILABLE

Front cover image of King Arthur and his knights
© 2017 Duncan Walker/iStock

Printed in the United States of America

*McFarland & Company, Inc., Publishers
Box 611, Jefferson, North Carolina 28640
www.mcfarlandpub.com*

Table of Contents

Introduction

I recently published a book entitled *British Religion from the Megaliths to Arthur: An Archaeological and Mythological Exploration*, in which among other things I attempted to trace the history of Arthur from prehistory to the 12th century and Geoffrey of Monmouth's *History of the Kings of Britain*. I was looking at Arthur from a Welsh perspective, at works written in Welsh or (in the case of Geoffrey of Monmouth) in Latin. This was in a sense just the beginning of the story of Arthur, for the court of King Arthur was soon adopted by the French poet Chrétien de Troyes, who created the most famous Arthurian knight, Lancelot, in his romance *Lancelot, the Knight of the Cart*, and whose unfinished *Perceval, the Story of the Grail* was taken up by another French writer, Robert de Boron, who transformed the Grail into the Holy Grail. Soon the story of Arthur expanded into the early 13th century prose epic, the *Lancelot-Grail*, which created a whole new Arthurian world with Lancelot, Galahad and the quest for the Holy Grail.

My main interest, however, is in seeing how the story of Arthur evolved in England, in the language we now call Middle English. After the Norman Conquest, Old English, the language of the Anglo-Saxons, suffered an eclipse, being replaced among the elite by Norman French. For a long time, only one English text survived, and that was the Peterborough version of the *Anglo-Saxon Chronicle*, which was recorded by the monks of Peterborough Abbey until 1154. Most literature after the Conquest was written in French, and one of the first literary texts in English was Layamon's *Brut*, a Middle English version of Geoffrey's *History of the Kings of Britain*.

Middle English literature began to flower in the 14th century, which saw a new version of the last days of Arthur, the *Alliterative Morte Arthure*, based on Geoffrey of Monmouth, but presenting a more ambiguous version of Arthur than that presented by Layamon. However, the most fascinating Arthurian romance of this period is *Sir Gawain and the Green Knight*, which focuses on the Arthurian hero Gawain, and his nemesis the Green Knight, an Arthurian villain like no other. This may have inspired three Arthurian romances set in Inglewood Forest (Cumbria) where Arthur is present but Gawain often plays the leading role.

As I trace the evolution of Arthur, I necessarily cover some of the ground covered in *British Religion from the Megaliths to Arthur*. This ground includes the 11th century Welsh tale *Culhwch and Olwen*, but here I focus on Arthur as "the leader of a band of heroes who live outside of society, whose main world is one of magical animals, giants and other wonderful happenings, located in the wild parts of the landscape,"[1] or as an outlaw comparable to the Irish hero Fionn (or Finn) mac Cumhaill.[2] But I also go into previously unexplored territory, with an investigation of the northern Romano-British hunter/warrior god, perhaps an ancestor of the later Welsh Arthur.

I also go over other ground not usually covered in accounts of Arthur. The figure of Arthur partly arose as a result of conflicts between the British of the "Old North" (northern England and Southern Scotland) and the emerging Anglo-Saxon kingdom of Northumbria. Here I examine what we know of these conflicts from literary sources such as the Welsh poem *Y Gododdin* and the *Triads of the Island of Britain*, in the encyclopedic edition by the late Rachel Bromwich.[3] But I also look at the Anglo-Saxon world, and Anglo-Saxon heroes, including Oswald, the warrior-saint of early Northumbria; the powerful man buried at Sutton Hoo in East Anglia; the warriors who accumulated the recently discovered Staffordshire Hoard; the Mercian soldier-saint Guthlac who spent his last years in the wild fens of south Lincolnshire; and Alfred the Great of Wessex, who defeated the Vikings and became in effect the first king of England.

Most of these Anglo-Saxon heroes were celebrated in Old English poetry or prose. Guthlac's *Life* was originally written in Latin but later translated into Old English; and the deeds of Alfred and his successors were recounted in the Old English *Anglo-Saxon Chronicle*, which was originally produced in Wessex (southern England) in the late 9th century. As the name implies, the *Chronicle* was mainly a history, but occasionally it includes poetry, like the *Battle of Brunaburh*, which celebrates a Wessex victory against the Vikings in 937. Much Anglo-Saxon literature was religious (saints' lives, homilies), or military (the *Battle of Brunaburh* and the *Battle of Maldon*, about another later encounter between Anglo-Saxons and Vikings). However there were also poems of exile like *The Wanderer* and *The Seafarer*, and the epic *Beowulf*, which is set in Scandinavia and describes Beowulf's battle with three monsters: Grendel, Grendel's Mother and a dragon. Although Anglo-Saxon literature was ended by the Conquest, it continued to influence Middle English literature, and we can't really understand *Sir Gawain and the Green Knight* without being aware of *Beowulf* and poems of exile like *The Wanderer*.

After the Conquest a new figure emerged in England, the figure of the outlaw, first represented by Hereward (later known as Hereward the Wake), who led a rebellion against the Norman invaders from the fens of Cambridgeshire and south Lincolnshire. Hereward may have been the model for Robin Hood, who emerged in the 14th century, at the time of the Hundred Years' War (1337–1453), the Black Death (1348–9 and 1361–2), and the Peasants' Revolt (1381), but was most popular in the 15th century, when England lost the Hundred Years' War and was plunged into the War of the Roses (1455–1487). Robin Hood may seem to have little in common with King Arthur, but there are connections: like the Welsh Arthur, Robin Hood operated in the wilderness (Sherwood Forest in Nottinghamshire), and was even associated with Inglewood Forest in Cumbria, the location of three late Arthurian tales. The Welsh Arthur fights monsters, and in one of the most bizarre of the Robin Hood tales Robin is pitted against a "monster," a bounty hunter called Guy of Gisborne, who is clad in a horse-hide.

Since this book shifts between Roman Britain, Anglo-Saxon England, Welsh Arthur, Norman Britain, English Arthur and Robin Hood, it might be a good idea to give an outline of the chapters to show how the book hangs together. As the title suggests, one of the unifying threads of this book is wilderness, and in Chapter 1 I look at resistance to Roman rule in Britain, especially in the frontier region around Hadrian's Wall, that is, large parts of Northumberland and southern Scotland as far north as the Firth of Forth and the Firth of Clyde. To the Romans this was in all senses a wilderness, so it is no surprise that the frontier peoples worshipped a hunter/warrior god, who may well have fed into the myth of Arthur.

In Chapter 2 I show that this frontier region of Hadrian's Wall came under the control of the Anglo-Saxon kingdom of Northumbria, which for a time extended as far north as East Lothian in the southeast of Scotland, and Dumfries and Galloway in the southwest of Scotland. The native British of course resisted Anglo-Saxon rule, and much of what we know of this resistance is to be found in the early Welsh poem *Y Gododdin* ("The Votadini"), which speaks of a battle at *Catraeth* (Catterick in North Yorkshire) fought by the Votadini of southeast Scotland in which a number of heroes died; and in the poems of the 6th century Welsh bard Taliesin, and the medieval Welsh *Triads of the Island of Britain*, which speak in particular of a certain Urien, who ruled over a kingdom called Rheged, located somewhere in northwest England and southwest Scotland. These heroes of the "Old North" haunted the later Welsh, and in some way became the basis for the later Welsh Arthur and the 12th century Norman Arthur of Geoffrey of Monmouth.

In Chapter 3 I explore the beginnings of the myth of Arthur. I first look for real Arthurs, among them a certain *Artur* who was the son of the king of Dal Riata in western Scotland, and discuss the origin of the name *Arthur*, which most likely means "Bear-Man." I then ask what bears meant in the Iron Age and Roman period, and examine the bear-hoods worn by Germanic warriors in the Roman army, and the evidence for Germanic soldiers serving in Roman Britain. I then pass on to the earliest mention of Arthur, in the 9th century *History of the Britons*, where he was depicted mainly as a warrior fighting Saxons, much like the heroes of the "Old North." Finally I look closely at the Welsh poem *Pa gur yv y porthaur?* ("What man guards the gate?"),[4] in which Arthur and his retinue are no longer fighting Saxons but various supernatural beings like witches and werewolves.

Chapter 4 is an exploration of the most substantial Welsh Arthurian tale, *Culhwch and Olwen*, which dates from the 11th century. In this tale Arthur is king with a court at Celliwig in Cornwall and retinue of courtiers, including Cei and Bedwyr (Sir Kay and Sir Bedivere of later romances). Arthur and his courtiers are constantly pitted against supernatural enemies— giants, witches, and the great boar Twrch Trwyth who had once been a (human) king. Arthur and his retinue operate in the wilderness, which links them to the Romano-British hunter/warrior gods and also to heroes of Anglo-Saxon England and later medieval English heroes.

In Chapter 5 I return to Anglo-Saxon England and survey some of the early English heroes: King Oswald, Northumbria's martyred warrior-saint; the East Anglian hero buried in a ship at Sutton Hoo in Suffolk; the warrior-kings of Mercia and the Staffordshire Hoard; and the Mercian soldier-saint Guthlac, who lived for many years in the wilderness of the fens of south Lincolnshire. I then turn to later Anglo-Saxon heroes, especially those who fought against the Vikings (Danes) between the 9th and 11th centuries; including the martyred king Edmund of East Anglia, and the Wessex king Æthelstan who defeated a large force of Vikings at the Battle of Brunaburh in 937. Not all late Anglo-Saxon heroes were warriors, and I conclude the chapter with two poems of exile and wilderness.

Chapter 6 deals with the most famous Anglo-Saxon legendary hero of all, Beowulf. The poem *Beowulf* concerns Beowulf's battles as a young man with the monster Grendel and subsequently with Grendel's Mother, and his final battle as an old man with a dragon guarding its treasure. The story clearly had resonances in Anglo-Saxon England: three names from *Beowulf* figure in the genealogies of the kings of Wessex, and a description of Hell in a late 10th century homily resembles the description of Grendel's Mother's mere (lake) in *Beowulf*. Beowulf may seem to have little to do with Arthur, but as I show, they are both linked to bears, Beowulf more closely than Arthur; and Beowulf must trek through the wilderness to fight Grendel's Mother, just as Arthur and his retinue often do battle in the wilderness.

In 1066 William of Normandy invaded England, defeated and killed the English king Harold at the battle of Hastings, and was crowned king in Westminster Abbey. Anglo-Saxon aristocrats and churchmen were replaced by Norman aristocrats and churchmen, and their French became the language of the elite. English ceased to be a literary language for around 150 years, and apart from the Peterborough version of the *Anglo-Saxon Chronicle*, which continued until 1154, there was no one left to speak for the English. Into this gap stepped the Norman cleric Geoffrey of Monmouth, with his Latin *History of the Kings of Britain*. In Chapter 7 I show how Geoffrey created a new British hero who defeated the Anglo-Saxons and created a great empire stretching from Ireland to Gaul (France). Geoffrey drew on the 9th century *History of the Britons* for Arthur's battles, and on a variety of other unknown sources for his depiction of Arthur's father Uther Pendragon, Arthur's wife Guinevere, and Mordred and Guinevere's betrayal of Arthur. With his *History* Geoffrey inspired French writers of the 12th and 13th century, and English writers of the 13th and 14th centuries: without Geoffrey's *History of the Kings of Britain* we would not have works like the *Alliterative Morte Arthure* and *Sir Gawain and the Green Knight*, which were able to bring back Anglo-Saxon themes into English writing.

In chapter 8 I examine two works in Middle English inspired directly by Geoffrey's *History*, Layamon's *Brut* and the *Alliterative Morte Arthure*. Layamon's *Brut*, dating from around 1200, is a Middle English retelling of Geoffrey *History*, but is does incorporate some Anglo-Saxon elements like the wilderness, and the violence of the battles owes more to *Beowulf* than to Geoffrey. The *Alliterative Morte Arthure* (14th century) strays further from Geoffrey, depicting Arthur as a flawed character brought down by overweening ambition. Some of the battle scenes are particularly graphic, most unlike Geoffrey's rather bloodless battle scenes.

The *Alliterative Morte Arthure* may well have been the last English work to draw solely on Geoffrey's *History*, and in Chapter 9 I analyze a work that owes more to the French Arthurian tradition and Anglo-Saxon literature than to Geoffrey. *Sir Gawain and the Green Knight* is reckoned to be one of the finest works of medieval English literature, and it confronts Gawain, a well-known Arthurian hero, with the Green Knight, a character unique in English literature. The poem owes much to French Arthurian literature: in real life the Green Knight is Bertilak de Hautdesert, who seems to be borrowed from the *Lancelot-Grail*, as is Bertilak's guest Morgan le Fay; but many elements of the poem, like the Green Knight's arrival at Camelot, and Gawain's journey through the "wilds of the Wirral," are apparently inspired by *Beowulf* and Anglo-Saxon poems of exile like *The Wanderer*.

I conclude my Arthurian investigations in Chapter 10, with three Arthurian tales set in Inglewood Forest, Cumbria, perhaps inspired by *Sir Gawain and the Green Knight*, which feature Arthur but often put Sir Gawain at the forefront of the action. Cumbria was probably part of the 5th/6th century kingdom of Rheged, and may well have been one of the regions of the "Old North" where stories of Arthur originated. Arthur may have begun as a hunter/warrior god, so it is fitting that late stories of Arthur should be set in a Cumbrian forest.

Medieval literature was not just about kings and knights, and after the Norman Conquest the outlaw became a recognized figure, initially in the shape of Hereward the Wake. Hereward resisted the Norman invasion from the fens of Cambridgeshire and south Lincolnshire, and by the 12th century he had been celebrated in a Latin romance. In the 14th and 15th century there was civil unrest in England as a result of the Hundred Years' War and the War of the Roses, and a new outlaw figure emerged—Robin Hood—living in the wilds of Sherwood Forest in Nottinghamshire. In Chapter 11 I explore the story of Hereward, trace the origins of Robin Hood, and examine two early Robin Hood tales, one typical and one decidedly untypical. In Chapter 12 I analyze the most substantial of the Robin Hood tales and examine a tale which does not concern Robin Hood but a band of outlaws living in Inglewood Forest, the same forest that was also a haunt of Arthur and Gawain.

With this final tale, the cycle of Arthurian romances and Robin Hood ballads turns full circle: Arthur began as a hunter/warrior god in Cumbria and Northumberland, and ends up frequenting Inglewood Forest in Cumbria, the same forest where my final Robin Hood ballad takes place.

1

Resistance to Roman Rule in Northern Britain and the Hunter/Warrior God

The Romans in Britain

Julius Caesar's Incursions into Southeast England

Britain first entered the history books in 55 and 54 BC, when the Roman general Julius Caesar, who was busy conquering Gaul at the time, launched two incursions into Britain and famously clashed with the British leader Cassivellaunus, who perhaps belonged to the Catuvellauni tribe of Hertfordshire. The clash between Caesar and Cassivellaunus obviously made an impression on the native Britons, since Cassivellaunus appears in Welsh mythology as Caswallawn, son of Beli. Caswallawn's opposition to the Romans is repeatedly expressed in the medieval compendium of Welsh mythology known as the *Triads of the Island of Britain*. According to Triad 35, Caswallawn pursued the retreating Romans out of Britain, and his army is one of the "Three Silver Hosts" which never returned. Triad 38 names Caswallawn's horse Meinlas ("Slender Grey"). Triads 67 and 71 depict Caswallawn as a lover, seeking Rome in the disguise of a cobbler in quest of Fflur ("Flora"), about whom almost nothing is known.[1] The name of Caswallawn's father Beli may be derived from *Belgios*, the god of the *Belgae*,[2] a collection of tribes who lived in northern France, Belgium and southeast England (Kent, Sussex, Hampshire, Hertfordshire and Essex).

The Roman Invasion of Britain

In AD 43 the Romans, with four legions commanded by Aulus Plautius, invaded Britain, and soon built a legionary fortress at Camulodunum (Colchester in Essex). The Roman invasion met with resistance from Caratacus, a

7

chief of the Catuvellauni of Hertfordshire. According to the Roman historian Tacitus in his *Annals* (early 2nd century AD), Caratacus resisted the Romans with the help of the Silures of southeast Wales and the Ordovices of north Wales; he was defeated in AD 51, and sought refuge with Cartimandua, queen of the Brigantes of North Yorkshire, who handed him over to the Romans.[3]

The Roman conquest was also jeopardized by the revolt of Boudica, queen of the Iceni of East Anglia: according to Tacitus, after the death of her husband Prasutagus, who was an ally of the Romans, Boudica "was scourged, and his daughters outraged." In response to this treatment at the hands of the Romans, Boudica, with the help of the Trinovantes of Essex, destroyed Camulodunum (Colchester), London and Verulamium (St. Albans) before being defeated by the Roman governor Suetonius Paulinus in AD 60 or 61.[4]

The Welsh continued to resist Roman rule, and in AD 61 the Roman governor Gaius Suetonius Paulinus prepared to attack the island of Mona (Anglesey in north Wales), which had a powerful population and was a safe haven for fugitives. The attack is described in blood-curdling detail by the Roman historian Tacitus.[5] The Romans crossed the Menai Strait that separates Anglesey from the mainland:

> On the shore stood the opposing army with its dense array of armed warriors, while between the ranks dashed women, in black attire like the Furies, with hair dishevelled, waving brands. All around, the Druids, lifting up their hands to heaven, and pouring forth dreadful imprecations, scared our soldiers by the unfamiliar sight, so that, as if their limbs were paralysed, they stood motionless, and exposed to wounds. Then urged by their general's appeals and mutual encouragements not to quail before a troop of frenzied women, they bore the standards onwards, smote down all resistance, and wrapped the foe in the flames of his own brands. A force was next set over the conquered, and their groves, devoted to inhuman superstitions, were destroyed. They deemed it indeed a duty to cover their altars with the blood of captives and to consult their deities through human entrails.

But we don't just have Tacitus's word for it that Anglesey was important to the Druids. In 1942 a hoard of over 150 objects of bronze and iron was discovered at a small lake called Llyn Cerrig Bach on the northwest of Anglesey, during construction of the RAF airfield at Valley.[6] The finds are "primarily military" and included eleven swords, eight spearheads and parts of a parade shield. Equipment from several chariots was also present, both the harness and parts of the structure:

> Up to 22 chariots can be recognised from the wheels discovered, but this might indicate the offering of wheels alone (which are known to have been sacred to one of the Celtic gods) rather than complete vehicles. Some items were locally manufactured, a few came from Ireland but a great many originated from southern England; a possible sign of trade, plunder captured from war or suggestive that the lake was more

than a shrine of local importance. The dates of the finds are also of interest. Some of the swords are of types current in the 2nd century BC, others are of later designs, but nothing later than AD 60 can be identified.

By AD 48 the Romans had established a legionary camp at Lincoln, and in AD 71 another camp was established at York. Occupation of the North proceeded rather slowly. In AD 72 or 73 the Romans established a fort at Carlisle in Cumbria (northwest England); between AD 69 and 75 a fort was constructed at Binchester in County Durham; and in around AD 90 the Romans established a fort at Corbridge in Northumberland.

Roman Invasions of Scotland

In AD 78 Agricola became governor of Britain and invaded Scotland, defeating a force of Scots at the Battle of Mons Graupius, whose location remains elusive. Agricola established a number of forts in Scotland, both in the east and west. Forts in the east included Newstead in the Scottish Borders (southeast Scotland), Elginhaugh in Midlothian (to the southeast of Edinburgh), Castlecary and Camelon to the west of Falkirk, Bochastle to the northwest of Stirling, Ardoch, Dunning and Inchtuthil in Perth and Kinross, and Dun and Stracathro in Angus; while forts in the west included Birrens, Dalswinton and Broomholm in Dumfries and Galloway (southwest Scotland), Crawford and Castledykes in South Lanarkshire (to the southeast of Glasgow), and Loudoun Hill in East Ayrshire (to the southwest of Glasgow).

However, for some reason these forts were abandoned, and the northern frontier of the Empire was fixed at Hadrian's Wall, which was begun in AD 122 and stretches 73 miles from Wallsend near Newcastle upon Tyne through the southern part of Northumberland and the northern part of Cumbria to Bowness on the Solway Firth, which separates England from Scotland.

Then in AD 142 the Emperor Antoninus Pius ordered the construction of the Antonine Wall, which ran some 39 miles from Bo'ness on the south bank of the Forth near Falkirk to Old Kilpatrick on the north bank of the Clyde in West Dunbartonshire, and many of the forts built during Agricola's invasion were brought back into use. The Wall was abandoned in 162, and hopes of conquering Scotland were abandoned for the next forty years or so. In 208 the Emperor Septimius Severus travelled to Britain and, together with his son and co-emperor, Caracalla, waged war on the Caledones, who may have lived around the Great Glen, in the area between Inverness and Fort William, and the Maeatae, who lived just beyond the Antonine Wall. His aim according to the contemporary historian Cassius Dio was to conquer the whole of the island, and he is recorded as reaching nearly the end of the island. The northern tribes submitted but then rebelled and it was while

Caracalla was putting down this revolt that his father died in York and the son abandoned the newly won territory, together with Roman forts, and returned to Rome.[7]

One of the most northerly of the Roman camps was at Kintore in Aberdeenshire. The camp at Kintore covered an area of around 109 acres and was first recorded in the middle of the 19th century. The camp was excavated between 2000 and 2006 in advance of a housing development. The excavated interior of the marching camp contained over 300 internal Roman features including rubbish pits, cooking ovens and evidence of structures. Dating evidence indicated that the site was occupied twice, the first in the 1st century AD and then again in the late 2nd or early 3rd centuries AD.[8] Evidently it was first used by Agricola and then later by Severus.

The Frontier Peoples of Roman Britain

In the 2nd century the Greco-Egyptian writer Ptolemy wrote his *Geography*, a compilation of geographical coordinates of all parts of the world known to the Roman Empire during this time. In his section on Scotland, Ptolemy names several tribes and their chief strongholds. In the far southwest were the *Novantae*, with their main stronghold at *Rerigonium*, though to be somewhere near Loch Ryan in Galloway[9]; and next to them, in Dumfriesshire, were the *Selgovae*.[10]

But the best known tribe living on the frontiers of Roman Britain were the *Votadini*, who lived in southeast Scotland. The name *Votadini* is related to Irish *fothad* "support," and to a character in Irish mythology called *Fothad*. In an 8th century text, Fothad Canainne was one of three sons born at a single birth and all named Fothad. His other name was *Caindia*, "Fair God." He never sat down at a feast without severed heads in front of him, thus illustrating his prowess as a warrior. He had a band of warriors and with them he waged constant war on Ailill Flan Bec of Munster. But then he fell in love with Ailill's beautiful wife, and made an assignation with her. They went off together, but Ailill pursued them with his warband, killed Fothad and decapitated him. The woman lifted up the head of her lover and it then sang a long, extempore poem to her, in which it bewailed its sad state, and instructed her on what to do with its possessions.[11]

In Roman times the main stronghold of the Votadini was the hillfort of Traprain Law in East Lothian. It first came to public attention in 1919 with the discovery of the Traprain Law Treasure, a hoard of fine Roman silverware. There were more than 100 objects—bowls, cups, flagons, coins, spoons, and mounts, some decorated with Christian scenes, others with rich and exotic Mediterranean motifs, handles in the form of dolphins and panthers, nearly all folded and cut up as if for melting down. The coins suggested a date for the hoard during the reign of Honorius, between AD 395–423.

During the first four centuries AD, Traprain Law was variously inside and outside the fluctuating boundaries of the Roman Empire, being located between Hadrian's Wall and the Antonine Wall. Several factors suggest that the Votadinian elite enjoyed a special relationship with Rome at this time, and had "apparently unequalled access to Roman goods of the highest quality." It is likely that the Votadini "had allied themselves with Rome and may even have been, at certain times, a buffer state on the edge of the Empire." In the decades around AD 400 a final rampart was erected at Traprain Law, and at more or less the same time the Traprain Law treasure was buried beneath the floor of a house. Both may well have been "signs of stressful times, for after 400 occupation appears quite abruptly to cease," coinciding with the end of Roman rule in Britain.[12]

Hunter/Warrior Gods in Northern Britain

Northern Britain was at the frontier of the Roman Empire, so it is probably not surprising that the most popular gods on both sides of Hadrian's Wall were hunter/warrior gods, which often took the form of a horned god. One of the earliest representations of the horned god in northern Britain comes from Aldborough in North Yorkshire—a bronze terret (ring on a horse harness) in form of a male bust. From the sides of the head "spring great horns, while a projection in the centre of the head may represent a third horn, or may be associated with the leaf-crown, now almost destroyed, which originally emerged from the back of the head. The face is moustached, this giving added severity to the drooping mouth; the eyes are enormous with large pupils which must have been enamelled at one time, the ferocity of the gaze emphasised by the furrowed brow." A date shortly before AD 71 has been proposed for this work.[13]

But most of the representations of the horned god belong to the Roman period. At Maryport Roman fort in Cumbria, several altars and reliefs in local sandstone "depict a horned god, his feet turned to the left or right of his body, and conveying an impression of movement and vigour. The features are invariably crude and rudimentary, in some cases only the eyes being portrayed. The horns are pronounced, and in one or two instances a Saint Andrews cross is figured on the breast of the deity. The weapons are especially interesting, consisting of a rectangular shield and a large knobbed spear. Here the horned god is frequently phallic...."[14]

Perhaps the best-known horned head in the region is the fine ram-horned head from Netherby Roman fort (also known as *Castra Exploratorum*) in the parish of Arthuret, to the north of Carlisle. This head "is fashioned from local red sandstone and is square rather than triangular in shape. The narrowed eyes are depicted by deep indentures in the stone which gives greater prominence to the jutting brows, while the powerful, clean-shaven chin, long narrow nose, and straight, slightly-parted lips give the countenance a grim, war-like aspect which is very arresting. The most striking feature however is the presence of two well-demarcated ram horns which curve boldly down towards the ears, below which they terminate."[15]

At Castlecary Roman fort near Falkirk, which was built during Agricola's campaign then rebuilt as part of the defenses' of the Antonine Wall, a sculptured stone dating to between 140 and 165 depicts a hunting scene with deer and archers within a wood. It was perhaps part of a decorative frieze for a shrine or temple dedicated to local woodland gods and goddesses.[16]

At the Roman fort of Risingham in Northumberland, to the north of Hadrian's Wall, a relief shows Silvanus Cocidius (a composite Roman and Celtic god) as a hunter with a hound, a deer and a tree. An altar from Risingham has an inscription to Cocidius and a hunting scene. Three figures of the horned god come from the Roman fort of High Rochester in Northumberland, also to the north of Hadrian's Wall. In each case "the god is naked, having extremely crude features, and with a pronounced phallus and horns. Another, and more sophisticated representation of the horned god as a Silvanus figure comes from near Carlisle. He is portrayed in relief on a small altar. His horns are well defined. He is naked apart from a cloak about his shoulders and has his left foot up on a rock, while he holds a small animal over an altar."[17]

There are numerous dedications to the god Cocidius in northern Britain. It has been suggested, says Ross,[18] that the name *Cocidius* "contains the root of the Welsh *coch*, 'red,' this being appropriate to a god of slaughter, and giving the name some such meaning as 'the Red One.'" However, this derivation is problematic, says Ross:

> One would expect gemination [lengthening] of the internal -c- if it were to be connected with the word *coch*, and the fact that it is consistently spelt with a single internal -c- argues against such an interpretation. On the other hand, the Celtic association of the colour *red* with warrior gods is undeniable, while the words for *red* in the Goidelic dialects, *dearg* and *ruadh* carry the meaning of the colour *red*, and also mean *strong, swift, turbulent*.

Ross then goes on to cite Irish gods related to Cocidius or connected with the color red:

> An Irish deity *Da Choc* or *Coca*, may be comparable with the north British god, and O'Rahilly cites examples of names of this type having ungeminated internal -c-. *Da Derga* in Ireland likewise may mean "the red god," while we also have another name

for the Dagda, *Ruad Rofhessa*, "The Red One of Great Wisdom"; in Gaul the god Rudiobus, whose name also contains the word for "red," is equated with the Roman Mars.

Two silver plaques dedicated to Cocidius come from the Roman fort at Bewcastle in Cumbria. Cocidius is represented as a warrior, armed in native fashion with a shield and a long, knob-ended spear, and wearing in one instance a curious pleated garment about his shoulders, resembling a double row of frills."[19] It is likely that in Roman times Bewcastle was called *Fanum Cocidii* ("Shrine of Cocidius"), and it remained a sacred place in the Christian period. The Anglo-Saxon Bewcastle Cross

> stands over 4m (14 feet) high in the churchyard at the south-west corner of the church. It has been much studied since it was first recorded in 1601. It has figures, inhabited vine scroll decoration, an inscription in runes and a sundial. There has been much debate about its date and function. It was thought to be late 7th century, but Rosemary Cramp now thinks that it was made probably in the early 8th century. It seems to have been set up to commemorate an individual and it may have been a focus for a cemetery or put in an existing burial ground. With its sundial (to work out the times for religious services) and its elaborate carving, it suggests that Bewcastle was a Northumbrian monastery at this time. The runic inscription implies there were people around who could read it.[20]

There are also dedications to Mars Cocidius at Bewcastle ("the sacred god, Mars Cocidius"), Old Wall near Carlisle, and at Stanwix Roman fort in Cumbria ("the god Mars Cocidius"). At Lancaster Roman fort (Lancashire) he appears as "the sacred god Mars Cocidius," and at Housesteads (Northumberland) as "Mars, the god Cocidius." He is invoked at Bankshead, near Lanercost Priory (Cumbria), as "Cocidius, god of soldiers."[21] At Ebchester Roman fort in County Durham there is an inscription to *Cocidius Vernostonus* ("Cocidius of the Alder Tree").

The most spectacular *Cocidius* or *Silvanus* (the Roman god of the forest) is the so-called Robin of Risingham, not far from Risingham Roman fort in Northumberland. Robin of Risingham is a figure cut in relief on a rock detached from a quarry cliff. Before mutilation, shortly before December 1819, the figure, wearing a tunic and holding a bow in its right hand and a hare in its left, stood to a height of approximately 4 feet. There was a panel above it and a rectangular block, probably an altar, to its right. The association of the figure with an ansate panel [a panel with stylized lugs or handles] is sufficient proof of its Roman date.[22]

Recently an ancient rock carving was uncovered near Chesters Roman Fort on Hadrian's Wall in Northumberland. The carving of a 16-inch-high figure, holding a shield in one hand and spear or sword in the other, was found at Carr Edge near the fort by a team of rock carving experts. The carving is thought by experts to be a representation of Cocidius, a Romano-British warrior god. Rock art project officer Tertia Barnett said: "We can date it from the Roman period by looking at the style of the carving and the stance of the figure. It is very similar to other Roman period carvings of the same deity in the area."[23]

A shrine was discovered in spring 1980 at Yardhope near Holystone, to the north of Hadrian's Wall in Northumberland, and excavated in June of that year by the Field Research Group of the Society of Antiquaries of Newcastle upon Tyne. The shrine is situated high on the south side of the narrow valley of the Holystone Burn in Upper Coquetdale (the valley of the River Coquet), at a height of 984 feet above sea level. On the west side of a narrow gulley faulting in the bed-rock has formed a natural chamber, almost square, with its entrance on the east. Carved on the face of the rock on the north side of the entrance, and framed in a mushroom-shaped niche, is the full frontal figure of the god, 12 inches high. Facing east, the figure stands with his feet slightly apart and his arms outstretched. In his right hand he holds a spear, in his left he brandishes the reverse of a small round shield. Apart from what appears to be a close-fitting cap or helmet, pulled low over his jutting brows, he is completely naked but non-phallic. Near his right hand, at the entrance, and carved out of the rock which forms the north wall of the shrine, is a narrow ledge, 16 inches long and 6 inches wide, which may have been used for a lamp or offerings from worshippers. Above the ledge, a groove chiseled along the top of the rock probably held supports for a sloping roof. The stone slab which formed the south side of the entrance abutted a natural rock outcrop which had been built up to a surviving height of 4 feet by dry-stone walling. Within the shrine, in the southeast corner, was a flue or chimney. The carving suggests a pre–Roman, Celtic, origin for the shrine, adopted in the later period.[24]

The End of Paganism

In AD 313 Christianity was legalized by the Emperor Constantine, and in 380 Christianity became the official state religion under the Emperor Theodosius. Christianity came to Britain just as the Roman Empire was disintegrating and Roman legions were withdrawing from Britain. Nature, as they say, abhors a vacuum, and the vacuum left by the Romans was soon filled by new settlers from Germanic lands on the North Sea coast, in what is now Lower Saxony—the people of England we now call the Anglo-Saxons. In the 6th and 7th centuries, the area around Hadrian's Wall, and parts of southern Scotland came under the control of the Anglo-Saxon kingdom of Northumbria. Northumbrian rule was resisted by the native British, and their resistance was commemorated in poetry and prose, some of it contemporary but much of it written several centuries later. This area under Northumbrian rule came to be known by the Welsh as the "Old North," and it is highly likely that the heroes of the "Old North" played an important role in the later stories of Arthur, as set down by the 12th century Norman priest Geoffrey of Monmouth.

2

The Kingdom of Northumbria

Resistance to Anglo-Saxon Rule in Northern Britain

The First Anglo-Saxon Settlers

In AD 407 the last Roman legions left Britain, in 410 Rome was sacked by the Germanic Visigoths under Alaric, and by 476 the Western Roman Empire had collapsed. In northern Gaul the Romans were replaced by the Germanic Franks, who came from land between the Lower and Middle Rhine in what is now Germany; in southern Gaul they were replaced by the Visigoths, who came from the southern Baltic, from the area around the Vistula River in what is now Poland; and in England the Romans were replaced by the Anglo-Saxons, who originated on the North Sea coast of Germany, between the rivers Elbe and Weser.

Information on Britain after the departure of the last Roman legions is scarce, and the best source we have for the period is a long sermon in Latin by the cleric Gildas entitled *On the ruin and conquest of Britain*. The date of this work is uncertain: it is usually said to have been written in the 540s, though it could well date to the 520s or even earlier. Nor is it known where Gildas wrote the work, though there seems to be a consensus that if it was written in Britain, it was probably written in Dorset, in southwest England. In the early part of his sermon, Gildas gives a brief history of Britain. He says that after the last Roman legions left, Britain was attacked by Picts and Scots (Irish), who occupied the north of Britain as far as Hadrian's Wall. Hoping for help from Rome, the inhabitants of Britain sent a letter (known as the "Groans of the Britons"), some time between AD 446 and 454, to Aetius, a Roman general who was fighting insurgents in Gaul at the time. This help was probably not forthcoming, so a council was held "to deliberate what means ought to be determined upon, as the best and safest to repel such fatal and frequent irruptions and plunderings by the nations mentioned above."[1]

The council along with the "proud tyrant" (*superbus tyrannus*) decided that "those wild Saxons, of accursed name, hated by God and men, should be admitted into the island, like wolves into folds, in order to repel the northern nations"[2] (Gildas does not mention the name of the "proud tyrant," but Bede calls him Vortigern). After the "proud tyrant" invited the Saxons to settle in England, says Gildas, they arrived in three "keels" (*cyulae*) and settled in the "eastern part of the island."

However, says Gildas, the Saxons were not satisfied with the terms of the treaty, and "devastated all the neighbouring cities and lands."[3] There was constant conflict until the British united under a leader called Ambrosius Aurelianus who defeated the Saxons at the Siege of Mons Badonicus (Mount Badon).

Gildas says that the Saxons settled in the "eastern part of the island," and the cemetery evidence supports this. The first Anglo-Saxon settlers practiced cremation, and there are early cremation cemeteries along the east coast of England, from East Yorkshire in the north to Suffolk in the south. These cemeteries include Sancton near Market Weighton in East Yorkshire; Cleatham and Elsham, both in Lindsey (North Lincolnshire); Loveden Hill near Grantham in the south of Lincolnshire; North Elmham in Norfolk; and Eye in Suffolk. Elsewhere there are mixed inhumation and cremation cemeteries: at Caistor St. Edmund in Norfolk (the site of the Roman town of *Venta Icenorum*, the tribal capital of Boudica's tribe, the *Iceni*); West Stow in Suffolk; Mucking on the Thames estuary in Essex; Ringlemere Farm, Woodnesborough near Sandwich in Kent; Bishopstone near Seaford in East Sussex; Highdown Hill near Worthing in West Sussex; Boscombe Down and Chessell Down on the Isle of Wight; and Winchester in Hampshire.

The Kingdom of Northumbria

In the Roman period Hadrian's Wall marked the boundary between the Roman Empire and northern Britain, and in the Anglo-Saxon period the frontier between Anglo-Saxon lands and northern Britain was formed by the kingdom of Northumbria. We know a great deal about early Northumbria thanks to Bede, a monk at the twin monasteries of Monkwearmouth on the River Wear near Sunderland and Jarrow on the River Tyne near Newcastle upon Tyne, and his *Ecclesiastical History of the English People*, written in Latin around 730. The name Northumbria (roughly, "Land North of the Humber") was probably devised by Bede to describe the amalgam of two kingdoms, Deira and Bernicia.

It is generally thought that the name Deira is British rather than Anglo-Saxon. The Celtic scholar John Koch says[4] that the Welsh form *Deifr* may well be derived from Brythonic *Dubria* "land of waters," related to Irish *dobur*, Welsh *dwfr*, "water."[5] The kingdom of Deira included east and northeast Yorkshire, between the Humber estuary and the River Tees. As John Koch points out,[6] the boundaries of early medieval Deira "do not correspond closely to those of known Romano-British divisions, such as the *civitas* of the Parisii or that of the Brigantes, nor to the *territorium* of the town and legionary fortress of York." As a result, it is difficult to know where a British kingdom of Deira may have been based, but one good candidate is the Roman fort and settlement at Catterick. One of the most interesting aspects of the site at Catterick is "its survival as a Roman town and settlement, which must have lasted well into the fifth century."[7] The best example of this is[8]

> Building VI, 8, which had been altered in the last decades of the fourth century, along with other buildings in Insula VII, when an apse was added to the open west end. This apsidal building remained in use long enough for occupation material to collect on its floors, after which it fell into decay, with soil accumulating round its walls and over its floor until little or no visible remains can have shown above the ground. Then, and only then, a new building was constructed on the same site, but with its wall aligned differently and now built entirely of timber with individual posts set in the ground or on flat blocks of stone. The time which elapsed between the construction of the apsidal building and this timber-framed house would seem to be long enough for the latter to be safely attributed to the fifth century, even though no direct dating evidence was found. But this was not the only house to show these easily distinguished structural features; several were found in Insula III, with fragments of others elsewhere. It would appear that a substantial Romano-British settlement still existed at Catterick, sheltered by its massive walls, at least in the first part of the fifth century.

Anglo-Saxon brooches have been found in Catterick, and an early medieval cemetery was discovered at Catterick Racecourse between 1993 and 1996 during work on the A1—there were 44 Anglian inhumations, dated to the period 450 to 550 from the brooches associated with the inhumations.[9]

Bernicia, the other kingdom of Northumbria, covered the present counties of Northumberland and Durham in England, and Berwickshire and East Lothian in Scotland, and corresponded, in part at least, to the territory of the Votadini (Welsh *Gododdin*). The name Bernicia is thought to derive from Brythonic *Bryneich* or *Brynaich*, and may mean "Land of the Mountain Passes" (see Old Irish *bern*, "mountain pass"). There are several mentions of Brynaich in early Welsh poetry, notably in the *Marwnad Cunedda* ("Death Song of Cunedda"), where the chief of the Votadini Cunedda is described as leading the "men of Brynaich," and in *Y Gododdin*, which speaks of "the army of Gododdin and Brynaich."[10] The quote from *Y Gododdin* implies that Brynaich was distinct from the land of the Gododdin, but gives no clue as to where it was located. One possibility is that Brynaich was based at Birdoswald, on Hadrian's Wall in Cumbria, near the border with Northumberland. Birdoswald Roman fort is situated in a commanding position on a triangular spur of land bounded by cliffs to the south and east overlooking a broad meander of the River Irthing. The fort was constructed from AD 117, first as a fort of turf and timber, and later as a larger stone fort. During the first half of the 3rd century there is evidence for rebuilding before the site was abandoned for a period, from the end of the 3rd century, and re-occupied in the early 4th century. During the late 4th/early 5th century, the south granary was converted for residential use. During the 5th century a sequence of timber buildings were erected on the site of the north granary. The site was possibly abandoned altogether by about 520.[11]

The first king of Anglo-Saxon Deira of which anything is known is Ælla. He is referred to by Bede[12] in the famous story about Pope Gregory (590–604). Seeing pale-skinned boys for sale in a market, he enquired who they were. Told they were from the island of Britain and were pagans, he asked from which nation, and was informed they were Angles. The pope remarked they deserved to be with the angels. Learning they were from the province of Deira, he said they should be delivered *de ira* ("from wrath"). Told that the king of that province was Ælla, Gregory, alluding to the name, said "Hallelujah, the praise of God the Creator must be sung in those parts." Little is known of Ælla, but he may have reigned from 559 to 588.

The first king of Bernicia is Ida, who is said to have reigned from 547 to 559, and founded the Northumbrian stronghold of Bamburgh in Northumberland. But the first Bernician king of whom much is known is Æthelfrith, the grandson of Ida, who became king in around 593 and ruled until 616. According to Bede,[13] Æthelfrith "ravaged the Britons more than all the great men of the English," and "conquered more territories from the Britons, either making them tributary, or driving the inhabitants clean out, and planting English in their places, than any other king or tribune." We know of two of Æthelfrith's battles, Degsastan and Chester. At Degsastan (location unknown), Æthelfrith fought against Aedan mac Gabrain, the king of Dal Riata (a Gaelic kingdom located on the hillfort of Dunadd in Argyll, western Scotland), in 603 and destroyed Aedan's army. At Chester in Cheshire (northwest England), Æthelfrith defeated and killed King Selyf of Powys in 615.[14]

For Bede, the story of Northumbria did not really begin until its conversion to Christianity. When the Anglo-Saxons first settled in England they were pagans, but they began converting to Christianity in 597 when St. Augustine, prior of the Abbey of St. Andrew's in Rome, was sent by Pope Gregory the Great to preach to the Anglo-Saxons of Kent. However, Christianity did not reach Northumbria until three decades later. In 624 the Northumbrian king Edwin, son of Ælla of Deira, married Æthelburh, the daughter of King

Æthelberht of Kent and the Merovingian (French) princess Bertha, and the sister of the then Kentish king Eadbald. Æthelburh was Christian, and when she went to Northumbria, she was accompanied by Paulinus, an Italian priest and member of the mission sent by Pope Gregory, who set about trying to convert Edwin to Christianity. As a result, Edwin held a council in 627 to decide whether to convert.[15]

The decision was made to convert, and Edwin was baptized in specially constructed timber church in the old Roman city of York. Then Paulinus spent thirty-six days in Yeavering, Northumberland, baptizing people in the River Glen, after which he moved on to Catterick in North Yorkshire, baptizing people in the River Swale.[16]

Catterick in North Yorkshire is the old Roman town that may have been an early stronghold of Deira. Yeavering, a small hamlet in the far north of Northumberland near the border with Scotland, is the site of an Anglo-Saxon palace that was excavated by Brian Hope-Taylor between 1952 and 1962. The site actually consists of the Iron Age hillfort of Yeavering Bell and a much smaller "whaleback hill" immediately to the north which contains the site of the Anglian palace named by Bede as *Ad Gefrin*. Hope-Taylor's excavations showed that a small henge monument was constructed on the whaleback during the late Neolithic/early Bronze Age and an early Bronze Age cremation cemetery is focused on an unusual monument which Hope Taylor interprets as a stone circle. The hillfort on Yeavering Bell is usually thought to date from the latter half of the 1st millennium BC, though a Late Bronze Age origin is possible. It may have been during the Late Iron Age that the so-called "Great Enclosure" was erected on the whaleback. This has been interpreted as a great stock enclosure, presumably of both functional and ceremonial significance. It was maintained throughout much of the life of the Anglian palace, which was erected immediately adjacent to it at some point during the latter half of the 6th century AD. The palace incorporated several large buildings, most notable of which were the great hall and a unique "theatre." The name *Gefrin* is Celtic, and can be translated as "Hill of the Goats." Interestingly, Hope Taylor found a goat's skull and a "ceremonial staff" decorated with what may have been a goat motif in what was apparently one of the most significant Anglian period burials at *Ad Gefrin*.[17] It seems likely that Yeavering was an important British ceremonial center that was taken over by the Anglo-Saxons of Bernicia in the 6th century AD.

Interestingly, the *History of the Britons*, composed in Latin in AD 829 and attributed to the Welsh monk Nennius, has a different story about the baptism of Edwin and his subjects[18]:

> Edwin, son of Aelle, reigned seventeen years, seized on Elmet, and expelled Cerdic, its king. Eanflaed, his daughter, received baptism, on the twelfth day after Pentecost, with all her followers, both men and women. The following Easter Edwin himself

received baptism, and twelve thousand of his subjects with him. If any one wishes to know who baptized them, it was Rhun son of Urien: he was engaged forty days in baptizing all classes of the Saxons, and by his preaching many believed on Christ.

Urien was a late 6th century ruler of Rheged, a British kingdom in northwest England and southwest Scotland. Elsewhere,[19] the *History of the Britons* says that Oswiu, king of Northumbria (642–670) had two wives, Rhianmellt, daughter of Royth, son of Rhun (clearly a British princess from Rheged), and Eanflæd, daughter of Edwin. In the Durham *Liber Vitae*, which probably dates from the 9th century, a register is provided of "queens and abbesses" of Northumbria, in which a lady called *Raegnmaeld* is listed first, followed by Oswiu's Anglo-Saxon wife Eanflæd—*Ragnamaeld* is thought to be an Anglo-Saxon version of Rhianmellt. It is likely that Oswiu married Rhianmellt some time in the 630s, before he married Eanflæd, which occurred between 642 and 645.[20] So it does seem plausible that Rhun at least played a part in the conversion of the Saxons, especially in the west of Northumbria, despite Bede's assertion[21] that the British "never preached the faith to the Saxons, or English, who dwelt amongst them." I should add that Bede rarely had a good word to say about the British, so some of his claims should be taken with the proverbial pinch of salt.

Edwin did not long survive his conversion to Christianity: in 633 he was killed by Penda of Mercia and Cadwallon ap Cadfan of Gwynedd (north Wales) at the Battle of Hatfield Chase, near Doncaster (South Yorkshire). Bede remarks, in a passage that helps explain his hostility to the British[22]:

At this time a great slaughter was made in the church or nation of the Northumbrians; and the more so because one of the commanders, by whom it was made, was a pagan, and the other a barbarian, more cruel than a pagan; for Penda, with all the nation of the Mercians, was an idolater, and a stranger to the name of Christ; but Cadwalla, though he bore the name and professed himself a Christian, was so barbarous in his disposition and behaviour, that he neither spared the female sex, nor the innocent age of children, but with savage cruelty put them to tormenting deaths, ravaging all their country for a long time, and resolving to cut off all the race of the English within the borders of Britain. Nor did he pay any respect to the Christian religion which had newly taken root among them; it being to this day the custom of the Britons not to pay any respect to the faith and religion of the English, nor to correspond with them any more than with pagans.

Edwin was succeeded as king of Bernicia by Eanfrith, son of the former king Æthelfrith, who was killed by Cadwallon ap Cadfan in 634. Eanfrith in turn was succeeded as king by his brother Oswald, who led an army against Cadwallon and defeated and killed him at the Battle of Heavenfield, near Hexham (Northumberland).

Not surprisingly, Cadwallon appears in a number of the *Triads of the Island of Britain*, as Cadwallawn. For example, Triad 29, "Three Faithful War-Bands of the Island of Britain" mentions "The War-Band of Cadwallawn son of Cad-fan, who were with him seven years in Ireland; and in all that time they did not ask him for anything, lest they should be compelled to leave him." He also appears in the *Annales Cambriae* ("Annals of Wales") in the entry for 629: "The besieging of king Cadwallon in the island of Glannauc"; the entry for 630: "On the Kalends of January the battle of Meigen; and there Edwin was killed with his two sons; but Cadwallon was the victor"; and the entry for 631: "The battle of Cantscaul in which Cadwallon fell." Glannauc is Priestholm, a small island off Anglesey; Meigen is Hatfield Chase; and Cantscaul "the young warrior's enclosure" is a "literal translation of Hagul-staldesham [Hexham], the nearest place to the site of the battle of Heavenfield which is likely to have been known to a Welsh chronicler."[23]

According to Rachel Bromwich, the contest between Cadwallon and Edwin "so impressed itself on the consciousness of Welsh poets that *Edwin* came to symbolize the typical Saxon enemy, though surprisingly, several Welsh rulers were later given his name."[24] After his conquest of the British kingdom of Elmet in West Yorkshire in 616, Edwin is said[25] to have conquered the "Mevanian islands," which have been taken to mean the islands of Man and Anglesey. The English conquest of Anglesey would explain why Cadwallon sought refuge in Ireland, as referred to in Triad 29. Historians have regarded the siege of the island of Glannauc as a prelude to Cadwallon's exile, and the island of Priestholm may have been Cadwallon's last stronghold on Welsh soil.[26]

The Legendary Heroes of the "Old North": The British Living on the Northern Borders of Northumbria

The Gododdin (Votadini)

We know from Bede that there was conflict between the Anglo-Saxons of Northumbria and the native Britons, but relatively little is known about the early history of what the Welsh called the "Old North" (*Yr Hen Ogledd*)—those parts of northern England and southern Scotland where the inhabitants spoke a language closely related to Welsh called Cumbric. We know from Welsh poetry that the northeast was dominated by the Votadini (Welsh *Gododdin*), and that the northwest was dominated by a kingdom called Rheged.

In post–Roman times the Votadini emerged as the heroes of the Welsh poem *Y Gododdin* ("The Votadini"), a series of elegies for warriors who fell in battle against vastly superior numbers. The *Gododdin* makes a passing reference to Arthur, stating that the warrior Gwawddur, who killed three hundred men, "fed black ravens on the rampart of a fort, though he was no Arthur." The warriors of the *Gododdin* were based at *Din Eidyn*, and the battle was fought at *Catraeth* (Catterick in North Yorkshire). *Din Eidyn* is thought to be the hill where Edinburgh Castle now stands. The area of Edinburgh Castle known as Mill's Mount produced the earliest finds and occupation features (cobbled surfaces and hearths) dated to the early centuries AD, providing tentative evidence for the existence of native Iron Age and Dark Age forts. The principal finds were Roman and native pottery and a fibula brooch dated to the 1st–2nd centuries, sealed by layers which produced a comb dated 7th–10th centuries AD.[27]

By the 4th century Christianity had come to Britain, and by the time Gildas wrote his long sermon *On the ruin and conquest of Britain*, all native Britons were Christians. There is some evidence for early Christianity in northeast England and southeast Scotland. In 1878 a tombstone in the name of *Brigomaglos* was discovered at the Roman fort of *Vindolanda* near Hexham in Northumberland. The name *Brigomaglos* can be interpreted to mean "High Lord" and the formula for the inscription is Christian. Vindolanda has also produced the remains of an early church which was located in 1998 inside the courtyard of the commanding officers residence. Further early Christian evidence from the site come most notably in the form of a portable Christian "altar" stone with an early Christian chi-rho symbol (the first two letters of the Greek *Christos*), recovered during the 1999 southern fort wall excavations.[28]

Close to Vindolanda is Housesteads Roman fort, which was built shortly after AD 122, and was in use until the 4th century. Immediate post–Roman activity at Housesteads is indicated by a cist burial in a water tank close to the north curtain wall. This may be associated with an apsidal structure nearby that is similar in size and form to a building at Vindolanda that has been identified as a church.[29]

In southeast Scotland, the early 6th century Yarrow Stone from the Scottish Borders to the west of Selkirk carries a Latin inscription: HIC MEMORIA PERPETUA. IN LOCO INSIGNISIMI PRINCIPES NVDI DVNOGENI. HIC IACENT IN TVMVLO DVO FILLI LIBERALI, "This is the eternal memorial: in this place lie the most illustrious *Nudus* and *Dumnogenus*. Here lie in the grave the two sons of *Liberalis*."[30] Rachel Bromwich (*Trioedd Ynys Prydein: Triads of the Island of Britain*) links this stone to Triad 2 of the *Triads of the Island of Britain*[31]:

> Tri Hael Enys Prydein
> Three Generous (Noble, Victorious) Men of the Island of Britain
>
> Nudd the generous, son of Senyllt,
> Mordaf the generous, son of Serwan,
> Rhydderch the Generous, son of Tudwal Tudglyd.

The three personal names in the triad denote three leading princes of the "Men of the North." Bromwich says she finds it impossible to dissociate *Hael* in the triad from the epithet *Liberali(s)* ("generous") in the Yarrow Stone, and believes that the inscription refers to an ancestor of Nudd the generous, son of Senyllt.[32] Nudd is also referred to in the poetry of the 6th century Welsh bard Taliesin, and his father Senyllt is mentioned in *Y Gododdin*.

The Kingdom of Rheged

The kingdom of Rheged is first mentioned in poems by Taliesin, who names a certain Urien as "The protector of Rheged."[33] The extent of Rheged is unclear, but Rachel Bromwich believes that it stretched "from Galloway (where the name of *Rheged* may have survived in *Dunragit* near Stranraer [= *Dun Recet*] *circa* 800 in the *Martyrology of Oengus*) over much of the Scottish Lowlands and Border country; and to the south it extended over Cumbria and the Lake District."[34] It is probable that the center of Rheged lay around the Solway estuary and included Carlisle in Cumbria, Annan in Dumfriesshire and the valley of the River Eden in Cumbria (the Eden rises in southeast Cumbria and flows near Penrith and through Carlisle to the Solway Firth). Bromwich notes that since in the Taliesin poems Urien "is also entitled *llyw Catraeth* "ruler of Catterick," this may be taken as evidence that *Rheged* at some period stretched as far south as North Yorkshire."[35] Bromwich adds that Urien was probably dead by the time of the *Gododdin* and that the battle at *Catraeth* commemorated in the *Gododdin* may well have been an attempt to regain lands that had formerly held by Urien.[36]

As I said, the center of Rheged probably lay around the Solway estuary, in Dumfries and Galloway, southwest Scotland, and Cumbria, northwest England If we look at Cumbria, there are several possible candidates for an early Rheged stronghold. Carlisle was the site of a Roman fort called *Luguvalium*, and may have been the capital of the local tribe, the Carvetii. Excavations in 2000 and 2001 in the central range of the fort have provided evidence for continued use of the headquarters building (*principia*), as well as building adjacent to the south side of the *via principalis* ("main street"), after the end of the 4th century.[37]

Another possible stronghold is Birdoswald Roman fort, which was occupied until around 520. Not far from Birdoswald is Netherby Roman fort, also known as *Castra Exploratorum*. *Castra Exploratorum* is a Roman fort at Netherby in Cumbria, in the parish of Arthuret. All above-ground remains have been destroyed by the building of Netherby Hall and the landscaping of the surrounding grounds, but the descriptions by antiquarians from Leland onwards, and the epigraphic evidence of a number of inscriptions, make it certain that a fort and substantial settlement existed here, probably with a port on the River Esk, since silted up. John Leland (mid–16th century) saw the "ruinous walls of marvellous buildings," and was told of rings and staples set in walls as if for the mooring of ships, whilst the early editions of Camden (late 16th century) refer to the "wonderful and large ruins of an ancient city." It seems reasonably certain that a fort was established here by the time of Agricola (77–85), guarding a road junction and crossing of the Esk, but the earliest definite evidence is an inscription which records construction carried out by the second legion in the time of Hadrian (117–138). Inscriptions of the 3rd century show that the fort became the headquarters of the frontier scouts in the re-organization by Caracella, being occupied by Cohors I Aelia Hispanorum around AD 211, with detachments on loan from the two legions of Upper Britain. The external bath-house was built around 222, and the rebuilding of a temple probably dates from about the same time. The latest direct dating evidence is a coin of Gordian (238–244), but it is reasonable to suppose that occupation continued well into the 4th century, as with the other four outpost forts of the Caracallan system.[38]

Netherby Roman fort is very close to the supposed site of the battle of Arfderydd (Arthuret), mentioned by the *Annales Cambriae* ("Annals of Wales") in its entry for 573. In a later version of the *Annals*, the battle is said to have been fought between the sons of Eliffer (Peredur and Gwrgi) and Gwenddolau, son of Ceidio. The entry goes on to say that Gwenddolau died and "Myrddin went mad." Myrddin is the character better known in Arthurian romances as Merlin, but in the Welsh tradition as *Myrddin Wyllt* ("Myrddin the Wild"). In a brief article, W.F. Skene drew attention to the apparent preservation of Gwenddolau's name in that of the *Carwinelow* burn which falls into the River Esk three miles north of Longtown in Cumbria, which itself is a mile north of Arthuret.[39] Chadwick suggested that Gwenddolau's stronghold was situated in Netherby Roman fort.[40]

The Welsh genealogies show that Peredur and Gwrgi belonged to the family of Coel Hen and were among the "Men of the North" who lived in the last half of the 6th century. Coel Hen ("Coel the Old," or "Coel the Ancestor") was the progenitor of a number of dynasties in the "Old North," including that of Urien Rheged. On the basis of genealogies, Coel Hen is believed to have been a dominant ruler or "Overlord" over much of northwest England and southern Scotland in the early 5th century.[41]

None of the Cumbrian sites sounds like the headquarters of a Dark Age kingdom, and more interest has focused on *Rerigonium*, a site mentioned in the 2nd century by Ptolemy, which is thought to have been near Loch Ryan in the Rhinns of Galloway, in the far southwest of Scotland. The location of *Rerigonium* ("Very Royal Place") is unknown, but it may have been on the eastern side of Loch Ryan in the vicinity of Innermessan farm.[42] No Dark Age site has been found at Innermessan, but in the 12th century Innermessan became the site of a motte and wooden castle, around which a small town developed—this reached its peak in the late Middle Ages, but by 1684 it was being described as a small village.[43]

To the south of Loch Ryan is Kirkmadrine church in the parish of Stoneykirk, where there was a Dark Age site. The present Kirkmadrine church was built in the 1800s, but three of the oldest Christian memorials surviving in Scotland have been found in or around the churchyard. The three memorials (known as Kirkmadrine 1, 2 and 3) may date from the mid-to-late 6th century AD. They have incised Latin inscriptions, and bear Greek chi-rho crosses. They commemorate priests or bishops. Kirkmadrine 1 reads: HIC IACENT S(AN)C(T)I ET PRAECIPUI SACER DOTES IDES VIVENTIUS ET MAVORIUS ("Here lie the holy and distinguished priests/bishops, namely Viventius and Mavorius"). Kirkmadrine 2 commemorates someone called Florentius. Kirkmadrine 3 has an allusion to a passage from the Book of Revelation: "The beginning and the end." It may not have been a burial marker and may, instead, have been located in an appropriate liturgical context at the church.[44]

There may not have been an early medieval stronghold near Loch Ryan, but along the coast to the east of the Rhinns of Galloway is the hillfort of Trusty's Hill, at Anwoth near Gatehouse of Fleet. Excavations carried out in 1960 revealed occupation relating to two periods. In the Iron Age, an area 50 feet by 80 feet on the summit was enclosed by a 4-foot-wide timber-laced stone wall. An oval stone guard-hut built in a natural hollow outside the entrance on the southeast and a massive rock-cut ditch across the neck of the promontory to the northeast also belong to this period. In the 6th–7th centuries AD, additional ramparts of poorer type with external revetment only were constructed outside the entrance, and possibly timber huts inside. A group of class I Pictish symbols are cut on a rock outcrop at the fort entrance, and now protected by an iron grille. The symbols are deeply incised, and are as follows: in the upper left-hand corner the double-disc ornament traversed by the Z-shaped floriated rod (usually called the double-disc and Z-rod); to the right, and separated by a natural fissure, a marine monster (possibly the so-called Pictish beast); and immediately below it a heart-shaped figure with incurvation terminating in spirals and surmounted with a conical spike; at the left-hand lower corner a human mask with two horns ending in spiral curves on the top of it.[45] Pictish symbols are usually found in eastern Scotland, and one of the only other sites in western Scotland with a Pictish symbol is the hillfort of Dunadd in Argyll and Bute, thought to be the stronghold of the Dark Age kingdom of Dal Riata. Interestingly, a Pictish symbol stone was also found in Edinburgh, near Edinburgh Castle, the home of the Votadini (*Gododdin*), suggesting that Pictish symbols were associated with royal capitals.

Recently the Galloway Picts Project and GUARD Archaeology excavated Trusty's Hill and found that it was a high-status site[46]:

> An abundance of domestic rubbish, including animal bones, a rotary quern, tools and a spindle whorl demonstrate that Trusty's Hill was once the home of a small community. There was also clear evidence, in the form of crucibles, a clay mould and iron slag, that metalworking and the production of high status jewellery was being carried out in part of the site. But the clincher for the Galloway Picts Team was the discovery of high status jewellery itself and even rarer pottery sherds from France. The pottery sherd not only dates to the seventh century AD, exactly the right time when Pictish Symbols were being carved in Scotland, but are so rare from this period that only people of the highest status—kings, princes, lords and bishops—acquired this pottery.

Not far from Trusty's Hill is Dumfries and Galloway's most famous early monastery, at Whithorn, which is said to have been founded by St. Ninian. St. Ninian is mentioned in the *Ecclesiastical History of the English People*: Bede says[47] that Ninian was "a most reverend bishop and holy man of the nation of Britons" who had been trained in Rome. The Episcopal see was named after St. Martin of Tours and his church was known as Candida Casa ("Shining House") because it was built from limestone (recent excavations have found spreads of burnt limestone, plaster and cement, possibly the remains of this limestone church). Excavations between 1984 and 1991 demonstrated that the site was in use from Roman times: finds include sherds of glass, pottery (both coarse ware and samian) and amphorae all largely belonging to the second or third centuries AD.[48] The 1984–1991 excavations concentrated on Northumbrian remains of AD 700–850 but also found evidence for the 5th to 7th centuries. Low-lying ground revealed a complex of curvilinear ditches, pits and stakeholes interleaved with waterborne silts which had been severely disturbed by 7th century moldboard plowing. A rich assemblage of finds include 9 sherds of A ware (6th century African Red Slipware made near Carthage in Tunis); B ware (amphorae from the eastern Mediterranean); D ware (cordoned bowls and bowls with internal rouletted or stamped ornament from northern or southern Gaul); E ware (6th–7th century jars, bowls and jugs in hard granular gray wares, probably produced in western or central France); numerous cone beaker sherds (cone beakers date from the 5th–6th century, and were produced in Frankish glass workshops in France, Belgium or Germany); and a scatter of possible Late Roman glass and pottery. An extensive 7th-century cemetery on higher ground contained at least 50 graves mostly laid out in regular rows. Graves include long cists with and without stone cover slabs.[49] One of the oldest objects found at Whithorn is the Latinus stone. Carved around AD 450, it was erected to Latinus and his unnamed daughter, and would have stood by an early Christian church and cemetery, pre-dating the later churches on the hilltop at Whithorn. The inscription on the stone is in Latin and when translated reads: "We praise you, the Lord! Latinus, descendant of Barrovados, aged 35, and his daughter, aged 4, made a sign here." There are traces of the Christian chi-rho symbol above the lettering, which might be the "sign" referred to in the inscription.[50]

East of Trusty's Hill is the hillfort known as the Mote of Mark at Rockcliffe. The hillfort was first defended with a stone-faced rampart in the 6th century AD, and was a center for the production of high-quality bronzes until the later 7th century, when the site was burnt and its defenses slighted. The Mote of Mark was a relatively high-status site, witnessed not only by its metalworking but by the presence of continental imports, notably E-ware and glass. The excavators did not regard the site as royal, seeing it instead as "the residence of a master smith rather than that of a lord who retained such a craftsman under his patronage."[51]

Kirkmadrine, Whithorn, Trusty's Hill and the Mote of Mark are all on the south coast of Dumfries and Galloway facing the Solway Firth, and together they could have constituted the core of the kingdom of Rheged, based in Galloway but making raids across the Solway Firth into Cumbria.

Early religious sites in Cumbria are hard to find, but one possible exception is the Roman fort of Maryport on the Solway Firth, where numerous images of the horned god were found. Excavations at Maryport between 2011 and 2013 found that a large number of Roman altars buried there (23 in all) had acted as foundations for postholes—a total of 64 postholes were uncovered. Two structures have been tentatively identified: a larger building to the west, and a smaller one to the east. The post-holes were sunk after the construction of a ring ditch, which contained fragments of Crambeck parchment ware, a type of off-gray pottery that dates to the late 4th century. About 22 yards north of the post pits is a cemetery. Seven graves in this cemetery were excavated, with six of them seemingly concentrated around a deeper, central burial. A minute fragment of textile—fleece—extracted from one grave was radiocarbon dated to between 240 and 340, while the upper fill of the central grave yielded a Valentinianic *nummus* coin, minted after 364. A couple of small, white quartz pebbles were found in the central grave; white quartz pebbles were also found in graves in the early Christian cemetery at Llandough near Cardiff in south Wales, and may be linked to a line in *Revelation* 2:17 (King James Version):

> He that hath an ear, let him hear what the Spirit saith unto the churches; To him that overcometh will I give to eat of the hidden manna, and will give him a white stone, and in the stone a new name written, which no man knoweth saving he that receiveth it.

Two early Christian-style tombstones are known from Maryport, dedicated to Rianorix and Spurcio, as well as a long-lost altar recut with a chi-rho monogram.[52]

Alt Clut (Dumbarton Rock)

Alt Clut, now known as Dumbarton ("Fort of the Britons"), is on the River Clyde to the west of Glasgow and is mentioned by Bede in his *Ecclesiastical History*. In describing the western of the two arms of the sea which divided the Picts from the Britons—that is, the Firths of Forth and Clyde—Bede writes "there is up to the present a strongly defended political centre of the Britons called Alcluith."[53] Elsewhere he calls it *urbs Alcluith* ("city of Alcluith"), and explains that *Alcluith* "means Clyde Rock in their language" (the language of the Britons; *Petra Cluit* in Latin) "because it is beside the river of that name."[54] Adomnan, in his *Life of St. Columba*, also mentions a "King Roderc, son of Tothal, who reigned on the Rock of Cluaith" (Clyde Rock). In AD 870, the Annals of Ulster record that two kings of the Norsemen, Olaf and Ivar, besieged the citadel for four months, and ultimately destroyed and plundered it, and this is the last we hear of the name.[55]

Dumbarton Rock, now the site of Dumbarton Castle, was excavated in 1974–1975 in the hope of finding the remains of the early medieval fortress, and a number of artifacts dating from the 6th to the 8th century were uncovered. There were the remains of Class B amphorae, representing a total of seven or eight amphorae in which wine had been imported from the Mediterranean in the 6th century AD. There were three sherds of Class E pottery—this consists of high-quality kitchen and tableware, suitable for high-status-households in the absence of any local pottery-production. It was imported from undiscovered centers in Gaul, beginning perhaps in the late 6th century AD, running through the 7th, and then for several decades at least into the 8th century as well. There were also six sherds of glass best defined as "Germanic," which might belong to the 6th and 7th centuries.[56]

No early religious site has been identified at Dumbarton, but recently an early monastic site has been identified on Inchmarnock, a small island off the west coast of Scotland, not far from the Firth of Clyde. Excavations were carried out near the remains of the 12th century chapel of St. Marnock which uncovered a probable earlier stone church and also a much earlier monastic settlement, specifically the detritus associated with a school-house where novices were taught to read and write, as well as compass-work and instruction in elementary design and decoration. A number of inscriptions were found, dating to the 7th and 8th centuries. One of the earliest pieces, recovered from the monastic enclosure ditch, is a rough water-worn slate cobble, possibly a prayer-stone, on which the name Ernan has been written no less than three times. Ernan is the saint's name, which is commemorated in the name Marnock, from the Gaelic familiar form of Mo-Ernan. Meanwhile, from the metal-working area near the church came a fragment of an incised slate board datable to around 750. On one side was a curvilinear cross-motif, set beside an ogham (early Irish) alphabet; on the other were two lines of almost identical Latin text, identifiable as a line of octosyllabic Hiberno-Latin verse: *adeptus sanctum praemium* ("having reached the holy reward"). This is a unique survival, a line of verse from a hymn that formed part of the *Antiphonary of Bangor*, a late 7th-century liturgical commonplace book from Northern Ireland. Another important find was the so-called "Hostage Stone," which appears to depict three armored warriors leading an ecclesiastical figure off to their boat.[57]

The most prominent ruler of Alt Clut was Rhydderch Hael, who flourished in the latter part of the 6th century. A reference to "Rhydderch son of Tudwal who ruled in Alt Clut" in the late 7th century *Life of St. Columba* attests that Rhydderch was reigning in Strathclyde during the life of the saint, who died in 597. The 9th century *History of the Britons* lists *Riderch hen* ("Rhydderch the Old") along with *Urbgen* (Urien Rheged), Gwallawc and Morcant as the four north-British rulers who opposed the Anglian successors of Ida, apparently fighting together as a confederacy.[58]

Northumbria and the Picts

Northumbria was the dominant Anglo-Saxon kingdom for much of the 7th century, but that was not to last. Oswiu died in 670, and was succeeded by his son Ecgfrith, who reigned for fifteen years before leading a disastrous campaign against the Picts. According to Bede,[59] Ecgfrith "rashly led his army to ravage the province of the Picts, greatly against the advice of his friends and particularly of Cuthbert, of blessed memory, who had lately been ordained bishop." The Picts, says Bede, "made a feigned retreat, and the king was drawn into a narrow pass among remote mountains, and slain, with the greater part of the forces he had led thither." Bede does not say where the battle occurred, but the Irish *Annals of Ulster* mention "The battle of Dun Nechtain on the 20th of May, a Saturday, that is, in which Ecgfrith son of Oswiu, king of the English, having completed the fifteenth year of his reign, was slain with a great body of his soldiers."[60]

Dun Nechtain has recently been identified as Dunachton in Badenoch (Inverness-shire), lying on the western shore of Loch Insh to the southeast of Inverness. Dunachton is certainly a narrow place surrounded by remote mountain, and therefore matches Bede's description.[61] There is evidence that Dunachton may have been significant in Pictish times: a symbol stone has been found there, which shows a deer's head.[62] According to the Irish *Annals of Tigernach* the Pictish commander at the battle of Dun Nechtain was Bredei, son of Beli, king of Fortriu,[63] which may have been based somewhere around Forres on the Moray Firth.[64]

It is unclear whether Northumbria ruled over the Picts north of the Firth of Forth, although Bede says that Abercorn in West Lothian was created as a bishopric for the Picts. At any rate, after the death of Ecgfrith, Northumbrian territory extended as far as the Forth. Recent excavations at Auldhame in East Lothian unearthed a Christian cemetery with burials as early as 650, and evidence for a timber church that was later replaced by a stone church. Some Anglo-Saxon artifacts were found there, as well as a glass inkpot, which are almost always associated with monasteries. Historical records show that St. Balthere (8th century) lived as a hermit on the Bass Rock in the Firth of Forth, returning to the mainland to discharge his pastoral responsibilities. As the nearest landing ground to the Bass Rock lies at Auldhame, it would make a logical setting for his monastery.[65]

The End of the "Old North"

It is likely that British resistance to Northumbrian rule ended in the 7th century: by the time Bede was writing his *Ecclesiastical History* there was a Northumbrian bishop at Lindisfarne (Northumberland); there were Northumbrian monasteries at Carlisle and Dacre (Cumbria), Melrose (Scottish Borders), and Abercorn (West Lothian); and Whithorn (Dumfries and Galloway) had become the seat of a Northumbrian bishop. The Welsh never forgot the "Men of the North," but in time the real northern warriors were replaced by a more mythical figure named Arthur. This Arthur started predominantly as a warrior fighting against the Saxons in the *History of the Britons*, but by the time of the Welsh poem *Pa gur yv y porthaur?* ("What man guards the gate?"), his enemies were not Saxons but supernatural foes like witches and werewolves.

3

Arthur and His Retinue in the Earliest Arthurian Texts

The Origins of Arthur

The "Men of the North" loomed large in Welsh history and mythology, and by the 9th century they had come to be represented by one man, Arthur, who probably combines one or more historical figures with the northern hunter/warrior god of the Roman period. Rachel Bromwich believes that Arthur "may have been the first and the most prominent of the many North-British heroes concerning whom traditions were brought south from the 'Old North' and from the ninth century onwards were freshly localized and elaborated in Wales." It is possible, says Bromwich, "that Arthur could have been in origin an early Romano-British opponent of the Anglian raiders and settlers in the Catterick area of Yorkshire." This would explain the reference to Arthur in *Y Goddodin*, which implies that Arthur was a warrior belonging to a generation that fought before the battle commemorated in the poem, which probably took place around AD 600.[1]

The name *Arthur* is attested in Britain from as early as the 6th century. A certain *Artur* or *Artuir*, son of Aedan mac Gabran, king of Dal Riata, is mentioned in three medieval documents. In Adomnan's *Life of St. Columba* (AD 700), Aedan asks Columba which of his three sons—Artur, Eochaid Find or Domangart—will succeed him; Artur is also mentioned in the genealogical section of the *History of the Men of Scotland* (650–700); and Artur's death is recorded in the *Annals of Tigernach* (AD 1088), in around AD 590 (he died fighting against the *Miathi*, or Maeatae, who lived in the Stirling-Falkirk are of eastern Scotland). Artur is a British name, and it is possible his mother was British.[2]

Further south there was an Arthur ap Pedr, a prince of Dyfed (southwest Wales) born around AD 570–580, and a St. Armel/Arthfael ("Bear-Prince") of Brittany, who flourished in the early 6th century.[3] Recently a slate with the name *Artognou* ("Bear-Knowing") etched on its was found in a 6th century context at Tintagel in Cornwall, the "capital" of the early medieval kingdom of Dumnonia (Devon and Cornwall).[4]

There are several possible explanations for the name Arthur, but the most plausible is that *Arthur* is derived from Brittonic (proto-Welsh) *Arto-uiros*, "Bear-Man." We have no real idea what bears signified to early medieval Britons, but there are some clues. In the Late Iron Age (100 BC to AD 43), cremated bodies were wrapped in bear skins. At Baldock in North Hertfordshire a roughly circular pit 5.24 feet in diameter was dug down into the solid chalk to a depth of nearly one foot. In it were placed "a large bronze cauldron, two bronze dishes, two bronze mounted wooden buckets, two iron firedogs, an Italian Dressel 1A amphora and part of a pig. The cremated body, much of which was recovered from the cauldron, had been wrapped in the skin of a brown bear since phalange bones of the beast were found mixed with those of the human occupant."[5] And at Welwyn Garden City, the cremated body of a man aged about thirty-five was wrapped in a bear skin—the grave also included five wine amphorae, a bronze Campanian pan, a silver cup of Italian origin, colored glass gaming beads, and an iron object which may have been the boss of a shield.[6]

However, this was not an English custom. Burial with bear skins first began in Germany, mostly in male graves, in an area associated with the Germanic Jastorf culture (6th–1st century BC). The oldest burial is one at Döhren in Saxony-Anhalt, northern Germany, which is dated to the second half of the 5th or to the 4th century BC; but most belong to the 1st century BC. They are found as far south as Tisice in the north of the Czech Republic, but are concentrated in central Germany (Thuringia and Hesse), and in northern Germany (Saxony-Anhalt, Mecklenburg–West Pomerania and Lower Saxony).[7] However, two burials with bear-claws are also found further west, at Clemency in Luxembourg, and at Neuwied/Heimbach-Weis near Koblenz in the Rhineland-Palatinate, western Germany.

Bears may have had a religious significance among prehistoric Germanic tribes, but it is equally possible that bears were valued because of their strength and fierceness. Trajan's Column in Rome was completed in AD 113 to commemorate the Emperor Trajan's victory in the Dacian Wars, and the historian Michael Speidel says that scene 36 on Trajan's Column depicts Germanic warriors[8] (the Batavi were a Germanic tribe from the Netherlands):

> On the relief, eight soldiers of the emperor's strike force wear Roman auxiliary uniforms: knee-breeches, tunics, mailshirts, and neckerchiefs. Their weapon of attack is the sword, with which Batavi tribesmen were wont to fight and with which, when they closed in for the shock attack, they stabbed their foes. Unlike other regular auxiliaries on the Column, however, these men sport strange headgear: four wear

openwork crossband helmets, two wear broad-pawed bearskins, two others narrow-pawed wolfskins. Most of them are bearded, while most regular soldiers on the Column are clean-shaven.

The wolfskins and bearskins seen here cover head and shoulders, leaving the arms free [...] Like Herakles, the warriors on the Column fasten their skins over the chest by crossing and knotting the animal's forelegs.

Speidel goes on to say[9] that in the mid–1st century AD bear-hoods came into use among regular non–Germanic Roman auxiliaries, worn by eagle-bearers, standard-bearers and musicians. P. Coussin, he says, believed that "Rome adopted bear-hoods from her northern neighbours. Roman soldiers who killed Germanic bear-warriors may have stripped off their hoods as trophies and worn them as badges of bravery." The earliest known bear-hooded Roman standard-bearer is Pintaius of cohors V Asturum, whose gravestone at Bonn dates to the reign of Claudius (AD 41–54). The next one is Genialis, image-bearer of cohors VII Raetorum, whose gravestone at Mainz dates to the time of Nero (AD 54–68).

By the 4th century there were Germanic soldiers serving in Roman Britain, as indicated by late 4th century metal buckles from leather belts with distinctive Germanic designs. Buckles of this kind have been found at Richborough Roman fort near Sandwich in Kent, where a full burial of a German soldier has been discovered; at the Roman fort of Bradwell-on-Sea in Essex; and also in several of the Roman towns, including London, Leicester and Winchester.[10] The Roman authorities may also have recruited Germanic warriors, not organized in regular military units, to reinforce the defenses of some Romano-British settlements. Roman pottery decorated to suit Germanic taste has been found at Caister Roman fort near Yarmouth in Norfolk, and at Colchester in Essex, Richborough, Aldborough in North Yorkshire, York, Ancaster in Lincolnshire, Brancaster in Norfolk and Leicester.

There is some evidence that bears were important in northern Britain in the Roman period. At the Roman fort of High Rochester in Northumberland there was a dedication, dating from AD 213, to a god called *Matunus*:

> To the god Matunus for the welfare of Marcus Aurelius ... reigning for the good of the human race, Gaius Julius Marcus, emperor's propraetorian legate, set up and dedicated this, under the charge of Caecilius Optatus, tribune.

According to the *Irish Language Dictionary*, *math* is an archaic word for "bear, replaced in Middle Irish by *mathgamain*"—so *Matunus* must be a bear-god.

A bear cameo made of sardonyx (an type of onyx) was found at the Roman fort of South Shields (Tyne and Wear); a jet bear was found in the grave of a child at the Roman fort of Malton, North Yorkshire; and a bear's tooth amulet was found at Chesters Roman fort, Northumberland.[11]

Arthur in the History of the Britons

Probably the first extended mention of Arthur was in the *History of the Britons*, supposedly composed by the Welsh monk Nennius and dated to the early 9th century. The work purports to treat Arthur as a historical figure—a warrior fighting against the Saxons—but also gives us glimpses of a more mythological Arthur, including Arthur the hunter. In Chapter 56 Nennius gives us an account of a series of battles that Arthur is supposed to have fought[12]:

> At that time the Saxons increased their numbers and grew in Britain. On Hengest's death, his son Octha came down from the north of Britain to the kingdom of the Kentishmen, and from him are sprung the kings of the Kentishmen. Then Arthur fought against them in those days, together with the kings of the British, but he was the *dux bellorum* ["leader in battles"]. The first battle was at the mouth of the river called Glein. The second, the third, the fourth and the fifth were on another river, called the Dubglas, which is in the country of Linnuis. The sixth battle was on the river called Bassas. The seventh battle was in Celyddon Forest, that is Cat Coit Celidon. The eighth battle was in Guinnion Fort, and in it Arthur carried the image of the holy Mary, the everlasting Virgin, on his shoulders, and the heathen were put to flight this day, and there was a great slaughter upon them, through the power of Our Lord Jesus Christ and the power of the holy Virgin Mary, his mother. The ninth battle was fought in the city of the Legions. The tenth battle was fought on the bank of the river called Tribruit. The eleventh battle was on the hill called Agned. The twelfth battle was on Badon hill and in it nine hundred and sixty men fell in one day, from a single charge of Arthur's, and no one laid them low save he alone, and he was victorious in all his campaigns.

Hengist of Kent is mentioned by Bede in his *Ecclesiastical History*,[13] and Octa is mentioned later.[14] Most of the battles that Arthur fought are unknown, but we can make educated guesses about most of them. The "river called Glein" may be the River Glen, a tributary of the River Welland in south Lincolnshire, or the River Glen in Northumberland, which flows past Yeavering, where Edwin, king of Northumbria, had a royal palace in the early 7th century.[15]

The "country of Linnuis" is the area of Lincolnshire now known as Lindsey, based on the Roman city of *Lindum* (Lincoln), which may have survived as a British kingdom into the first half of the 6th century.[16] This became the Anglo-Saxon kingdom of Lindsey, which was incorporated into Mercia in the 7th century; the last king was Aldfrith, and one of his ancestors is listed as Cædbæd, whose name is at least partly Celtic (the element *Cæd-* is related to Welsh *cad*, "battle").[17]

The *Cat Coit Celidon*, or Battle of the Caledonian Forest, may not be a real battle but a mythical one, which forms the subject of a poem attributed to the Welsh bard Taliesin called *The Battle of the Trees*.[18] This deeply obscure poem tells the story of a battle between animated trees that probably takes place in the Caledonian Forest in Scotland—here are a few lines to give a flavor of the poem[19]:

> Alder, pre-eminent in lineage, attacked in the beginning;
> Willow and rowan were late to the army;
> Thorny plum was greedy for slaughter;
> Powerful dogwood; resisting prince;
> Rose-trees went against a host in wrath ...
> Elm because of its ferocity did not budge a foot:
> It would strike in the middle, on the flanks, and in the end ...
> Swift and mighty oak: before him trembled heaven and earth;
> Fierce enemy of warriors, his name in wax tablets.

Arthur is mentioned once in the poem, in these enigmatic lines[20]:

> Druids, wise one, prophesy to Arthur;
> There is what is before, they perceive what has been.

The city of the Legions is probably the Roman legionary fort of Chester, where Æthelfrith of Northumbria (593–616) fought a battle against the kingdom of Powys, killing the king of Powys Selyf Sarffgadau. At the time, Chester was in territory associated with the British kingdom of Powys and was perhaps the seat of a branch of the royal dynasty of the Cadelling, whose representatives were prominent in the battle. Under their rule, too, the area was ecclesiastically important. The city was probably the scene of a synod of the British Church shortly after 600, and just to the south there seems to have been an early mother church at Eccleston. Further south was the great monastery of Bangor (Flintshire), 1,200 of whose monks were allegedly slaughtered by the Northumbrians at the battle of Chester as they prayed for a British victory.[21]

Tribruit seems to be the same as *Tryfrwyd*, mentioned in the Welsh poem *Pa gur yv y porthaur?* ("What man guards the gate?"), where the battle involves Bedwyr (Sir Bedivere in later romances) and a certain Manawydan (see below for further discussion of this poem). The site of *Tryfrwyd* is unknown, but O.G.S. Crawford, the pioneer of aerial surveys in archaeology, believed that the battle was fought on the River Forth at the Fords of Frew, to the west of Stirling between Gargunnock and Kippen. This was a key crossing point, regarded as a gateway between the Lowlands and the Highlands.[22] This would be an appropriate place for Manawydan, whose name may be linked to *Manaw Gododdin*, which lay on the south side of the Firth or Forth.[23]

Agned is sometimes called *Bregouin*, and may be the Roman fort of *Bremenium* at High Rochester in Northumberland—a poem written by the Welsh bard Taliesin mentions "The battle of Cellawr Brewyn'" fought by the northern British ruler Urien Rheged.[24] *Cellawr Brewyn* is "Cells of Bremenium," implying there were monks at *Bremenium*. No early religious site is known at *Bremenium*, though churches have been found at other Roman forts, including *Vindolanda* and Housesteads, both in Northumberland.

Badon hill is mentioned in the 6th century sermon by Gildas, *On the ruin and conquest of Britain*, as the siege of Badon Hill, in which the Britons, led by Ambrosius Aurelianus, prevailed over the Saxons—or as Gildas says (Chapter 26), "almost the last great slaughter inflicted upon the rascally crew."[25] Badon is usually placed in the south of England, at Bath in Somerset or Badbury Rings in Dorset, but it could equally be in Lincolnshire. Baumber near Horncastle in Lindsey was *Badeburg* in the Domesday Book of 1086. Horncastle, a fortified Roman "small town," is considered to be part of the Late Roman defenses of the east coast and "one of the leading settlements in the Lincoln area," so a battle at Baumber—at a high point on the Roman road from Lincoln to Horncastle—would not be at all implausible.[26]

Apart from the city of Legions and Badon, these battles belong more to legend and folklore than they do to history, and the legendary status of Arthur is underlined in a section on the "wonders of Britain,"[27] in which Nennius tells us:

> There is another wonder in the region called Buelt. There is a heap of stones, and one stone laid on the heap having upon it the footmark of a dog. When he hunted the swine Troynt, Cabal, which was a dog of the warrior Arthur, impressed the stone with the print of his foot, and Arthur afterwards collected a heap of stones beneath the stone in which was the print of his dog's foot, and it is called Carn Cabal. And people come and take away the stone in their hands for the space of a day and a night, and on the next day it is found on its heap.

Buellt, now Builth or Builth Wells is in Powys, mid–Wales, not far from the border with Herefordshire. Here Arthur is seen as a hunter rather than a warrior, and is associated with a dog called Cabal ("Horse"), and with the "swine Troynt," who features in the 11th century prose tale *Culhwch and Olwen*. Carn Cabal is actually a mountain near Builth Wells called Carngafallt, where four Middle Bronze Age gold torcs were found hidden under a small heap of stones.[28]

A second wonder also features Arthur, this time in Ercing (now Archenfield in western Herefordshire):

> a tomb is located there next to a spring called Licat Amr; and the name of the man who is buried in the tomb was called Amr. He was the son of Arthur the soldier, and Arthur himself killed and buried him in that very place. Men come to measure the grave, and find it sometimes six feet in length, sometimes nine, sometimes twelve, sometimes fifteen.

This may refer to a tumulus called Wormelow Tump (now destroyed), which is near Gamber Head Spring, just to the south of Wormelow.

Arthur in "Pa gur yv y porthaur?"
("What man guards the gate?")

One of the oldest texts in which Arthur is an identifiable character is the Welsh poem *Pa gur yv y porthaur?* ("What man guards the gate?"), which dates to the 9th or 10th century. The poem begins as dialogue between Arthur and Glewlwyd[29]:

> What man guards the gate?
> Glewlwydd Great-Grip.
> Who wants to know?
> Arthur and Cei the Fair.
> Who goes with you?
> The best men in the world.
> You will not come into my house,
> unless you vouch for them.
> I will name them,
> and you shall know them.

Arthur then names two more people:

> Mabon son of Modron,
> servant of Uthir Pendragon.

Mabon, son of Modron, appears in the later prose tale *Culhwch and Olwen*; and Uther Pendragon is Arthur's father in Geoffrey of Monmouth's 12th century *History of the Kings of Britain*. The name Modron is derived from Matrona, the goddess of the River Marne in France, whose sanctuary was at Balesmes-sur-Marne in northeastern France, near the source of the river.[30] In Triad 70 of the *Welsh Triads*, Modron is said to be the mother of Owain, the son of Urien Rheged. Mabon is the Welsh version of the god Maponos ("Divine Boy" or "Divine Son"), from Gaulish *mapos* "young boy, son." Maponos is mentioned in inscriptions from Gaul (Bourbonne-les-Bains in Haute-Marne, northeastern France, and Chamalières in Auvergne, central France), but is mainly attested along Hadrian's Wall, at Brampton in Cumbria, at Corbridge in Northumberland, at Ribchester in Lancashire, and at Vindolanda in Northumberland. In France the most interesting inscription is the Gaulish inscription from Chamalières in Auvergne, which requests help from Maponos in a military revolt. In Britain the most interesting artifact is a silver crescent found at Vindolanda Roman fort near Hexham in Northumberland, with the inscription *Deo Mapono*, "to the god Maponos." There is also a relief at Vindolanda showing Maponos flanked by Sol and Luna (Sun and Moon), and at Ribchester, Maponos is depicted with a hunter goddess.[31]

The name Maponus may be preserved in Lochmaben, Dumfries and Galloway, and, in the Lochmaben Stone in the parish of Gretna, also in Dumfries and Galloway. The Lochmaben Stone (also known as the Clochmabenstane—*cloch* in Gaelic means "stone") is sited 270 yards from the edge of the River Esk at the head of the Solway Firth. The stone itself is a coarse granite erratic, 9 feet, 6 inches high and 6 feet across at its widest point. Another, smaller granite boulder lies 26 yards north-northeast of the Clochmabanestane on the line of the present field boundary.

The ONB (Ordnance Survey Name Book) states that the two stones are all that remains of a stone circle consisting of nine stones, and an earlier reference in the OSA (Old Statistical Account) of 1841 describes "a number of white stones placed upright circling half an acre of ground in an oval form." The Clochmabenstane is first recorded in 1398, when it is mentioned as a location for the settlement of frontier disputes. The stone has been identified with the *Locus Maponi* referred to in the Ravenna Cosmography dating to the 7th century.

In February 1982 the stone fell over and was investigated by Anna Crone.[32] A trench was opened up just north of the fallen stone revealing a shallow ovoid pit full of rounded stones. The stones sealed a gray sandy clay which contained a small concentration of charcoal, which was radiocarbon dated to around 2525 BC, in the late Neolithic. The earliest date for a stone circle comes from Newgrange in Ireland: there the passage grave has been dated to 2585 BC, and it has been argued that the stone circle surrounding the mound is contemporary with it. The stone circle at Stenness, Orkney has been dated to 2536 BC by material from the surrounding henge ditch.

Arthur then names another of his retinue:

> Manawydan son of Llyr,
> whose counsel has been deep:
> Manawyd escaped
> with broken shields from Tryfrwyd.

Manawydan is the hero of the Third Branch of the *Mabinogion*, a collection of medieval Welsh tales written between 1060 and 1200; Tryfrwyd is Tribruit, one of Arthur's battles in the *History of the Britons*. Manawydan, son of Llyr, is related to the Irish god Manannan mac Lir, and in both cases the name *Llyr/Lir* implies that they have some connection with the sea. Rachel Bromwich says that the name *Manawydan* "is evidently related to the territorial name *Manaw*, applied in early times both to the Isle of Man and to the region of *Manaw Gododdin* which lay along the southern shore of the Firth of Forth."[33] Bromwich says that the Welsh *Manawydan* undoubtedly corresponds with the Irish sea-god *Manannan mac Lir*, "who in euhemerized form is associated with the Isle of Man in *Cormac's Glossary* (*circa* 900)":

[He was] a celebrated merchant who was in the Isle of Man. He was the best pilot that was in the west of Europe. He used to know by studying the heavens [i.e., using the sky] the period which would be the fine weather and the bad weather, and when each of these two times would change.

In other Irish tales (*The Voyage of Bran, The Sick-Bed of Cu Chulainn*) Manannan's mythological character is more fully apparent: he presides over the Otherworld island to which Bran and Cu Chulainn are invited.

As Bromwich says, the relationship between *Manannan mac Lir* and *Manawydan fab Llyr* is most unclear, but she believes that both are derived from the same root—Welsh *Manaw*, Irish *Mana, Manu. Manawydan* is based on the nominative case, while *Manannan* is derived from the genitive case, and in support Bromwich cites two Scottish place-names, *Clackmannan* and *Slamannan*[34] (Clackmannan, or "Stone of Manaw" is to the east of Stirling in the Forth Valley, while Slamannan is to the south of Falkirk on the River Avon).

Arthur also mentions another of his men:

> Mabon son of Mellt [Lightning],
> who stained with blood the grass.

Mabon, son of Mellt, also appears in *Culhwch and Olwen. Mellt* means "Lightning," and O'Rahilly compares the name to the Gaulish tribe called the *Meldi*, who gave their name to the commune of Meaux, to the northeast of Paris.[35]

The poem then goes on to the exploits of Arthur and his men:

> Cei would beseech them,
> while killing them three by three.
> At the loss of Celli,
> a fierce defense was gotten;
> Cei would plead with them,
> while he cut them down.
> Though Arthur was laughing,
> blood was flowing
> in the hall of Afarnach,
> fighting with the witch-hag.
> He pierced Penn Palach ["Cudgel-Head"]
> in the dwellings of Dissethach.
> On the mountain of Eidyn
> he fought were-dogs [dogheads].
> By the hundred they fell,
> they fell by the hundred,
> before Bedwyr Bedrydant:
> on the sandbanks of Tryfrwyd,
> Fighting with Garwlwyd [Rough-Grey]—
> fierce was his spirit
> with sword and shield.

Cei and Bedwyr are the Sir Kay and Sir Bedivere of later Arthurian romances. *Celli* may be Arthur's court of *Celliwig* (Welsh *Kelli Wic*), which features in

Culhwch and Olwen, or it could conceivably be *Calleva* (Silchester in Hampshire), the Romano-British capital of the Atrebates tribe, which probably remained in British hands until the 6th century. Cei may be derived from the Roman name *Caius*, or it may be linked to Irish *cai* or *coi*, words which are explained in *Cormac's Glossary* as equivalent to Irish *conair* "path, way."[36]

The "mountain of Edinburgh" is the site of Edinburgh Castle where the Gododdin/Votadini had a Dark Age stronghold. Garwlwyd ("Rough-Grey") sounds like a character in the medieval *Triads of the Island of Britain* (Triad 32) called Gwrgi ("Man-Dog") Garwlwyd, who "used to make a corpse of one of the Cymry every day, and two on each Saturday so as not to slay on Sunday." *Garwlwyd* probably signifies a wolf, and Gwrgi Garwlwyd is likely to be a werewolf.

> An army was worthless against Cei in battle:
> he was a sword in battle;
> his hand took hostages.
> He was a stern captain of the host
> in the defense of his land.
> Bedwyr son of Bridlaw:
> nine hundred in defense,
> six hundred in attack
> was his leading the fight worth.
> I had some fine young men:
> it went better when they were there.
> Before the kings of Emrys,
> I saw Cei charge:
> the taker of spoils,
> the tall man was angry.
> Heavy was his vengeance,
> bitter was his fury.
> When he drank from a horn,
> he would drink for four;
> when he came into battle,
> he would kill like a hundred.
> Unless God himself should perform it,
> Cei could not be killed.
> Cei the Fair and Llacheu
> used to start the battles,
> rushing against the pain of blue-tipped spears.

Llacheu is one of Arthur's sons, and is mentioned in the 10th century *Dialogue of Gwydno Garanhir and Gwyn ap Nudd*[37]:

> I have been where Llacheu was slain
> the son of Arthur, awful [/marvelous] in songs
> when ravens croaked over blood.

The Early Arthur

In the *History of the Britons*, Arthur is depicted as a warrior fighting against the Saxons, while in *Pa gur?* his enemies seem to be more often supernatural beings than human foes. In *Pa gur?* he acquired a retinue, including Cei and Bedwyr, and as time passed, and the Anglo-Saxons became a fact of life, Arthur and his retinue took on giants and supernatural boars as well as witches in the most developed of the Welsh Arthurian tales, *Culhwch and Olwen*. Arthur became a king and, as befits a king, he had a court at Celliwig in Cornwall. But appearances can be deceptive, and despite the court and the Cornish location, Arthur and his retinue operated in the wilderness, often in the "old North," and the tale is peopled with characters from the *Gododdin*.

4

Arthur and His Retinue
in the Welsh Arthurian Tale
Culhwch and Olwen
Warriors in the Wilderness

Culhwch Visits Arthur's Court

Culhwch and Olwen is a prose tale dating from the 11th century, and is
the longest Arthurian tale before Geoffrey of Monmouth composed his *History of the Kings of Britain* in the early 12th century. As the story opens, Cilydd,
son of Cyleddon Wledig or Celyddon Wledig (possibly "lord of the Caledonian forest" in Scotland), takes as his wife Goleuddydd ("Light of the Day"),
daughter of Amlawdd Wledig. Cilydd or *Kilyd* "comrade, companion" was
the father of one of the warriors mentioned in the *Gododdin*[1]; Amlawdd may
be borrowed from a Breton king called *Anblaud*, named in a 12th century life
of the saint as the maternal grandfather of St. Illtud.[2]

Goleuddyd then became pregnant[3]:

> But from the time she grew with child, she went mad, without coming near a
> dwelling. When her time came upon her, her right sense came back to her; it came
> in a place where a swineherd was keeping a herd of swine, and through terror of the
> swine the queen was delivered. And the swineherd took the boy until he came to the
> court. And the boy was baptized, and the name Culhwch given to him because he
> was found in a pig-run.

This story is no doubt linked to the fact that Culhwch's name means "slender
pigling."[4] However, the storyteller reassures us, "the boy was of gentle lineage:
he was first cousin to Arthur," since Arthur's mother was Eigyr or Igraine,
another daughter of Amlawdd Wledig.

Not long after this, Goleuddydd grew sick and died. Some years later,
Cilydd decided to remarry, and was advised to choose the wife of king Doged;

so they killed the king and carried off his wife and daughter (there is a saint called Doged, commemorated in the church of Llandoged in Conwy, north Wales). When the new queen was introduced to Culhwch, she suggested that Culhwch marry her daughter. Culhwch said he was too young to wed, so the queen swore a destiny on him—that he would not find a wife until he won the hand of Olwen, the daughter of Ysbaddaden ("Hawthorn") the Chief of Giants. Culhwch immediately fell in love with Olwen on hearing her name, and his father advised him to seek help from his cousin Arthur.

Culhwch then journeyed to Arthur's court, where he immediately was confronted by a surly porter/gatekeeper (like the one in *Pa gur?*) who refused to admit him. But Culhwch threatened him:

> If thou open it not I will bring dishonors upon thy lord and ill report upon thee. And I will raise three shouts at the entrance of this gate, so that it shall not be less audible on the top of Pengwaedd in Cornwall and in the depths of Dinsel in the North, and in Esgeir Oerfel in Ireland. And every woman with child that is in this court shall miscarry, and such of them as are not with child their wombs shall turn to a burden within them, so that they may never bear child from this day forth.

Eventually the porter consulted Arthur, and Culhwch was admitted. Culhwch then asked Arthur to trim his hair, and Arthur agreed, trimming Culhwch's hair with a gold comb and scissors of silver. The significance of the hair-cutting, "as a recognition and acceptance of consanguinity," is made clear from a passage in the *History of the Britons*, Chapter 39, relating to Vortigern's treatment of his son, a boy born by incest with Vortigern's own daughter (Vortigern is the "proud tyrant" mentioned by Gildas). The boy is placed in the care of St. Germanus, who receives him with the following words[5]:

> "I will be a father to thee, and I will not let thee go until there be given to me a razor with scissors and a comb, and it is permitted to thee to give these to thy carnal father." And thus it was done. And the child obeyed Germanus, and went to his grandfather—that is his carnal father—Guorthegirn, and the boy said to him, "Thou art my father, shear my head and comb my hair." And he was ashamed and remained silent, and would not reply to the child, but rose up, and was very angry.

Once this was done, Culhwch asked Arthur for a favor, and Arthur asked Culhwch to say who he was:

> "[I am] Culhwch son of Cilydd son of Cyleddon Wledig, by Goleuddydd daughter of Anlawdd Wledig, my mother." Quoth Arthur: "True it is. Thou art then my first cousin. Name what thou wilt, and thou shalt have it, whatever thy mouth and thy tongue shall name. God's truth thereon to me, and the truth of thy kingdom's thou shalt have it gladly." "My claim on thee is that thou get me Olwen daughter of Ysbaddaden Chief Giant. And I invoke her in the name of thy warriors."

Culhwch then asked for his favor in the name of a long list of warriors in Arthur's court, including Cei, Bedwyr, Gwyn, son of Nudd, Gwalchmei, son of Gwyar (the Gawain of later literature), Gwenhwyvar Chief of Queens (the Guinevere of later tradition), and Lludd Llaw Eraint ("Lludd Silver-Hand"), Manawydan, son of Llyr, and the 6th century bard Taliesin.

Gwyn, son of Nudd, and Lludd Siver-Hand are both linked to the god Nodens, who is best known in Britain from the Romano-British temple at Lydney Park in Gloucestershire. Lydney Camp is a Late Iron Age promontory fort on the west bank of the Severn close to the Welsh border, established in or just before the 1st century BC. In the 2nd and 3rd centuries AD the Romano-British population there were engaged in iron-mining, and in the late 3rd or early 4th century the hillfort became the site of a Romano-British temple. The presiding deity at Lydney "is named as Nodens on the single curse tablet from the site and on two other metal plaques from the site as Mars Nodons and Nudens Mars." Among the votive objects (ritual deposits) found at the site are dog figurines—some are "highly schematic," but one figurine, possibly of an Irish wolfhound, is "amongst the most accomplished pieces of bronze sculpture from Roman Britain." Other ritual offerings include "the bone representation of a woman and a hollow bronze arm." The "discovery of an oculist's stamp (to be stamped into cakes of eye medicine)" suggests the presence of a healer at the temple.[6] Given the fact that the temple was built on an iron mine, it seems possible that Nodens was an underworld deity connected with mining. Nodens appears in Irish mythology as Nuada, a legendary Irish king who lost a hand or arm in a battle, and had it replaced by a silver hand or arm—which explains the epithet "Silver-hand."

The Search for Olwen

After Culhwch asked for his favor, Arthur sent out messengers to find Olwen, but after a year had passed, they had still not found her. So Cei said that he and Culhwch would go in search of her:

> Cei had this peculiarity, nine nights and nine days his breath lasted under water, nine nights and nine days would he be without sleep. A wound from Cei's sword no physician might heal. A wondrous gift had Cei: when it pleased him he would be as tall as the tallest tree in the forest. Another peculiarity had he: when the rain was heaviest, a handbreadth before his hand and another behind his hand what would be in his hand would be dry, by reason of the greatness of his heat; and when the cold was hardest on his comrades, that would be to them kindling to light a fire.

Arthur also asked Bedwyr to accompany Culhwch and Cei—"although [Bedwyr] was one-handed, three warriors could not shed blood faster than he on the field of battle. Another property he had; his lance would produce a wound equal to those of nine opposing lances." In addition he called on Cynddylig the Guide; Gwrhyr the Interpreter of Tongues; Gwalchmei, son of

Gwyar, his sister's son, "because he never returned home without achieving the adventure of which he went in quest. He was the best of footsoldiers and the best of knights"; and Menw, son of Teirgwaedd, "for should they come to a heathen land he might cast a spell over them, so that none might see them and they see every one."

Culhwch, Cei and the others set out and came to a wide open plain where they saw a huge fort. They eventually met a shepherd, who told them that the fort belonged to Ysbaddaden Chief of Giants. Culhwch gave the shepherd a gold ring, and he took the ring home to his wife. She recognized the ring, for she was the sister of Culhwch's mother, and when Culhwch approached their house, she ran out to greet Culhwch. Culhwch told his aunt that he had come to see Olwen, and she said that Olwen came there very Saturday to wash her head. But Culhwch asked that she be summoned, and she was duly sent for. Culhwch said he wished to marry her, but she told him that her father would die on the day she married. Culhwch and his five companions then went to Ysbaddaden's fortress and Culhwch told him he wished to marry his daughter. The giant told them to come back the next day:

> They rose, and Ysbaddaden Chief Giant snatched at one of the three poisoned stone-spears which were by his hand and hurled it after them. And Bedwyr caught it and hurled it back at him, and pierced Ysbaddaden Chief Giant right through the ball of his knee. Quoth he, "Thou cursed savage son-in-law! I shall walk the worse up a slope. Like the sting of a gadfly the poisoned iron has pained me. Cursed be the smith who fashioned it, and the anvil on which it was wrought, so painful it is!"

The six companions returned the next day and once more asked for the giant's daughter Olwen. The giant said he needed consult Olwen's great-grand-parents, and the six stood up:

> As they arose he took hold of the second stone-spear which was by his hand and hurled it after them. And Menw son of Teirgwaedd caught it and hurled it back at him, and pierced him in the middle of his breast, so that it came out in the small of his back. "Thou cursed savage son-in-law! Like the bite of a big-headed leech the hard iron has pained me. Cursed be the forge wherein it was heated. When I go uphill, I shall have tightness of chest, and belly-ache, and a frequent loathing of meat." They went to their meat.

The men returned once more the next day and again asked for Olwen. Ysbaddaden asked them to raise up the forks—his eyelids had fallen over the balls of his eyes—so he could look at his future son-in-law:

> They arose, and as they arose he took the third poisoned stone-spear and hurled it after them. And Culhwch caught it and hurled it back, even as he wished, and pierced him through the ball of the eye, so that it came out through the nape of the neck. "Thou cursed savage son-in-law! So long as I am left alive, the sight of my eyes will be the worse. When I go against the wind they will water, a headache I

shall have, and a giddiness each new moon. Cursed be the forge wherein it was heated. Like the bite of a mad dog to me the way the poisoned iron has pierced me."

Finally the Giant agreed that Culhwch could marry his daughter, but only on condition that he complete a series of impossible-sounding tasks. The list of tasks is long, and many of them are connected to the hunt for the great boar Twrch Trwyth (the "swine Troynt" in the *History of the Britons*). Culhwch's task is to get the comb, razor, and scissors that are between the ears of Twrch Trwyth, son of Taredd Wledig: only with these will the giant be able to brush his hair. However, before the hunt for Twrch Trwyth can begin, a number of other tasks must be completed. Culhwch must obtain Drudwyn, the "whelp of Greid son of Eri," the leash of Cors Hundred-claws, and the collar of Canhastyr Hundred-hands. Then, says the giant:

> There is no huntsman in the world can act as houndsman to that hound, save Mabon son of Modron, who was taken away when three nights old from his mother. Where he is unknown, or what his state is, whether alive or dead.

Culhwch's Tasks

Once the Giant had set Culhwch all his tasks, he and his companions set off and came to a great fort, the home of Wrnach the Giant (Ysbaddaden has asked for Wrnach's sword). The porter (gatekeeper) refused to let them in, so Cei told the porter he was a "furbisher of swords." The porter told Wrnach, and he said he needed Cei's services, and Cei went in alone. He began polishing the giant's sword. The giant asked Cei if he had an assistant—Cei said he did, and Bedwyr was admitted. Once he was finished his work, Cei gave Wrnach the sword—Cei then said the scabbard needed repairing, took the scabbard and sword, and plunged the sword into the giant's head.

After this they returned to Arthur's court, and decided to search for Mabon, son of Modron. But first Arthur and his men had to find Mabon's kinsman Eidoel son of Aer: he was in prison guarded by Glivi (from Latin *Glevum* "Gloucester"), who agreed to release him. The men then advised Arthur to go home, for "you cannot proceed with your host in quest of such small adventures as these." Arthur then told Gwrhyr Interpreter of Tongues, Cei, Bedwyr and Eidoel to go in search of Mabon. In order to find Mabon, son of Modron, Arthur and his men sought the help of a number of animals, starting with the Blackbird of Cilgwri. According to Bromwich and Evans,[7] *Cilgwri* is likely to be the Wirral peninsula in northwest England, which is referred to as *Killgury* in Camden's *Britannia* (1587). The Blackbird told them:

"When I first came here, there was a smith's anvil in this place, and I was then a young bird; and from that time no work has been done upon it, save the pecking of my beak every evening, and now there is not so much as the size of a nut remaining thereof; yet the vengeance of Heaven be upon me, if during all that time I have ever heard of the man for whom you inquire."

So the Blackbird directed them to the representative of an older race of animals, the Stag of Rhedynfre. Rhedynfre means "Fernhill" or "Brackenhill"—this could be in Aberdaron, at the tip of the Llyn peninsula in northwest Wales, or it could be the original name of Farndon in Cheshire (Old English *fearn-dun*), just to the south of Chester in northwest England—which would bring it relatively close to the Wirral.[8] The Stag told them:

"When I first came hither, there was a plain all around me, without any trees save one oak sapling, which grew up to be an oak with an hundred branches. And that oak has since perished, so that now nothing remains of it but the withered stump; and from that day to this I have been here, yet have I never heard of the man for whom you inquire."

So the stag directed them to the representative of an even older race of animals, the Owl of Cwm Cawlwyd, possibly *Llyn Cowlyd*, a lake between Capel Curig and Llanwrst in Gwynedd.[9] The Owl said to them:

"If I knew I would tell you. When first I came hither, the wide valley you see was a wooded glen. And a race of men came and rooted it up. And there grew there a second wood; and this wood is the third. My wings, are they not withered stumps? Yet all this time, even until to-day, I have never heard of the man for whom you inquire."

So the owl directed them to the representative of a still older race of animals, the Eagle of Gwern Abwy, possibly *Bodernabwy* near Aberdaron.[10] The Eagle said to them:

"I have been here for a great space of time, and when I first came hither there was a rock here, from the top of which I pecked at the stars every evening; and now it is not so much as a span high. From that day to this I have been here, and I have never heard of the man for whom you inquire, except once when I went in search of food as far as Llyn Llyw. And when I came there, I struck my talons into a salmon, thinking he would serve me as food for a long time. But he drew me into the deep, and I was scarcely able to escape from him. After that I went with my whole kindred to attack him, and to try to destroy him, but he sent messengers, and made peace with me; and came and besought me to take fifty fish spears out of his back. Unless he know something of him whom you seek, I cannot tell who may. However, I will guide you to the place where he is."

Llyn Llyw, or "Shining Lake" is a pool situated on the Severn estuary,[11] on the border between Gloucestershire and southeast Wales.

So they went thither; and the Eagle said, "Salmon of Llyn Llyw, I have come to thee with an embassy from Arthur, to ask thee if thou knowest aught concerning Mabon the son of Modron, who was taken away at three nights old from his mother." "As much as I know I will tell thee. With every tide I go along the river upwards, until I come near to the walls of Gloucester, and there have I found such wrong as I never found elsewhere; and to the end that ye may give credence thereto, let one of you go thither upon each of my two shoulders." So Kai and Gwrhyr Gwalstawd Ieithoedd went upon the two shoulders of the salmon, and they proceeded until they came unto the wall of the prison, and they heard a great wailing and lamenting from the dungeon. Said Gwrhyr, "Who is it that laments in this house of stone?" "Alas, there is reason enough for whoever is here to lament. It is Mabon the son of Modron who is here imprisoned; and no imprisonment was ever so grievous as mine, neither that of Lludd Llaw Ereint, nor that of Greid the son of Eri."

After finding where Mabon was imprisoned, the men returned to Arthur, who raised an army, and went to Gloucester; while Arthur's warriors assaulted the fort, Cei broke into the fort and escaped with Mabon on his back.

The "oldest-animal" format of this story is not unique to *Culhwch and Olwen*. In a fragment attributed to the early Greek poet Hesiod, it is reckoned that the crow lives nine human generations, the stag four times as long as a crow, the raven three times as long as a stag, the date-palm nine times as long as a raven, and the Nymphs ten times as long as the date-palm.[12] The Hesiod verses were often quoted in late antiquity and more than once rendered into Latin, so could have been known to anyone with a classical education.[13] However, "neither Classical learning nor any other form of horizontal transmission can account for the extraordinary parallel" between *Culhwch and Olwen* and an episode in the *Mahabharata*, the Indian epic composed between 800 and 400 BC. In the *Mahabharata*, it is related that the royal seer Indradyumna fell from heaven because no one any longer remembered him. He asked the sage Markandeya if he recognized him. Markandeya did not, but told him that there was an owl in the Himalaya who was older than himself and might know him. They went there. The owl said that he did not recognize Indradyumna, but that there was a crane living by a lake who was older than him. The crane was also unable to identify the seer, but said there was a tortoise in the lake who was even older than him and might know more. The tortoise was summoned and after much reflection recognized the seer, who had formerly built his fire altars on the tortoise's back.[14]

Some of the tasks that followed were accomplished as if by chance:

And as Gwythyr son of Greidawl was one day journeying over a mountain, he heard a wailing and a grievous lamentation, and these were a horrid noise to hear. He sprang forward in that direction, and when he came there he drew his sword and smote off the anthill level with the ground, and so saved them from the fire. And they said to him, "Take thou God's blessing and ours, and that which no man can ever recover, we will come and recover it for thee." It was they thereafter who came

50   **Warriors and Wilderness in Medieval Britain**

with the nine hestors [18 bushels] of flax seed which Ysbaddaden Chief Giant had named to Culhwch, in full measure, with none of it wanting save for a single flax seed. And the lame ant brought that in before night.

Ysbaddaden had asked for flax seeds so that he could grow flax and make a veil for Olwen.

As Cei and Bedwyr were sitting on top of Pumlumon on Carn Gwylathyr, in the highest wind in the world, they looked about them and they could see a great smoke towards the south, far off from them, and not blowing across with the wind. And then Cei said, "By the hand of my friend, see yonder the fire of a warrior." They hastened towards the smoke and approached thither, watching from afar as Dillus the Bearded was singeing a wild boar. Now he was the mightiest warrior that ever fled from Arthur. Then Bedwyr said to Cei, "Dost know him?" "I know him," said Cei; "that tis Dillus the Bearded. There is no leash in the world that may hold Drudwyn the whelp of Greid son of Eri, save a leash from the beard of him thou seest yonder. And that too will be of no use unless it be plucked alive with wooden tweezers from his beard; for it will be brittle, dead." "What is our counsel concerning that?" asked Bedwyr. "Let us suffer him," said Cei, "to eat his fill of meat and after that he will fall asleep." Whilst he was about this, they busied themselves making tweezers. When Cei knew for certain he was asleep, he dug a pit under his feet, the biggest in the world, and he struck him a blow mighty past telling, and pressed him down in the pit until they had entirely twitched out his beard with the tweezers; and after that they slew him outright.

Pumlumon or Plynlimon is the highest point of the Cambrian Mountains in the west of Wales.

Cei and Bedwyr then returned to Celliwig in Cornwall, Arthur's court, and presented him with a leash made from the beard of Dillus. Inspired by this gift, Arthur sang this *englyn* (a short poem of three or four lines):

> Cei made a leash
> From Dillus' beard, son of Eurei.
> Were he alive, thy death he'd be.

And because of this Cei grew angry, so that it was with difficulty the warriors of this Island made peace between Cei and Arthur. But nevertheless, neither for Arthur's lack of help, nor for the slaying of his men, did Cei have aught to do with him in his hour of need from that time forward.

Celliwig probably means "forest grove," implying that Arthur's court was in a woodland location.

The story of the accomplishment of the tasks is halted for a short time because Arthur is needed to settle a dispute:

A short while before this Creiddylad daughter of Lludd Silver-hand went with Gwythyr son of Greidawl; and before he had slept with her there came Gwyn son of Nudd and carried her off by force. Gwythyr son of Greidawl gathered a host, and he came to fight with Gwyn son of Nudd. And Gwyn prevailed, and he took prisoner

Greid son of Eri, Glinneu son of Taran, and Gwrgwst the Half-naked and Dyfnarth his son. And he took prisoner Pen son of Nethawg, and Nwython, and Cyledyr the Wild his son, and he slew Nwython and took out his heart, and compelled Cyledyr to eat his father's heart; and because of this Cyledyr went mad. Arthur heard tell of this, and he came into the North and summoned to him Gwyn son of Nudd and set free his noblemen from his prison, and peace was made between Gwyn son of Nudd and Gwythyr son of Greidawl. This is the peace that was made: the maiden should remain in her father's house, unmolested by either side, and there should be battle between Gwyn and Gwythyr each May-calends for ever and ever, from that day till doomsday; and the one of them that should be victor on doomsday, let him have the maiden.

Gwythyr ("Victor"), son of Greidawl ("Fierce"), appears in northern genealogies; Gwrgwst the Half-naked is named as a grandson of Coel Hen, one of the men of the "Old North"; Nwython (the British equivalent of Pictish Nechtan) is mentioned in the *Gododdin*.[15] The name *Cyledyr* can be compared to CULIDORI on a 5th century inscribed stone at Llangefni in Anglesey, north Wales ("The grave of Culidor, here he lies, and of his wife Orvita, the son of Secundus").[16]

Earlier Ysbaddaden had said the Culhwch must get hold of Gwyn, son of Nudd, "whom God has placed over the brood of devils in Annwn, lest they should destroy the present race"; clearly the fight between Gwyn and Gwythyr was a fight between darkness (winter) and light (summer).

The next task involved killing a boar:

After this Arthur went to the North and caught Cyledyr the Wild; and he went after Ysgithyrwyn Chief Boar. And Mabon son of Mellt went, and the two dogs of Glythfyr Ledewig in hand, and Drudwyn the whelp of Greid son of Eri. And Arthur himself took his place in the hunt, and Cafall, Arthur's dog in his hand. And Cadw of Prydain mounted Llamrei, Arthur mare, and he was the first to bring the boar to bay. And then Cadw of Prydein armed him with a hatchet, and boldly and gallantly set upon the boar and split his head in two. And Cadw took the tusk. It was not the dogs which Ysbaddaden had named to Culhwch which killed the boar, but Cafall, Arthur's own dog.

As I said earlier, *Mellt* means "Lightning," and is related to *Mjollnir*, the hammer of the thunder-god Thor in Norse mythology.[17] Cadw of Prydein, according to his name, comes from Pictland, which extended from Fife in eastern Scotland to the Moray Firth in the Highlands of northeast Scotland.

Cadw, also known as Caw, is best known as the father of St. Gildas: both *Lives* of the saint agree that Cadw/Caw ruled somewhere in Scotland. He also appears in the 11th century *Life of St. Cadoc*. The *Life* tells how on a visit to Scotland "the saint and his followers exhumed the bones of an enormous giant, whom St. Cadog miraculously resuscitated, and by doing so won the giant a temporary respite from hell."[18] The giant names himself as *Caw* and tells how he had ruled formerly "beyond mount *Bannauc.*" *Bannauc* is "an ancient Welsh name for a mountain in Scotland. It survives today only in the name of the 'Bannock' Burn" (a stream near Stirling). According to Kenneth Jackson, "*Bannog* is a range of uplands … which almost entirely blocks the narrow neck-land of Scotland between Stirling and Dumbarton.… Strategically [it is] one of the most significant mountain barriers in Scotland, forming the southern boundary of Pictland in the west."[19]

After this Arthur and his men set out on the hunt for the great boar Twrch Trwyth. An equivalent of Twrch Trwyth is to found in Irish mythology. A list of the members of the mythical *Tuatha De Danann* ("People of the Goddess Danu") in the *Lebor Gabala Erenn* ("Book of the Taking of Ireland") gives "Brigid the woman-poet, it was she who possessed Fe and Menn, the two royal oxen.… And with them was Torc Triath, king of the boars of Ireland." Again, in *Cormac's Glossary* the term *Orc Treith* is explained as "Name for a king's son." These two sources are at least as old as the 9th century *History of the Britons*.[20]

The hunt for Twrch Trwyth was an epic event:

> Then Arthur summoned unto him all the warriors that were in the three Islands of Britain, and in the three Islands adjacent, and all that were in France and in Armorica, in Normandy and in the Summer Country, and all that were chosen footmen and valiant horsemen. And with all these he went into Ireland. And in Ireland there was great fear and terror concerning him. And when Arthur had landed in the country, there came unto him the saints of Ireland and besought his protection. And he granted his protection unto them, and they gave him their blessing. Then the men of Ireland came unto Arthur, and brought him provisions.

After this Arthur went to Esgeir Oerfel where the great boar lived with his seven piglets. The Irish fought him, but he laid waste a fifth of Ireland; Arthur's men fought with him, but could not get the better of him; then Arthur fought him for nine days and nights without killing even one piglet. The warriors asked Arthur who he was, and he told them that Twrch Trwyth "was once a king, and that God had transformed him into a swine for his sins":

> Arthur sent Gwrhyr Interpreter of Tongues to seek to have a word with him. Gwrhyr went in the form of a bird and alighted above the lair of him and his seven young pigs. And Gwrhyr Interpreter of Tongues asked him, "For His sake who made thee in this shape, if you can speak, I beseech one of you to come and talk with Arthur." Grugyn Silver-bristle made answer. Like wings of silver were all his bristles; what way he went through wood and meadow one could discern from how his bristles glittered. This was the answer Grugyn gave: "By Him who made us in this shape, we will neither do nor say aught for Arthur. Harm enough hath God wrought on us, to have made us in this shape, without you too coming to fight us." "I tell you, Arthur will fight for the comb, the razor and the shears which are between the two ears of Twrch Trwyth." Said Grugyn, "Until first his life be taken, those treasures will not be taken. And tomorrow in the morning we will set out hence and go into Arthur's country, and there we will do all the mischief we can."

The name *Grugyn* is mentioned in the *Gododdin*, in this line: "Grugyn's shield, before battle's bull its front was shredded"[21]; the comb, razor, and scissors between the ears of Twrch Trwyth "appear to symbolize his royal status,"[22] which would explain why he is unwilling to give them up.

The boar and his seven young pigs then swam to Wales and fought against Arthur and his men for many days, causing great slaughter. Finally Arthur and his men managed to force Twrch Trwyth into the Severn:

> And first they laid hold of his feet, and soused him in Severn till it was flooding over him. On the one side Mabon son of Modron spurred his horse and took the razor from him, and on the other Cyledyr the Wild, on another horse, plunged into Severn with him and took from him the shears. But or ever the comb could be taken he found land with his feet; and from the moment he found land neither dog nor man nor horse could keep up with him until he went into Cornwall.

They then pursued the boar to Cornwall, where they finally succeeded in getting the comb. Twrch Trwyth was driven into the deep sea, and was never seen again.

After this epic battle, Arthur returned to Celliwig to bathe and rest, then prepared himself for the last task, getting the blood of the Very Black Witch from the head of the Valley of Grief in the uplands of Hell (the giant Ysbaddadden needs this to prepare his beard for shaving):

> Arthur set out for the North and came to where the hag's cave was. And it was the counsel of Gwyn son of Nudd and Gwythyr son of Greidawl that Cacamwri and Hygwydd his brother be sent to fight with the hag. And as they came inside the cave the hag grabbed at them, and caught Hygwydd by the hair of his head and flung him to the floor beneath her. And Cacamwri seized her by the hair of her head, and dragged her to the ground off Hygwydd, but she then turned on Cacamwri and dressed them down both and disarmed them, and drove them out squealing and squalling. And Arthur was angered to see his two servants well nigh slain, and he sought to seize the cave. And then Gwyn and Gwythyr told him, "It is neither seemly nor pleasant for us to see thee scuffing with a hag. Send Long Amren and Long Eiddil into the cave." And they went. But if ill was the plight of the first two, the plight of those two was worse, so that God knows not one of the whole four could have stirred from the place, but for the way they were all four loaded on Llamrei, Arthur's mare. And then Arthur seized the entrance to the cave, and from the entrance he took aim at the hag with Carnwennan his knife, and struck her across the middle until she was as two tubs. And Cadw of Prydein took the witch's blood and kept it with him.

The North and the Wilderness in Culhwch and Olwen

There are strong signs that *Culhwch and Olwen* was originally a tale from northern Britain. Culhwch is the son of Cilydd (a character from the

Gododdin), who is the son of Celyddon Wledig, probably "Lord of the Caledonian Forest." Mabon, son of Modron, who was rescued from a dungeon in
Gloucester, was in Roman times associated with Hadrian's Wall in Northumberland and Cumbria, and the Lochmaben Stone in Dumfries and Galloway.
Mabon's mother Modron is said to the mother of Owain of Rheged. Two of
the animal-helpers who enable Culhwch and his companions to find Mabon
may come from the North—the Blackbird from the Wirral, and the Stag from
Farndon in Cheshire. Gwyn, son of Nudd, and Gwythyr, son of Greidawl,
apparently live in the North. Arthur hunted the boar Ysgithyrwyn in the
North with his dog Cafall and with the help of Cadw or Caw of Pictland—
this may be an earlier version of the more famous hunt for Twrch Trwyth.
Although Twrch Trwyth is associated with Ireland, Wales and Cornwall, the
boar Grugyn is a warrior in the *Gododdin*. Finally, the Very Black Witch
apparently lived in the north, and Arthur was again accompanied by Cadw
or Caw of Pictland.

   If *Culhwch and Olwen* was originally a northern tale, why is his court
at *Celliwig* in Cornwall? At the time, of course, Cornwall was the only remaining Celtic part of England, so it was a natural place for Arthur. However,
the *Triads of the Island of Britain* tell a slightly different story. According to
Triad 1, "The Three Tribal Thrones of the Island of Britain," Arthur held sway
at three locations:

> Arthur as Chief Prince in Mynyw [= St. David's], and Dewi as Chief Bishop, and
> Maelgwn Gwynedd as Chief Elder;
>   Arthur as Chief Prince in Celliwig in Cornwall, and Bishop Bytwini as Chief
> Bishop, and Caradawg Strong-Arm as Chief Elder;
>   Arthur as Chief Prince in Pen Rhionydd in the North, and Gerthmwl Wledig as
> Chief Elder, and Cyndeyrn Garthwys as Chief Bishop.

The first two thrones are St. David's in Pembrokeshire (Wales) and Celliwig
in Cornwall; Dewi is St. David, the patron saint of Wales, Maelgwn is a 6th
century king of Gwynedd. Caradawg Strong-Arm first appears briefly in
Chrétien de Troyes' *Érec et Énide* (12th century); the Life of St. Padarn (also
12th century) associates Caradawg Strong-Arm with the colonization of Brittany, and the 13th century *Livre de Carados* ("Book of Caradawg") depicts
him as a king ruling in Vannes (southern Brittany). But it is the third throne
that is of interest here. *Pen Rhionydd* probably refers to the Rhins of Galloway,
and Cyndeyrn Garthwys is St. Kentigern, the late 6th century apostle of the
kingdom of Strathclyde.[23] Celliwig is a forest location, and may have originally
referred to the Caledonian Forest, which, for Welsh writers, was in the western lowlands of Scotland. In *Pa gur?* the poet describes "the loss of Celli,"
and this applies much more to the "Old North" than to Cornwall, which was
never really "lost."

Arthur may have been partly based on a northern hunter god, so it is not surprising that the wilderness plays a significant role in *Culhwch and Olwen*. Culhwch's mother went mad and spent some time in the wilderness before giving birth to Culhwch; Cei and Bedwyr saw Dillus the Bearded while they were on top of Pumlumon, or Plynlimon mountain; and Arthur's court is Celliwig ("forest grove"). The scholar Oliver Padel says that in early Welsh tales Arthur was very clearly "the leader of a band of heroes who live outside of society, whose main world is one of magical animals, giants and other wonderful happenings, located in the wild parts of the landscape."[24] And Thomas Green calls the Welsh Arthur "a pan-Brittonic folkloric hero, a peerless warrior of giant-like stature who leads a band of superhuman heroes that roam the wild places of the landscape."[25]

The Celtic scholar Simon Young sees the Welsh Arthur as an outlaw, and compares him to the Irish hero Fionn (or Finn) mac Cumhaill.[26] Fionn was originally an Irish or Celtic deity, and "in all recorded traditions of him he appears consistently as the adversary and conqueror of malevolent supernatural beings, but he acts rather as a human hero who has a very special and very familiar association with the Otherworld." In the earliest written tradition "he is already portrayed as the leader of a fraternity of free-lancing warriors known by the term *fian*." The principal occupations of this roving brotherhood "were hunting and fighting. In contrast to the protagonists of the other great heroic cycle, that of Cu Chulainn and the men of Ulster, the *fian* area rootless and restless collection of men who have severed their tribal affiliations and given themselves up to the hazardous freedom of the great no man's land that lies beyond the borders of organized society. They roam at will through Ireland and Gaelic Scotland, fighting and hunting and trysting. They are in constant and close association with nature and they continually cross and re-cross the blurred boundary between the secular and supernatural world."[27]

The stories of Fionn were known in Scotland in the medieval period—they are referred to briefly in John Barbour's Early Scots epic *The Bruce* (1375). John Bellenden's 1531 translation of Hector Boece's *Historia Gentis Scotorum* ("History of the Scottish People") narrates the following of Finn mac Cumhaill[28]:

> It is said that Fyn Makcoule, the son of Coelus, Scottis man, was in thir days, ane man of huge stature, xvij cubiits in hicht, and wes ane grete huntar, and richt terribil, for huge quantite, to the pepill, of quhom are mony wlgare fabillis, amang ws, nocht unlyke to thir gestis quhilkis are rehersit of King Arthure. And because his dedis is nocht autorist by attentik autouris, I will rehearse nothing therof ...
>
> [It is said that Finn MacCool, the son of Coelus, a Scottish man, was in their days a man of huge stature, 16 cubits in height, and was a great hunter, and was very terrible, for huge quantity, to the people, of whom are many vulgar fables among us,

not unlike the deeds which are related of King Arthur. And because his deeds are not authorized by authoritative writers, I will relate nothing thereof] ...

However, in the *Book of the Dean of Lismore*, compiled in the first quarter of the 16th century somewhere in eastern Perthshire, there are numerous tales of Finn, in Gaelic rather than English.

So if Arthurian tales were influenced by tales of Fionn mac Cumhaill, then this influence most likely came by way of the Irish-speaking kingdom of Dal Riata in western Scotland, presumably by way the British kingdom of Alt Clut/Dumbarton Rock.

The Celtic scholar John Koch observes: "In Irish genealogical doctrine, Nuadu is mentioned as the great-grandfather of Finn mac Cumail. There is a parallel in the mythological figure Gwynn ap Nudd from Welsh legendary prose texts, since the Welsh name *Gwynn* is the cognate of early Irish *Find*, modern Irish *Fionn*."[29] Certainly Gwynn is something of an outlaw in the Creiddylad episode, he is associated with the Otherworld, and he participates in the hunt for the magical boar Twrch Trwyth.

Meanwhile in England ...

Culhwch and Olwen marks the high point of early Arthurian literature, but before we can go any further in the story of Arthur, we need to look at what was happening in the Anglo-Saxon world, which knew nothing of Arthur but certainly had its own heroes. These included early heroes like the martyred king and saint Oswald of Northumbria, the East Anglian warrior buried in a ship at Sutton Hoo in Suffolk, and the soldier-saint Guthlac, who lived for many years in the wild fens of south Lincolnshire. Later heroes were mainly warriors who fought against the Vikings between the 9th and 11th century, including the Wessex king Æthelstan who defeated the Vikings at the Battle of Brunaburh in 937, but also nameless individuals in poems like *The Wanderer*, exiled in the wilderness like St. Guthlac, and meditating on their solitary state.

5

Anglo-Saxon England
Warriors, Saints, Exile and Wilderness

Oswald: Northumbria's Warrior-Saint

While Arthur was developing as a hero in the "Old North" and Wales, Anglo-Saxon England was producing its own heroes. As I said earlier, after Edwin, Northumbria's first Christian king, was killed by Penda of Mercia and Cadwallon ap Cadfan of Gwynedd at the battle of Hatfield Chase, he was succeeded by Oswald, son of Æthelfrith of Bernicia, who led an army against Cadwallon and defeated and killed him at the Battle of Heavenfield, near Hexham in Northumberland.

Oswald had spent several years in exile in the kingdom of Dal Riata in western Scotland where he converted to Christianity, no doubt under the influence of the monastery of Iona, founded in the 6th century by St. Columba. The stronghold of Dal Riata was at Dunadd in Argyll and Bute. Dunadd was an Iron Age hillfort refortified and occupied between the 6th and the 8th centuries. Excavations of the hillfort have uncovered a wide range of exotic items including imported Continental pottery and glass and raw materials from as far as the Mediterranean, showing that Dunadd was a high-status site.[1] The monastery on the island of Iona, off the west coast of Scotland, was founded in 563 by the Irish monk St. Columba. Columba is mentioned briefly by Bede[2]:

> In the year of our Lord 565, when Justin, the younger, the successor of Justinian, had the government of the Roman empire, there came into Britain a famous priest and abbot, a monk by habit and life, whose name was Columba, to preach the word of God to the provinces of the northern Picts, who are separated from the southern parts by steep and rugged mountains.

The monastery of Iona existed until about the turn of the 8th–9th centuries when the wooden complex was destroyed by Norse raiders. Nothing remains above ground of the original monastery except possibly the vallum, the bank and ditch that enclosed the monastery, and the cell on Tor Abb said to have been used by St. Columba. Excavations have shown that the Columban monastery, which consisted of about a dozen huts and a small church, lay in the vicinity of the early 13th century abbey. A few grave-slabs of the 7th and 8th centuries, generally simple incised or outline crosses, still survive from the early monastery.[3] Columba died in 597, and by 700 he was being venerated as a saint.

Bede was a great admirer of Oswald, and records a pious act that Oswald performed on the eve of the Battle of Heavenfield[4]:

> The place is shown to this day, and held in much veneration, where Oswald, being about to engage, erected the sign of the holy cross, and on his knees prayed to God that he would assist his worshipers in their great distress. It is further reported, that the cross being made in haste, and the hole dug in which it was to be fixed, the king himself, full of faith, laid hold of it and held it with both his hands, till it was set fast by throwing in the earth and this done, raising his voice, he cried to his army, "Let us all kneel, and jointly beseech the true and living God Almighty, in his mercy, to defend us from the haughty and fierce enemy; for He knows that we have undertaken a just war for the safety of our nation." All did as he had commanded, and accordingly advancing towards the enemy with the first dawn of day, they obtained the victory, as their faith deserved. In that place of prayer very many miraculous cures are known to have been performed, as a token and memorial of the king's faith; for even to this day, many are wont to cut off small chips from the wood of the holy cross, which being put into water, men or cattle drinking thereof, or sprinkled with that water, are immediately restored to health.

Adomnan in his *Life of St. Columba*, written around AD 700, also mentions Oswald's piety, but his story does not involve a cross. On the eve of the Battle of Heavenfield, says Adomnan, Oswald had a vision of St. Columba, "beaming with angelic brightness, and of figure so majestic that his head seemed to touch the clouds," who announced to the king[5]:

> "March out this following night from your camp to battle, for on this occasion the Lord has granted to me that your foes shall be put to flight, that your enemy Cadwallon shall be delivered into your hands, and that after the battle you shall return in triumph, and have a happy reign." The king, awaking at these words, assembled his council and related the vision, at which they were all encouraged; and so the whole people promised that, after their return from the war, they would believe and be baptized, for up to that time all that Saxon land had been wrapt in the darkness of paganism and ignorance, with the exception of King Oswald and the twelve men who had been baptized with him during his exile among the Scots.

With his ties to Iona, it is no surprise that Oswald should establish a monastery and bishopric on the island of Lindisfarne in Northumberland, with the Iona monk Aidan as the first bishop. Nothing remains of the Anglo-Saxon church and monastery but a collection of 51 complete or fragmentary Anglo-Saxon carved stones. One 9th-century stone sculpture clearly shows a violent attack by armed men, brandishing Viking-style swords and battle axes,[6] no doubt inspired by the attacks of the 9th century which led to the formation of a Danish kingdom based in York.

Like his predecessor Edwin, Oswald was killed fighting against Penda of Mercia, at the Battle of Maserfield (possibly Oswestry in Shropshire) in 642. According to Bede,[7] Oswald died a pious and bloody death. As he died,

> he prayed to God for the souls of his army. Whence it is proverbially said, "Lord, have mercy on their souls, said Oswald, as he fell to the ground." His bones, therefore, were translated to the monastery which we have mentioned [that is, Lindisfarne], and buried therein: but the king that slew him commanded his head, hands, and arms to be cut off from the body, and set upon stakes. But his successor in the throne, Oswiu, coming thither the next year with his army, took them down, and buried his head in the church of Lindisfarne, and the hands and arms in his royal city.

The royal city, which "has taken its name from Bebba, one of its former queens,"[8] is Bamburgh in Northumberland. Nothing remains of Anglo-Saxon Bamburgh but the Bowl Hole cemetery (6th–8th century),[9] the Bamburgh Sword, and a gold plaque known as the Bamburgh Beast (both 7th century).[10]

After his death at Maserfield, Oswald soon came to be venerated as a saint, as Bede makes clear[11]:

> How great his faith was towards God, and how remarkable his devotion, has been made evident by miracles since his death; for, in the place where he was killed by the pagans, fighting for his country, infirm men and cattle are healed to this day. Whereupon many took up the very dust of the place where his body fell, and putting it into water, did much good with it to their friends who were sick. This custom came so much into use, that the earth being carried away by degrees, there remained a hole as deep as the height of a man. Nor is it to be wondered that the sick should be healed in the place where he died; for, whilst he lived, he never ceased to provide for the poor and infirm, and to bestow alms on them, and assist them.

East Anglia and the Ship-Burial at Sutton Hoo

The kingdom of East Anglia included the modern counties of Norfolk and Suffolk, and perhaps parts of Cambridgeshire. The first king of East Anglia of whom anything is known is Rædewald, who ruled from 599 to 624. He converted to Christianity around 605, but his Christianity was obviously lukewarm, for as Bede says,[12] "in the same temple he had an altar to sacrifice to Christ, and another small one to offer victims to devils." Bede also says[13] that Rædwald was the fourth king that "had the sovereignty of all the southern provinces that are divided from the Northern by the river Humber."

Rædwald may have been the high-status individual buried at Sutton Hoo, near Woodbridge in Suffolk, in the famous ship-burial. In 1939 Mrs. Edith Pretty, a landowner at Sutton Hood, Suffolk, asked archaeologist Basil Brown to investigate the largest of many Anglo-Saxon burial mounds on her property. Inside, he made one of the most spectacular archaeological discoveries of all time. Beneath the mound was the imprint of a 88.5-foot-long ship. At its center was a ruined burial chamber packed with treasures: Byzantine silverware, sumptuous gold jewelry, a lavish feasting set, and most famously, an ornate iron helmet. Tiny fragments showed that rich textiles once adorned the walls and floor, along with piles of clothes ranging from fine linen over-shirts to shaggy woolen cloaks and caps trimmed with fur.[14]

No trace of a body was found during the 1939 excavation of the Sutton Hoo ship burial. Analyses of soil samples for residual phosphate (a chemical left behind when a human or animal body has completely decayed away), taken in 1967 during the British Museum's excavations, support the idea that a body was originally placed in the burial chamber, but had totally decayed in the acidic conditions at the bottom of the ship. A group of coins found inside the purse in the grave provide some clues about who was buried in the ship. There were 37 Frankish gold tremisses, three coin-sized blanks and two ingots. The most recent work on the coins suggests that they were struck between around AD 610–635. This provides an approximate period during which the burial probably took place.[15] There is no evidence that the person buried at Sutton Hoo was Rædwald, but he was certainly the most powerful and most overtly pagan of the East Anglian kings of the period.

A ship burial is described in the Old English poem *Beowulf*, set in pagan Denmark and Sweden. When Scyld Scefing, the ancestor of the legendary Scylding kings of Denmark died[16]

> His warrior band did what he bade them
> when he laid down the law among the Danes:
> they shouldered him out to the sea's flood,
> the chief they revered who had long ruled them.
> A ring-whorled prow rode in the harbour,
> ice-clad, outbound, a craft for a prince.
> They stretched their beloved lord in his boat,
> laid out by the mast, amidships,
> the great ring-giver, Far-fetched treasures
> were piled upon him, and precious gear.
> I never before heard of a ship so well furbished
> with battle-tackle, bladed weapons
> and coats of mail. The massed treasure

was loaded on top of him: it would travel far
on out into the ocean's sway.

No early ship burials are known from Denmark, but they are known from
Vendel in Uppland, southern Sweden. Excavations in the late 19th century
revealed 14 graves in and just beyond the southeast corner of Vendel churchyard. Several of the burials were contained in boats up to 30 feet long, and
were richly furnished with arrangements of weapons (including fine swords),
helmets, cauldrons and chains, beads, shields, and tools. The helmets from
Graves 1, 12 and 14 bear close comparison to the helmet from the early 7th
century ship-burial at Sutton Hoo, with die-stamped plaques depicting scenes
of warriors. The shield from Grave 12 at Vendel is also very comparable to
the Sutton Hoo shield, and has a stamped metal strip mount which is actually
die-linked to an equivalent piece at Sutton Hoo.[17]

The Warriors of Mercia ... and a Saint in the Wilderness

The name *Mercia* is a Latinization of Old English *mierce*, "border-peo-
ple," from Old English *mearc* "border," referring perhaps to people living in
Herefordshire, Shropshire and Cheshire, on the border between the Anglo-
Saxons and the Welsh kingdom of Powys. The first Mercian king of whom
anything is known is Penda, who first entered history in 633, when, with his
Welsh ally Cadwallon ap Cadfan, king of Gwynedd, he defeated and killed
Edwin of Northumbria at the Battle of Hatfield Chase. Bede (Book 2, Chapter
20) calls Penda "a most warlike man of the royal race of the Mercians, and
who from that time governed that nation twenty-two years with various success."[18]

In 642, Penda defeated and killed Oswald of Northumbria at the Battle
of Maserfield; Welsh sources imply that this time he was assisted by Cynd-
dylan, the ruler of the Welsh kingdom of Powys. In 655 Penda attacked King
Oswiu of Northumbria with "thirty legions, led on by most noted commanders," including Æthelhere, king of East Anglia,[19] and Cadafael king of
Gwynedd.[20] He besieged Oswiu at *Iudeu* (location unknown), where Oswiu
offered him a great deal of treasure in return for peace. Then for some reason
Penda and his army moved south, and Penda was killed at the Battle of the
Winwæd, possibly somewhere along the River Went, which rises near Feath-
erstone in West Yorkshire, and flows into the River Don a few miles from
Doncaster in South Yorkshire. Most of Penda's leaders were killed, including
Æthelhere. As Bede says: "The battle was fought near the river Winwæd, which
then, with the great rains, had not only filled its channel, hut overflowed its

banks, so that many more were drowned in the flight than destroyed by the sword."[21]

The 7th century history of Mercia was placed under the spotlight by the discovery of the Staffordshire Hoard. In 2009 a huge hoard of Anglo-Saxon gold and silver metalwork was found in a field outside the village of Hammerwich in Staffordshire, to the southwest of Lichfield, the seat of the bishops of Mercia. The hoard consists of over 3,500 pieces, comprising up to 11 pounds of gold and 2.9 pounds of silver. Most of the items in the hoard appear to be military, and most were made in the first half of the 7th century. The weaponry includes many finely worked silver and gold sword decorations removed from weapons, including 66 gold sword hilt collars and many gold hilt plates, some with inlays of cloisonné garnet in zoomorphic designs, and 86 sword pommels. The only items in the hoard that are not military are two (or possibly three) crosses; the largest of these may have been an altar or processional cross. One of the most intriguing items in the hoard is a small strip of gold inscribed on both sides with a quotation from the Old Testament (*Numbers* 10:35) in Latin which translates as "Rise up, Lord, may Your enemies be scattered and those who hate You be driven from Your face." Rivet holes show that it was originally fastened to another, larger object, possibly a reliquary or the cover of a Bible. The weaponry, which was chopped up, comes from different regions of England, and was probably collected over several decades.[22] Dating the hoard is difficult. The weaponry dates from the first half of the 7th century, but the gold strip probably dates from the late 7th or early 8th century. The inscription on the strip is a prayer for spiritual protection invoked against the torment of demons by the desert father St. Anthony, and was re-employed for this purpose by the early 8th century Mercian warrior-turned-hermit St. Guthlac, and by the 10th century Archbishop of Canterbury St. Dunstan. Significantly, it was also quoted around 700 in a consoling prophecy by Guthlac to King Æthelbald (716–757): Æthelbald was at that time in exile and was comforted by the hermit saint who assured him that he would come to power without bloodshed.[23]

Penda was a pagan, but in 653, while Penda was still king of the Mercians, the Middle Angles of the East Midlands, who were ruled by Penda's son Peada, converted to Christianity. As Bede says of Peada[24]:

> Being an excellent youth, and most worthy of the title and person of a king, he was by his father elevated to the throne of that nation, and came to Oswiu, king of the Northumbrians, requesting to have his daughter Alchflaed given him to wife; but could not obtain his desires unless he would embrace the faith of Christ, and be baptized, with the nation which he governed. When he heard the preaching of truth, the promise of the heavenly kingdom, and the hope of resurrection and future immortality, he declared that he would willingly become a Christian, even though he should be refused the virgin; being chiefly prevailed on to receive the faith by

King Oswiu's son Alhfrith, who was his relation and friend, and had married his sister Cyneburh, the daughter of King Penda.

So Peada was baptized by Bishop Finan at the royal estate called "At the Wall" (possibly Newcastle-upon-Tyne). Peada returned home, bringing with him four priests, including Cedd and Adda, and Betti, who were English, and Diuma, who was Irish. They preached to the Middle Angles, with Penda's tacit approval:

> Nor did King Penda obstruct the preaching of the word among his people, the Mercians, if any were willing to hear it; but, on the contrary, he hated and despised those whom he perceived not to perform the works of faith, when they had once received the faith, saying, "They were contemptible and wretched who did not obey their God, in whom they believed."

One of Mercia's most famous early saints was Guthlac, the saint who comforted the future king Æthelbald when he was in exile. Guthlac (673–714) was born into the Mercian nobility and became a soldier at the age of 15. After nine successful years, he rejected the warrior life and became a monk at the monastery of Repton in Derbyshire. After living under monastic rule for several years, he withdrew to Crowland, a secluded, desolate, spot on an "island" (actually, a gravel peninsula) in the fens of south Lincolnshire, to pursue the life of the religious hermit. About 740, scarcely twenty-five years after the saint's death, Ælfwald, King of the East Angles (713–749), commissioned Felix to write Guthlac's *Life*, which was translated into Old English in the 11th century. Here Guthlac's wilderness retreat is described in some detail[25]:

> There is in Britain a fen of immense size, which begins from the river Granta [Cam] not far from the city which is named Grantchester [Cambridge]. There are immense marshes, now a black pool of water, now foul running streams, and also many islands, and reeds, and hillocks, and thickets, and with manifold windings wide and long it continues up to the north sea.

Guthlac decided he would live there and asked the inhabitants about a suitable place to live:

> Whereupon they told him many things about the vastness of the wilderness. There was a man named Tatwine who said he knew an island especially obscure, which ofttimes many men had attempted to inhabit, but no man could do it on account of manifold horrors and fears, and the loneliness of the wide wilderness; so that no man could endure it, but every one on this account had fled from it. When the holy man Guthlac heard these words, he bid him straightway show him the place, and he did so; he embarked in a vessel, and they went both through the wild fens till they came to the spot which is called Crowland.

There Guthlac made his home[26]:

> There was on the island a great mound raised upon the earth, which some of yore men had men had dug and broken up in hopes of treasure. On the other side of the mound a place was dug, as it were a great water-cistern. Over the cistern the blessed man Guthlac built himself a house at the beginning, as soon as he settled in the hermit-station. Then he resolved he would use neither woollen nor linen garment, but that he would live all the days of his life in clothing of skins, and so he continued to do.

Guthlac's "great mound" sounds like a Neolithic or Bronze Age barrow, or burial mound. It is known that there was a Bronze Age barrow cemetery constructed along the axis of the gravel peninsula, on a line running northeast from Crowland Abbey to Anchorage Field.[27]

A year after Guthlac died, the grave was opened and the body found incorrupt. The Guthlac cult began, centered on his shrine at Crowland, to which his sister Pega had given his psalter and scourge. It soon became popular, with Wiglaf, king of Mercia (827–840), and Ceolnoth, archbishop of Canterbury (who was cured of ague by the saint in 851), among its devotees.[28]

Wessex and the Fight Against the Vikings

Wessex Emerges from the Shadow of Mercia

Judging from Bede's *Ecclesiastical History of the English People*, Northumbria was the dominant Anglo-Saxon kingdom in the 7th century, at least until 685, when Ecgfrith was defeated and killed by the Picts at the battle of Dun Nechtain. By the time Bede died in 735, Mercia, a kingdom centered on Tamworth and Lichfield in Staffordshire (West Midlands), had become the dominant force in England under three strong kings, Æthelbald (716–757), Offa (757–796) and Coenwulf (796–821). After the death of Coenwulf, Wessex, which originally covered Hampshire, Wiltshire, Somerset and Dorset, emerged as the strongest kingdom, and led the fight against Danish (Viking) raiders and invaders in the 9th century.

Wessex emerged as a kingdom in the 7th and early 8th century, with bishoprics at Winchester (Hampshire) and Sherborne (Dorset), and monasteries at Wimborne Minster (Dorset), Malmesbury (Wiltshire), and Glastonbury (Somerset). However, after the abdication of King Ine in 726, Wessex seems to have been dominated by Mercia, and it was not until the reign of king Egbert (802–839) that Wessex emerged from Mercia's shadow. Egbert's predecessor was Beorhtric (786–802), and in its entry for 839, the *Anglo-Saxon Chronicle* (late 9th century till 1154) says[29] of Egbert: "before he was king, Offa. king of Mercia, and Beorhtric, king of Wessex, put him to flight from the land of the English to the land of the Franks for 3 years; and Beorhtric helped Offa because he had his daughter as his queen"—all of which suggests that Offa and Beorhtric saw Egbert as a threat. On his accession in 802, the *Chronicle* reports[30]:

> Ealdorman Æthelmund rode from the Hwicce across at Kempsford; the Ealdorman Weohstan met him with the Wiltshire men; and there was a big battle, and both ealdormen were killed there and the Wiltshire men took the victory.

The Hwicce were a sub-kingdom of Mercia based in Winchcombe, Gloucestershire; and Kempsford is in Gloucestershire on the Thames, on the border with Wiltshire. The "Wiltshire men" are in Old English the *Wilsaete*, literally, "those who dwell by the River Wyle," referring to the old Wiltshire capital of Wilton, now overshadowed by its larger neighbor Salisbury.

The first years of Egbert's reign were otherwise uneventful, apart from the entry for 815, when the *Chronicle* notes: "King Egbert spread devastation in Cornwall from east to west." In 821, Coenwulf, the last of Mercia's three great rulers, died and Mercia entered a period of instability with two short-lived kings, Ceolwulf and Beornwulf. In 825, says the *Chronicle*, King Egbert and King Beornwulf fought at Ellendun ("Elder-bush Down"), and "Egbert took the victory; and a great slaughter was made there." The location of Ellendun is not known for certain, but it is generally thought to be somewhere near Swindon in Wiltshire. After Egbert defeated the Mercians at Ellandun[31]:

> he sent his son Æthelwulf from the army, and Ealhstan his bishop, and Wulfheard his ealdorman, to Kent with a great troop, and they drove Baldred the king north over the Thames; and the inhabitants of Kent turned to him—and the Surrey men and the South Saxons and East Saxons—because earlier they were wrongly forced away from his relatives. And, for fear of the Mercians, the same year the king and the nation of the East Angles sought King Egbert as their guardian and protector; and that year the East Angles killed Beornwulf, king of the Mercians.

Æthelwulf was Egbert's only known son, and Ealhstan was bishop of Sherborne in Dorset.

In 829, says the *Chronicle*, Egbert "conquered the Mercian kingdom, and all that is south of the Humber, being the eighth king who was sovereign of all the British dominions" (the first seven being the kings listed by Bede). The *Chronicle* also says that Egbert "led an army against the Northumbrians as far as Dore, where they met him and offered terms of obedience and subjection" (Dore is a village in south Yorkshire, probably then on the border between Mercia and Northumbria). Egbert's domination of Mercia did not last long, for two years later, says the *Chronicle*, "Wiglaf recovered his Mercian kingdom."

Early Viking Attacks
and the "Great Heathen Army"

It was during Egbert's reign that the Vikings began attacking England. In 834 the "heathens" attacked the Isle of Sheppey in Kent, and the following year, says the *Chronicle*, Egbert fought with "thirty-five pirates" at Carhampton in west Somerset, but the Danes "remained masters of the field." These attacks continued through the reign of Egbert's son Æthelwulf (839–858), his son Æthelbald (858–860), Æthelbald's brother Æthelberht (860–865), and Æthelberht's brother Æthelred (865–871).

The Viking attacks became more serious in 865, with the arrival of the "Great Heathen Army." In 865, according to the *Chronicle*, "came a large heathen army into England, and fixed their winter-quarters in East Anglia." The Great Heathen Army crossed into Northumbria and in 866 captured York. In the following year the Danes went into Mercia and fixed their winter headquarters at Nottingham. The Mercian king Burgred appealed to Æthelred for help, and the two besieged Nottingham, and made peace with the Danes. In 870 the Danes conquered the kingdom of East Anglia and destroyed the monastery of *Medeshamstede* (Peterborough). The *Anglo-Saxon Chronicle* records in its entry for 870[32]:

> Here the raiding-army went across Mercia into East Anglia, and took winter-quarters at Thetford; and in that year St Edmund the king fought against them and the Danish took the victory, and killed the king and conquered all that land, and did for all the monasteries to which they came. At the same time they came to Peterborough: burned and demolished, killed abbot and monks and all that they found there, brought it about so that what was earlier very rich was as it were nothing.

In 986 or 987 the monks of Ramsey in Cambridgeshire commissioned Abbo of Fleury, a monk from Fleury Abbey near Orléans in France who was living in Ramsey at the time, to write a Latin life of Edmund, the *Passio Sancti Eadmundi*. Abbo relates that the Danish leader captured Edmund at a place called *Hæglesdun*, had him tied to a tree, scourged, shot at with arrows, and finally beheaded. To prevent a decent burial, the Danes threw the saint's head into a thicket in *Hæglesdun* wood. Christians in the neighborhood buried the body and when peace was restored searched for the head. Eventually the head attracted their attention by calling "here, here, here," and they found it between the paws of an immense wolf, which was guarding it from other wild animals. The people took the head back to their village and fitted the head back on the body—the two miraculously reunited. The villagers buried the perfect uncorrupt body, which began to work miracles, and built a simple church over it.[33] Eventually the body was translated to Bury St. Edmunds in Suffolk; Abbo says it was perfect but had, as a sign of martyrdom, a thin red line like a thread of silk around its neck.[34]

Then in 871 the Danish army entered Reading. King Æthelred and his brother Alfred led their army to Reading and fought the Danes, but could not defeat them. Four nights later, Æthelred and Alfred again fought the Danes at Ashdown in Berkshire, and the Danes were defeated. Then two weeks later Æthelred and Alfred fought with the Danes at Old Basing near Basingstoke in Hampshire, and this time the Danes were victorious. Two months later Æthelred and Alfred again engaged the Danes at *Meretune*, the location of which is uncertain. Heahmund, bishop of Sherborne was killed, and Aethelred died shortly after, though it is not clear whether this was a result of the battle. He was buried in Wimborne Minster (Dorset).

Æthelred was succeeded by his brother Alfred, and within a month, as the *Chronicle* records, "King Alfred fought against all the Army with a small force at Wilton, and long pursued them during the day; but the Danes got possession of the field."

The Vikings at Repton (Derbyshire)

In 873–874 the Great Heathen Army overwintered at Repton in Debyshire. In the 1970s Martin Biddle and his wife uncovered the Viking-defended compound and probable slipway at Repton, constructed by the Vikings during 873–874. The D-shaped enclosure was open on the northwest side where the River Trent formed the boundary. St. Wystan's Church was incorporated in the southeast side, in effect providing a defended gateway to the enclosure. Five Viking inhumations lay to the northwest of the church, within the enclosure, and two lay south of the church on the line of the enclosure bank.

The most significant grave was the skeleton of a 35 to 45-year-old man, nearly 6 feet tall, lying in a grave north of the church which was originally marked by a 12-inch square wooden post which may once have been carved and painted. In an abutting grave was a second male inhumation; he was aged around 20, and was, perhaps, a retainer to his older companion. The elder male was a person of obvious importance, who seems to have died in a battle or skirmish, perhaps with the Anglian locals around the time of the Trent Valley incursion. The warrior had fallen from a blow to the skull, and whilst on the ground had been dispatched with a sword-cut that had severed the femoral artery. He was buried in true pagan fashion; round his neck was leather belt around his waist had been secured with a decorated copper-alloy buckle, and by his left side was an iron sword in a fleece-lined wooden scabbard covered with leather, with another copper-alloy buckle holding a suspension-strap for the sheath. By the sword hilt was a folding iron knife, plus a second knife with a wooden handle, whilst halfway down the scabbard was an iron key. Between the thighs was the tusk of a wild boar and lower down, perhaps originally in a bag or box, was the humerus of a jackdaw.[35]

As part of their operations in the village, the Biddles investigated 250-year-old reports of a mass burial discovered around 1686 by a laborer named Thomas Walker who was seeking stone in a close west of the church. Between 1980 and 1986 the Biddles investigated the site, finding the disordered bones of some 264 individuals whose defleshed bones had originally been stacked, charnel-wise, against the walls of the inner or easterly room of the building, which was probably constructed as a mausoleum to hold the body of the Mercian monarch Æthelbald who died in AD 757. It was in a ruinous state in 873 when the Vikings cut it down to ground level and floored the eastern room with a thick layer of marl. The central burial and the mass bone deposit was laid directly on this layer as a single deliberate act. When Walker stumbled upon this collective burial he had rummaged among the bone stack, dismantled the primary burial and subsequently taken away much of the stonework of the walls. Biddle's careful reinvestigation found many items missed by the earlier delvers, including a fine iron axe, a sword blade, two large seaxes, a key, chisel, and five silver pennies, all minted between 872–874, and securely dating the deposit to the Viking occupation of Repton between 873–874. The central "coffin" might well have been a slab-built cist, with the collective bones neatly stacked around it, completely filling up the wall space around the coffin. Heavy timber joists had then been laid on the tops of the cut-down walls to form a roof subsequently covered with flat slabs. The sunken structure had then been sealed by a low stone cairn, the cairn itself masked by a mound of pebbles edged by a kerb of upright stones. Careful clearing of the area around the rectangular barrow revealed four sunken pits which may have served for organic offerings; they were later filled with stones. Finally, at the southwest corner of the heap was a large pit containing four juvenile skeletons, one accompanied by a sheep's jaw. A square hole lined with upright stones on the south side of the hollow may have held a timber grave marker. The carefully arranged interments must represent human sacrifices associated with the closing of the tumulus. Of the bones piled in the eastern chamber, 82 percent were male, and of the 69 skulls rescued, only one was over 45 years old. The male bones were all robust in appearance, and suggest a Scandinavian population such as the Viking host which wintered in the Repton area at the time suggested by the coin evidence found within the barrow.

It is obvious that the burial mound must have housed some outstanding Viking figure, who died during that winter and was interred with blatant pagan rites and accompanied by some 250 fellow-warriors whose excarnated (de-fleshed) bones seem to have been disinterred to accompany the great man in death. They were probably soldiers who had died during the campaign, subsequently exhumed and piled in the chamber to lie with the body of their leader. The Biddles believe that the man buried there was Ivar the

Boneless, possibly the brother of Healfdeane, one of the leaders of the Viking force at Repton in 873–874. Ivar was noted as a man of exceptional cruelty and ferocity, and his nickname may indicate that he lacked legs, or may simply mean that he was long-legged or tall. The Viking force split into two in 874 and the occasion may have prompted the high status, elaborate and complex burial in the cairn placed on the bluff above the Trent at Repton. The entombment is without parallel in Europe during the Viking age, and it is interesting that one saga notes that Ivar died and was buried in England "in the manner of former times," an allusion to the fact he was interred in a barrow.[36]

To the east of Repton, in Heath Wood, Ingleby, are the remains of a Viking barrow cemetery. The cemetery was in use during the late 9th to early 10th centuries AD and includes 59 barrows laid out in four spatially distinct groups. The barrows are circular or sub-circular in shape and vary in height from 8 inches to 4 feet, 8 inches and in diameter, from 20 feet to over 42 feet. Some were constructed with an encircling ditch and others without. Approximately a quarter of the mounds have been excavated. The excavations have shown that although cremation burials are contained within some of the mounds, others are empty. The most common artifact to be found during the excavation was nails, being found in five of the fifteen mounds excavated and all but one of the cremation burials. The nails represent what remained of ships planking, upon which some of the burials were laid. This was a traditional, early Viking custom and ranks the burials amongst the earliest Viking graves in the British Isles.[37]

King Alfred Defeats the Vikings

In 876, the Great Heathen Army[38]

> stole away from the West Saxon Army into Wareham [Dorset]. And the king made peace with the raiding-army, and they swore him oaths on the sacred ring, which earlier they would not do to any nation, that they would quickly go from his kingdom; and then under cover of that, they stole away from the army by night—the mounted raiding-army into Exeter.

This "sacred ring" is mentioned in the Icelandic *Eyrbyggja Saga* (The Saga of the People of Eyri), which is preserved in manuscripts dating from the 13th and 14th centuries: "[on the altar of the temple] lay a solid ring weighing twenty ounces, upon which people had to swear all their oaths. It was the business of the temple priest to wear this ring on his arm at every public meeting."

In 878, the Danes launched a surprise attack on the royal estate at Chippenham, northwest Wiltshire, where Alfred was staying. As the *Chronicle* says:

> Here the raiding-army stole away in midwinter after Twelfth Night to Chippenham, and over-rode and occupied the land of Wessex, and drove many of the people across the sea, and the greatest part of the others they over-rode—and they turned to them—except for Alfred the king, and he with a small troop went through woods and into swamp fastnesses.

Alfred managed to escape and sought refuge at Athelney, an island in the Somerset Levels, where he later established a monastery. The place-name Athelney has been translated as "isle of the aethelings" and is traditionally the place where Æhelwine (son of Cynegils, the first Christian king of Wessex) lived as a hermit in the mid–7th century. From there Alfred was able to rally local fyrds, or militias, from Somerset, Wiltshire and Hampshire. In May 878 Alfred met the combined militias of Somerset, Wiltshire and "that part of Hampshire which is on this side of the sea"[39] (that is, west of Southampton Water), at *Egbert's Stone* east of Selwood, and fought the Danes at *Ethandun* (possibly Edington, near Westbury in Wiltshire). He defeated them and pursued them to Chippenham, where he starved them into submission. Guthrum, the leader of the Danes, surrendered to Alfred, and agreed to convert to Christianity. Some weeks later, according to the *Chronicle*, Guthrum and 29 of his men were baptized at Aller near Athelney, and this baptism was further celebrated at the royal estate of Wedmore in Somerset. Following this celebration, Guthrum and the Danes left Wessex and returned to East Anglia.

In the same year, or perhaps in 880, after the death of the Mercian king Ceolwulf II, Alfred and Guthrum signed a treaty which divided up the kingdom of Mercia: Alfred would rule West Mercia, while Guthrum would incorporate East Mercia into an enlarged kingdom of East Anglia—the Danish lands now included Essex, East Anglia, the Kingdom of York (Northumbria between the River Tees and the Humber), the so-called Five Boroughs (the Mercian towns of Derby, Leicester, Lincoln, Nottingham and Stamford in the East Midlands), and some towns to the south like Northampton, Bedford and Cambridge. Alfred also had control of the Mercian city of London. After this Alfred began styling himself "King of the Anglo-Saxons" as well as King of Wessex.

Edward the Elder and the Five Boroughs

Alfred died in 899 and was succeeded by his eldest son Edward, usually referred to as Edward the Elder. From the time of Edward well into the 11th century, the history of England is marked by almost continuous conflict between the English and the Danes, who not only controlled large parts of northern England at the time, but also the kingdom of Dublin in Ireland.

Edward's succession did not happen smoothly. Edward's cousin Æthelwold, the son of King Æthelred, rose in revolt and seized Wimborne and

Christchurch, both in Dorset. Edward marched to Badbury near Wimborne and offered battle, but Æthelwold refused to leave Wimborne. Then under cover of night, Æthelwold fled Wimborne and joined the Danes in Northumbria, who "received him as their king."[40] In 901, Æthelwold came with a fleet to Essex, which submitted to him. The following year he encouraged the Danes of East Anglia to rise up, so that they "overran all the land of Mercia, until they came to Cricklade, where they forded the Thames" (Cricklade is in the far north of Wiltshire). Edward then ravaged East Anglia, and ordered his forces to return home. But the Kentish men refused to obey the order, and engaged the Danes in battle: the Danes were victorious, but Æthelwold was killed.

After the last king of Mercia died, Æthelred (who may have been descended from Æthelbald of Mercia) took control of West Mercia, but soon acknowledged the lordship of King Alfred. Æthelred died in 911, and was replaced by his wife Æthelflæd, the daughter of King Alfred, who is commonly referred to as the Lady of the Mercians. For the next several years, the Lady of the Mercians and Edward concentrated on regaining lands lost to the Danes. In 913, according to the *Chronicle*, Edward went with some of his forces into Essex, to Maldon, and "camped there while they made and strengthened the stronghold of Witham; and a good part of the people who were earlier under the control of Danish men submitted to him."[41] In 917, Æthelflæd, Lady of the Mercians, conquered the town of Derby, one of the Five Boroughs that had been under Danish control, and in 918 she conquered Leicester, another of the Five Boroughs. In 919, Edward conquered Bedford, which had also been under Danish control.

But Edward's greatest successes came in 920 and 921. In 920, he captured Towcester (Northamptonshire) and the Danish fortress of Colchester (Essex). Then as the *Chronicle* records: "Jarl [Earl] Thurferth and the holds [hereditary landowners] turned to him, together with all the raiding-army which belonged to Northampton, as far north as the Welland, and sought him as their lord and protector"[42] (in other words, the Danes of Northamptonshire and south Lincolnshire submitted to Edward). Later that year, Edward went with the West Saxon army to Colchester and "improved the stronghold and restored it where it was broken down earlier." Then "a great tribe, both in East Anglia and Essex, that was before under the control of the Danes, turned to him."

In 921 Edward went with his army to Stamford (Lincolnshire), and "ordered the stronghold to be made on the south side of the river; and all the people who belonged to the more northerly stronghold [the Danes] submitted to him and sought him as their lord."[43] Then from there he went to Nottingham (one of the Five Boroughs) and "captured the stronghold and ordered it to be improved and occupied, both with Englishmen and Danish; and all the people that was settled in the land of Mercia, both Danish and English, turned to him."[44]

The Fight for Northumbria

Edward died in 924, and was succeeded by his son Æthelstan. In 925 "King Æthelstan and Sihtric king of the Northumbrians came together at Tamworth ... and Æthelstan gave away his sister to him." The following year Sihtric, the Danish king of Dublin, and his brother Guthfrith led a fleet from the Viking settlement of Dublin to retake York, but were unsuccessful.

In 937, Æthelstan and his half-brother Edmund defeated Anlaf (Olaf Guthfrithsson, King of Dublin), at the Battle of Brunaburh (possibly Bromborough in the Wirral, northwest England). Æthelstan's enemies included not only Olaf Guthfrithsson of Dublin, but also Constantine, king of Alba (Scotland north of the River Forth), and Owen, king of Strathclyde, which at the time was based in Govan, now a district of Glasgow. The battle was celebrated in an Old English poem, which glorifies the West Saxons[45]:

> In this year King Aethelstan, Lord of warriors,
> ring-giver to men, and his brother also,
> Prince Eadmund, won eternal glory
> in battle with sword edges
> around Brunanburh. They split the shield-wall,
> they hewed battle shields with the remnants of hammers.
> The sons of Eadweard, it was only befitting their noble descent
> from their ancestors that they should often
> defend their land in battle against each hostile people,
> horde and home. The enemy perished,
> Scots men and seamen,
> fated they fell. The field flowed
> with blood of warriors, from sun up
> in the morning, when the glorious star
> glided over the earth, God's bright candle,
> eternal lord, till that noble creation
> sank to its seat. There lay many a warrior
> by spears destroyed; Northern men
> shot over shield, likewise Scottish as well,
> weary, war sated.
> The West-Saxons pushed onward
> all day; in troops they pursued the hostile people.
> They hewed the fugitive grievously from behind
> with swords sharp from the grinding.
> The Mercians did not refuse hard hand-play to any warrior
> who came with Anlaf over the sea-surge
> in the bosom of a ship, those who sought land,
> fated to fight. Five lay dead

on the battle-field, young kings,
put to sleep by swords, likewise also seven
of Anlaf's earls, countless of the army,
sailors and Scots. There the North-men's chief was put
to flight, by need constrained
to the prow of a ship with little company:
he pressed the ship afloat, the king went out
on the dusky flood-tide, he saved his life.
Likewise, there also the old campaigner through flight came
to his own region in the north—Constantine—
hoary warrior. He had no reason to exult
the great meeting; he was of his kinsmen bereft,
friends fell on the battle-field,
killed at strife: even his son, young in battle, he left
in the place of slaughter, ground to pieces with wounds.
That grizzle-haired warrior had no
reason to boast of sword-slaughter,
old deceitful one, no more did Anlaf;
with their remnant of an army they had no reason to
laugh that they were better in deed of war
in battle-field—collision of banners,
encounter of spears, encounter of men,
trading of blows—when they played against
the sons of Eadweard on the battle field.

Departed then the Northmen in nailed ships.
The dejected survivors of the battle,
sought Dublin over the deep water,
leaving Dinges mere
to return to Ireland, ashamed in spirit.
Likewise the brothers, both together,
King and Prince, sought their home,
West-Saxon land, exultant from battle.
They left behind them, to enjoy the corpses,
the dark coated one, the dark horny-beaked raven
and the dusky-coated one,
the eagle white from behind, to partake of carrion,
greedy war-hawk, and that gray animal
the wolf in the forest.

Æthelstan died in 939, and was succeeded by his half-brother Edmund. Anlaf (Olaf Guthfrithsson), the King of Dublin who was defeated at Brunaburh, invaded and occupied Northumbria and the Five Boroughs of Mercia. Anlaf/Olaf died in 942, and Edmund reconquered the Five Boroughs. This victory was also celebrated in verse, in the *Chronicle* entry for 942[46]:

Here King Edmund, lord of the English,
guardian of kinsmen, beloved instigator of deeds,

conquered Mercia, bounded by the Dore,
Whitwell Gap and the Humber river,
broad ocean-stream; five boroughs:
Leicester and Lincoln,
and Nottingham, likewise Stamford also
and Derby. Earlier the Danes were
under Northmen, subjected by force
in heathens' captive fetters,
for a long time until they were ransomed again,
to the honour of Edward's son,
protector of warriors, King Edmund.

In 944, Edmund reconquered Northumbria and expelled King Anlaf (Olaf III) Sihtricsson, also known as Amlaíb Cuarán, and King Raegnals Guthfrithsson. In 946 Edmund was murdered, stabbed by a certain Leof at Pucklechurch, south Gloucestershire.

Edmund was succeeded by his brother Eadred. In 948 he launched an attack on Northumbria because "they had taken Eric for their king" (this was Eric Bloodaxe, a Norwegian who may have been King of Norway). Another version of the *Chronicle* says that Eric replaced Amlaíb Cuarán, who had become king in 949. At any rate, In 954 the Northumbrians expelled Eric, and Eadred became undisputed ruler of Northumbria.

The Welsh Prophesy of Britain

Not surprisingly, the Welsh were happy to see their Anglo-Saxon neighbors being attacked and occupied by the Vikings, and some time in the first half of the 10th century there appeared a poem called the *Armes Prydein*, or the *Prophecy of Britain*, which predicts a time when the Anglo-Saxons will be driven out by "an alliance between the Welsh and the men of Dublin [Vikings],/the Irish of Ireland, Anglesey and Pictland,/the men of Cornwall and Strathclyde."[47] The Welsh will be led by Cadwaladr king of Gwynedd (655–682), and Cynan, the ancestor of all the kings of Brittany.[48] Very little is known about Cadwaladr, and it is possible he was confused with his father Cadwallon.[49] The battle against the Anglo-Saxons will be a bloody one[50]:

The muse foretells that the day will come,
When the men of Wessex meet for counsel,
In one chorus, with one counsel, and England will burn,
In the hope that our beautiful hosts will be put to shame;
But the foreigners will have to set out into daily flight.
They do not know where they are wandering, where they are going,
    where they will be.
They will attack in battle like the bear from the mountain,

To avenge the blood of their comrades.
There will be a blow from a spear, continuous bloodletting;
The kinsman [of ours] will not spare his opponent's body.
There will be heads split open, emptied of brain.
There will be widowed wives and riderless horses.
There will be terrible crying before the onslaught of the attackers,
And many severed hands before the armies separate.
Messengers will meet death
When the corpses stand so tightly that they stand up against each other …

Interestingly, the *Prophecy* makes no mention of Arthur, but puts the obscure Cadwaladr in charge of the Welsh forces.

Æthelred the Unready
and King Cnut of Denmark

Northumbria may have returned to English control, but it was not long before Vikings began attacking England once more. In 978 Æthelred, known as Æthelred the Unready, became king, and in 980, Southampton (Hampshire) was plundered by the "pirate army, and most of the population slain or imprisoned." In the same year, the Isle of Thanet (Kent) was overrun, and Cheshire "was plundered by the pirate army of the North." In 981 Padstow (Cornwall) was plundered, and there were raids along the coasts of Devon and Wales. In 982, "three ships of the pirates" plundered Portland (Dorset). In 991, Anlaf (Olaf Tryggvason, later King of Norway) launched an attack: Ipswich (Suffolk) was plundered, and "very soon afterwards was Alderman Britnoth slain at Maldon. In this same year it was resolved that tribute should be given, for the first time, to the Danes, for the great terror they occasioned by the sea coast. That was first 10,000 pounds" (note that this means 10,000 pounds of silver). The Battle of Maldon in Essex ended with an English defeat; the battle is commemorated in the Old English poem of the same name. Here is an extract from the poem, in which the Anglo-Saxon leader Byrhtnoth confronts the Vikings[51]:

> Then Byrhtnoth marshalled his soldiers,
> riding and instructing, directing his warriors
> how they should stand and the positions they should keep,
> and ordering that their shields properly stand firm
> with steady hands and be not afraid.
> Then when he beheld that people in suitable array,
> he dismounted amid his people, where he was most pleased to be,
> there amid his retainers knowing their devotion.

Then a Viking messenger told Byrhtnoth that the Vikings would withdraw if the English gave them treasure, but Byrhtnoth was unwilling:

Byrhtnoth spoke, his shield raised aloft,
brandishing a slender ash-wood spear, speaking words,
wrathful and resolute did he give his answer:
"Hear now you, pirate, what this people say?
They desire to you a tribute of spears to pay,
poisoned spears and old swords,
the war-gear which you in battle will not profit from.
Sea-thieves messenger, deliver back in reply,
tell your people this spiteful message,
that here stands undaunted an Earl with his band of men
who will defend our homeland,
Aethelred's country, the lord of my
people and land. Fall shall you
heathen in battle! To us it would be shameful
that you with our coin to your ships should get away
without a fight, now you thus far
into our homeland have come.
You shall not so easily carry off our treasure:
with us must spear and blade first decide the terms,
fierce conflict, is the tribute we will hand over."

In 993 the Vikings attacked Bamburgh in Northumberland and the River Humber, which separates Yorkshire from Lincolnshire. In 994 Anlaf/Olaf and King Swein Forkbeard of Denmark attacked London, but they suffered heavy losses and left, attacking instead the coasts of Essex, Kent, Sussex and Hampshire. King Æthelred and his councilors agreed to offer the Vikings tribute and supplies if they would stop their attacks. They agreed, and took up winter-quarters in Southampton, where "they were fed by all the subjects of the West Saxon kingdom" and given "16,000 pounds in money." Then King Æthelred sent Bishop Ælfheah of Winchester and Alderman Æthelweard, who "led Anlaf with great pomp to the king at Andover. And King Æthelred received him at episcopal hands, and honoured him with royal presents. In return Anlaf promised, as he also performed, that he never again would come in a hostile manner to England"[52] (although the *Chronicle* is unclear on this point, it seems that Anlaf/Olaf was confirmed as a Christian in the ceremony at Andover in Hampshire).

However, in 997 a Viking army attacked the coast, from Cornwall to the Severn Estuary and Wales. In the same year they entered the River Tamar, on the border between Cornwall and Devon, attacking the fortified town of Lydford (Devon) and destroying Tavistock Abbey in Devon. In 998 the Viking army entered the River Frome, which flows into Poole Harbour near Wareham, and attacked Dorset. The Vikings made the Isle of Wight their base, and took supplies from Hampshire and Sussex. In 999 the Vikings sailed up the Thames and the Medway to Rochester (Kent), and laid waste most of west Kent. In 1001 there was "a great commotion in England in consequence of an invasion by the Danes, who spread terror and devastation wherever they went, plundering and burning and desolating the country with such rapidity, that they advanced in one march as far as the town of Alton; where the people of Hampshire came against them, and fought with them."[53] Then the Vikings went west into Devon, and were joined by Pallig, a Dane in the service of Æthelred who deserted his lord. After this, they burned Kingsteignton in the south of Devon, and attacked Pinhoe and Broad Clyst (both in Devon), after which they proceeded east to the Isle of Wight, and burned down Waltham in Hampshire. In response to this, the king made peace with the Vikings and paid them a tribute of 24,000 pounds.

Then on St. Brice's Day (November 13) in 1002, Æthelred ordered the massacre of all Danes in the kingdom, because he believed they were plotting to kill him. Danes had been settled in England for over a century, and perhaps Æthelred's decree only applied to new arrivals[54]:

> Certainly some Danes were killed, and not only men. In Oxford threatened Danish families broke into St Frideswide's church for sanctuary and resisted the local people's efforts to evict them. The local people then burned the place down and the Danes were presumably burned alive with it. This is mentioned in a charter Æthelred issued to St Frideswide's in 1004, in which he recalled his order for "a just extermination" of all the Danes in England, who had "sprouted like a cockle amongst the wheat." His decree had been issued, he claimed, on the advice of all his leading men and magnates.

In 2008 archaeologists digging in the grounds of St. John's College, Oxford found a mass grave—the remains of 37 people[55]:

> All the bodies in the grave appear to have been male (though two were too young for their sex to be determined), and most were between 16 and 25 years old. As a group, they were tall, taller than the average Anglo-Saxon at the time, and strong, judging by the large muscle-attachment areas of their bones. Despite their physical advantages, all these men appear to have met violent ends. One had been decapitated, and attempts at decapitation had seemingly been made on five others. Twenty-seven suffered broken or cracked skulls. The back and pelvic bones of 20 bodies bore stab marks, as did the ribs of a dozen others. A number of the skeletons had evidence of charring, indicating that they were burned prior to burial.

Analysis of the bones and teeth showed that the victims had diets with a substantial amount of seafood—somewhat more than is found in the diets of the local population at the time. The bones were radiocarbon dated to 960–1020, so the people buried there could well have been victims of the St. Brice's day Massacre.

Perhaps in retaliation for the massacre, King Swein Forkbeard attacked England in 1003, destroying Exeter, and plundering and burning the royal town of Wilton in Wiltshire. The following year Swein returned, plundering and burning Norwich and Thetford (Norfolk). In 1006 the Vikings returned after midsummer and sacked Sandwich in Kent; Æthelred recruited an army from Wessex and Mercia, which fought against the Vikings throughout the autumn, but without success. After November 11, the Vikings returned to their base on the Isle of Wight; at Christmas they proceeded through Hampshire into Berkshire, and burned Wallingford in Oxfordshire, then returned to their ships, passing through Winchester. In 1007, a tribute if 36,000 pounds was paid to the Viking army, together with provisions supplied from all parts of England.

In 1009 the army of the Swedish Viking Thorkell the Tall came to Sandwich and headed for Canterbury, but the men of Kent made peace with them and gave them 3,000 pounds. The army then turned toward the Isle of Wight, and burned and plundered widely in Sussex, Hampshire and Berkshire. After November 11, the army returned to Kent and took up winter quarters along the Thames, receiving supplies from Kent and Essex. From there they attacked London and burned Oxford. In 1010, the army marched into East Anglia, which they plundered and burned for three months. By 1111, the army had overrun East Anglia, Essex, Middlesex, Oxfordshire, Cambridgeshire, Hertfordshire, Buckinghamshire, Bedfordshire, half of Huntingdonshire, much of Northamptonshire and, to the south of the Thames, Kent, Sussex, Surrey, Berkshire, Hampshire, and much of Wiltshire. Finally, in 1012, the king paid the Viking army 48,000 pounds in tribute.

In 1013, Swein Forkbeard of Denmark came with his fleet to Sandwich, and soon entered the Humber and River Trent, and sailed up the Trent to Gainsborough (Lincolnshire). Earl Uhtred and all the Northumbrians submitted to him, as did the people of Lindsey (north Lincolnshire), the people of the Five Boroughs, and "all the army to the north of Watling Street" (that is, in the old Danelaw). Swein then moved south to Oxford and Winchester, which submitted to him; London at first refused to submit, but submitted after Swein went to Bath (Somerset) and received the submission of all the western shires of Wessex. Æthelred went into exile in Normandy, the homeland of his wife Emma, the sister of Richard II, Duke of Normandy.

Swein died in early 1014, and the Danes declared his son Cnut as king. Meanwhile, the English recognized Æthelred as king, and he landed in Lindsey (Lincolnshire) with an army that "plundered and burned, and slew all the men that they could reach." After the death of Swein, Olaf Haraldsson, the future king of Norway (1015–1028), apparently attacked London and destroyed London Bridge. This event is not mentioned in the *Anglo-Saxon Chronicle*, but the oldest Norse saga about Olaf Haraldsson does mention it[56]:

> Yet you broke [destroyed] the bridge[s] of London,
> Stout hearted warrior,
> You succeeded in conquering the land.
> Iron swords made headway
> Strongly urged to conflict;

Ancient shields were broken,
Battle fury mounted.

After his death Olaf was venerated as a saint, and six churches in London were dedicated to him, including one in Southwark, very close to the bridge he is supposed to have pulled down.[57]

After Swein died, Cnut fled to Denmark, but returned in 1015 and conquered most of England. Æthelred died in 1016, and the English recognized his son Edmund Ironside as king. Edmund and Cnut clashed at the Battle of Assandun in Essex, and Cnut was victorious. The two kings met at Alney near Deerhurst in Gloucestershire, and made a treaty: Edmund was to rule over Wessex, and Cnut would govern the rest of England. Shortly afterwards, Edmund Ironside died in mysterious circumstances, and Cnut married Emma, the widow of King Æthelred.

The Last Anglo-Saxon King

Cnut died in 1035, and was succeeded in Denmark by Harthnacut, son of Cnut and Emma, and in England by Harthnacut's half-brother Harold Harefoot. Harold died in 1040, and Harthnacut assumed the throne of England as well as Denmark. He died in 1042, and was succeeded by his half-brother Edward the Confessor, the son of Æthelred and Emma of Normandy, and step-son of Cnut, who was to be virtually the last Anglo-Saxon king.

Heroes in Exile

The *Battle of Brunaburh* and the *Battle of Maldon* give the impression that the only heroes in Anglo-Saxon England were warriors. However, as the 11th century Old English *Life of St. Guthlac* shows, there was another kind of hero—the hero exiled in the wilderness. One of the most famous poems of exile is *The Seafarer*, which probably dates from the 10th century. Here are the opening lines[58]:

> May I of my own self   1
> Truth's song reckon,
> Tell of my traverse,
> How I oft endured
> Days of hardship
> Times of trouble,
> Bitter the breast-care
> That I suffered,
> Known at my keel   5
> Many a care's hold,

Dread wave-fall
When wary night-watch
Found me often
There at the ship's stem,
Wave-tossed, by cliff-wall.
Cold-fettered
My feet
Frost-bound
In cold clasp, 10
Where cares seethed then
Hot at the heart;
Hunger within tore
The sea-weary soul.

This knows he not
Who on land
Lives lightly,
How I care-wretched
On ice-cold ocean
Weathered winter 15
In ways of exile,
Bereft of my brethren,
Hung with ice-shards;
Hail showers flew.
There I heard naught
But sea roaring,
Ice-cold wave.
Whiles the swan's song
Had I for pleasure; 20
Gannet's clamour,
Curlew's crying,
For men's laughter;
The mew's singing
For mead-drinking.

The other famous poem of exile is *The Wanderer*, which also dates from the 10th century. Here is an extract from the poem[59]:

Oft I alone must 8
Utter my sadness,
Each day before dawn.
Living there's none,
No man, to whom
I'd clearly speak
My innermost mind.
I know among
Men the custom 12
Truly is noble,
That a man his

Thoughts fast bind,
Hiding his mind-hoard,
Whatever he thinks.
For weary spirit may not
Withstand fate's ways,
Nor does a sad heart   16
Offer men aid.
Thus oft the glory-bound
Bind fast their
Drear thoughts
In their own breast.

So I, wandering,
Bereft of my homeland,
Far from my kinsmen,   20
Oft in wretchedness,
My innermost feelings
Am forced to fetter,
Over these long years
Since my lord I buried
Deep in the dark earth,
And from there, dully,
Went winter-freighted   24
Over the icy waves,
Seeking, hall-bereft,
Some giver of treasure;
Where I, far or near,
Might find one
In mead-hall, who
Knew my own clan,
Or might console me,   28
I, the friendless one,
Win with his welcome.
He who suffers it
Knows how sorrow
Makes cruel companion
To one who goes light
Of all loving friends.
Wandering wreathes him   32
Not the winding gold,
A frozen spirit, now,
Not the fruits of earth.
Halls of the warriors
He recalls, gold-giving:
How in youth his lord,
Ever treasure's friend,
Won him to wining.   36
Dead now all joyfulness!

Beowulf, Anglo-Saxon England's Most Famous Hero

The Battle of Brunaburh extols the virtues of the warrior, and *The Seafarer* laments the fate of the hero exiled in the wilderness, but the most famous Anglo-Saxon poem, *Beowulf*, presents us with a peerless warrior battling monsters—Grendel, Grendel's Mother, and a fire-breathing dragon—rather than ordinary mortals, and a depiction of the wilderness that was so well known in Anglo-Saxon England that it was used in a depiction of Hell in a late 10th century homily. Beowulf and Arthur may seem to have nothing in common, but in fact they are both descended from bears: Arthur's bear-ancestors are so remote that he has lost all characteristics of the bear, while Beowulf's bear-ancestors are so close that Beowulf is able to kill Grendel with his powerful bear-hug. However, there is one episode in *Beowulf* that highlights a distant relationship between Beowulf and the Arthur of *Culhwch and Olwen*.

6

Beowulf, an Anglo-Saxon Mythical Hero

The Poem Beowulf

The *Battle of Brunaburh* and the *Battle of Maldon* show us warrior heroes, and *The Seafarer* and *The Wanderer* show us heroes in the wilderness, but the most complete hero of Anglo-Saxon England was undoubtedly the mythical hero Beowulf. There is no agreement on when, where or for whom the poem *Beowulf* was composed; all we know for certain is that it was composed some time between the 8th century and the early 11th century. The only manuscript we have dates from around AD 1000, and is written mainly in the West Saxon (Wessex) dialect of Old English, with some features of the Anglian (Northumbrian and Mercian) dialect.

The poem begins with Hrothgar, the pagan king of the Danes, building a mead-hall at Heorot. Hrothgar belonged to the royal family called Scylding, and according to Scandinavian tradition, the seat of the Scyldings was at Lejre near Roskilde on the island of Zealand, just across the sea from Angeln, the traditional home of the Angles. The remains of a Viking hall complex was uncovered southwest of Lejre in 1986–1988 by Tom Christensen of the Roskilde Museum. Wood from the foundation was radiocarbon-dated to about 880. It was later found that this hall was built over an older hall which has been dated to 680. In 2004–2005, Christensen excavated a third hall located just north of the other two, which was built in the mid–6th century, and was about 164 feet long.[1] The third hall could well correspond to Hrothgar's mead hall.

But the building of the mead-hall did not go unnoticed by the forces of darkness, in the translation by the late Irish poet Seamus Heaney[2]:

> Then a powerful demon, a prowler through the dark,
> nursed a hard grievance. It harrowed him
> to hear the din of the loud banquet

> every day in the hall, the harp being struck
> and the clear song of a skilled poet
> telling with mastery of man's beginnings,
> how the Almighty made the earth
> a gleaming plain girdled with waters;
> in His splendour He set the sun and moon
> to be earth's lamplight, lanterns for men,
> and filled the broad lap of the world
> with branches and leaves; and quickened life
> in every other thing that moved.
> So times were pleasant for the people there
> until finally one, a fiend out of hell,
> began to work his evil in the world.
> Grendel was the name of this grim demon
> haunting the marches, marauding round the heath
> and the desolate fens; he had dwelt for a time
> in misery among the banished monsters,
> Cain's clan, whom the Creator had outlawed
> and condemned as outcasts. For the killing of Abel
> the Eternal Lord had exacted a price:
> Cain got no good from committing that murder
> because the Almighty made him anathema
> and out of the curse of his exile there sprang
> ogres and elves and evil phantoms
> and the giants too who strove with God
> time and again until He gave them their reward.

Beowulf may be set in pagan times, but it refers to *Genesis*: the poets sing of "man's beginnings/how the Almighty made the earth," and Grendel belongs to "Cain's clan," the descendants of Cain who was cursed for having killed his brother Abel.

> So, after nightfall, Grendel set out
> for the lofty house, to see how the Ring-Danes
> were settling into it after their drink,
> and there he came upon them, a company of the best
> asleep from their feasting, insensible to pain
> and human sorrow. Suddenly then
> the God-cursed brute was creating havoc:
> greedy and grim, he grabbed thirty men
> from their resting places and rushed to his lair,
> flushed up and inflamed from the raid,
> blundering back with the butchered corpses.

After this massacre, Heorot was abandoned, and stood empty for twelve years. Hrothgar and his men turned to pagan gods:

> Sometimes at pagan shrines they vowed
> offering to idols, swore oaths

> that the killer of souls might come to their aid
> and save the people. That was their way,
> their heathenish hope; deep in their hearts
> they remembered hell. The Almighty Judge
> of good deeds and bad, the Lord God,
> Head of the Heavens and High King of the World.
> was unknown to them. Oh, cursed is he
> who in time of trouble has to thrust his soul
> in the fire's embrace, forfeiting help;
> he has nowhere to turn. But blessed is he
> who after death can approach the Lord
> and find friendship in the Father's embrace.

Then Beowulf, a warrior from the court of Hygelac, king of the Geats from Geatland (Götland in Sweden), hears of Hrothgar's troubles and sails to Denmark to help him. After a feast at Heorot, Beowulf and his companions stay in the mead-hall and wait for Grendel:

> In off the moors, down through the mist-bands
> God-cursed Grendel came greedily loping.
> The bane of the race of men roamed forth,
> hunting for prey in the high hall.
> Under the cloud-murk he moved towards it
> until it shone above him, a sheer keep
> of fortified gold. Nor was that the first time
> he had scouted the grounds of Hrothgar's dwelling—
> although never in his life, before or since.
> did he find harder fortune or hall-defenders.

Then Grendel entered the mead-hall:

> He saw many men in the mansion sleeping,
> a ranked company of kinsmen and warriors
> quartered together. And his glee was demonic,
> picturing the mayhem: before morning
> he would rip life from limb and devour them,
> feed on their flesh; but his fate that night
> was due to change, his days of ravening
> had come to an end. Mighty and canny,
> Hygelac's kinsman was keenly watching
> for the first move the monster would make.

Then Grendel struck and Beowulf responded:

> he grabbed and mauled a man on his bench,
> bit into his bone-lappings, bolted down his blood
> and gorged on him in lumps, leaving the body
> utterly lifeless, eaten up,
> hand and foot. Venturing closer,

his talon was raised to attack Beowulf
where he lay on the bed, he was bearing in
with open claw when the alert hero's
comeback and armlock forestalled him utterly.
The captain of evil discovered himself
in a handgrip harder than anything
he had ever encountered in any man
on the face of the earth. Every bone in his body
quailed and recoiled, but he could not escape.
He was desperate to flee to his den and hide
with the devil's litter, for in all his days
he had never been clamped or cornered like this.
Then Hygelac's trusty retainer recalled
his bedtime speech, sprang to his feet
and got a firm hold. Fingers were bursting,
the monster back-tracking, the man overpowering.
The dread of the land was desperate to escape,
to take a roundabout road and flee
to his lair in the fens. The latching power
in his fingers weakened; it was the worst trip
the terror-monger had taken to Heorot.
And now the timbers trembled and sang,
a hall-session that humbled every Dane
inside the stockade: stumbling in fury,
the two contenders crashed through the building.

Finally, Beowulf was victorious:

Then an extraordinary
wail arose, and bewildering fear
came over the Danes. Everyone felt it
who heard that cry as it echoed off the wall,
a God-cursed scream and strain of catastrophe,
the howl of the loser, the lament of the hell-serf
keening his wound. He was overwhelmed,
manacled tight by the man who of all men
was foremost and strongest in the days of this life.
[…]
Then he who had harrowed the hearts of men
with pain and affliction in former times
and had given offence also to God
found that his bodily powers failed him.
Hygelac's kinsman kept him helplessly
locked in a handgrip. As long as either lived,
he was hateful to the other. The monster's whole
body was in pain, a tremendous wound
appeared on his shoulder. Sinews split
and the bone-lappings burst. Beowulf was granted

the glory of winning; Grendel was driven
under the fen-banks, fatally hurt,
to his desolate lair. His days were numbered,
the end of his life was coming over him,
he knew it for certain; and one bloody clash
had fulfilled the dearest wish of the Danes.

But Beowulf retained a trophy of Grendel: "the hand the hero displayed/ high up near the roof: the whole of Grendel's/ shoulder and arm, his awesome grasp." Grendel also left other traces of his passing:

The bloodshot water wallowed and surged,
there were loathsome upthrows and overturnings
of waves and gore and wound-slurry.
With his death upon him, he had dived deep
into his marsh-den, drowned out his life
and his heathen souls: hell claimed him there.

Grendel may have been dead, but his mother was still alive. Grendel's mother

monstrous hell-bride, brooded on her wrongs.
She had been forced down into fearful waters,
the cold depths, after Cain had killed
his father's son, felled his own
brother with a sword. Branded an outlaw,
marked by having murdered, he moved into the wilds,
shunned company and joy. And from Cain there sprang
misbegotten spirits, among them Grendel,
the banished an accursed, due to come to grips
with that watcher in Heorot waiting to do battle.

Some time after Beowulf killed Grendel, a great feast was held at Heorot to honor Beowulf. Now his mother

had sallied forth on a savage journey,
grief-racked and ravenous, desperate for revenge.
She came to Heorot. There inside the hall,
Danes lay asleep, earls who would soon endure
a great reversal, once Grendel's mother
only by as much as an amazon warrior's
strength is less than an armed man's
when the hefted sword, its hammered edge
and gleaming blade slathered in blood,
razes the sturdy boar-ridge off a helmet.
Then in the hall, hard-honed swords
were grabbed from the bench, many a broad shield
lifted and braced; there was little thought of helmets
or woven mail when they woke in terror.

The hell-dam was in panic, desperate to get out,
in mortal terror the moment she was found.
She had pounced and taken one of the retainers
in a tight hold, then headed for the fen.

This retainer, Aeschere, was Hrothgar's dearest friend, and he was heartbroken at his loss. Beowulf was summoned, and told where he might find Grendel's mother:

"I have heard it said by my people in hall,
counsellors who live in the upland country,
that they have seen two such creatures
prowling the moors, huge marauders
from some other world. One of these things,
as far as anyone can ever discern,
looks like a woman; the other, warped
in the shape of a man, moves beyond the pale
bigger than any man, an unnatural birth
called Grendel by the country people
in former days. They are fatherless creatures,
and their whole ancestry is hidden in a past
of demons and ghosts. They dwell apart
among wolves on the hills, on windswept crags
and treacherous keshes [causeways], where cold streams
pour down the mountain and disappear
under mist and moorland. A few miles from here
a frost-stiffened wood waits and keeps watch
above a mere; the overhanging bank
in a maze of tree-roots mirrored on its surface.
At night there, something uncanny happens:
the water burns. And the mere-bottom
has never been sounded by the sons of men.
On its bank, the heather-steppe halts:
the hart in flight from pursuing hounds
will turn to face them with firm-set horns
and die in wood rather than dive
beneath its surface. That is no good place.
When wind blows up and stormy weather
makes clouds scud and the skies weep,
out of its depths a dirty surge
is pitched towards the heavens. Now help depends
again on you and on you alone.
The gap of danger where the demon waits
is still unknown to you. Seek it if you dare.
I will compensate you for settling the feud
as I did last time with lavish wealth,
coffers of coiled gold, if you come back."

Hrothgar and Beowulf set out to find Grendel's mother, following the tracks she had left:

> He went in front with a few men,
> good judges of the lie of the land,
> and suddenly discovered the dismal wood,
> mountain trees growing out at an angle
> above grey stones: the bloodshot water
> surged underneath. It was a sore blow
> to all of the Danes, friends of the Shieldings,
> a hurt to each and every one
> of that noble company when they came upon
> Aeschere's head at the foot of the cliff.
> Everybody gazed as the hot gore
> kept wallowing up and an urgent war-horn
> repeated its notes: the whole party
> sat down to watch. The water was infested
> with all kinds of reptiles. There were writhing sea-dragons
> and monsters slouching on slopes by the cliff,
> serpents and wild things such as those that often
> surface at dawn to roam the sail-road
> and doom the voyage. Down they plunged,
> lashing in anger at the loud call
> of the battle-bugle. An arrow from the bow
> of the Geat chief got one of them
> as he surged to the surface: the seasoned shaft
> stuck deep in his flank and his freedom in the water
> got less and less. It was his last swim.
> He was swiftly overwhelmed in the shallows,
> prodded by barbed boar-spears,
> cornered, beaten, pulled up on the bank,
> a strange lake-birth, a loathsome catch
> men gazed at in awe.

Then Beowulf put on his chainmail and helmet and plunged into the water. Grendel's mother seized him and carried him to her underwater hall.

> The gallant man
> could see he had entered some hellish turn-hole
> and yet the water did not work against him
> because the hall-roofing held off
> the force of the current; then he saw firelight,
> a gleam and flare-up, a glimmer of brightness.

Beowulf tried to kill Grendel's mother with his sword, but failed to do so. Grendel's mother tried to kill him with a knife, but it could not penetrate his chainmail.

> Then he saw a blade that boded well,
> a sword in her armoury, an ancient heirloom
> from the days of the giants, an ideal weapon,
> one that any warrior would envy,
> but so huge and heavy of itself
> only Beowulf could wield it in battle.
> So the Shieldings' hero, hard-pressed and enraged,
> took a firm hold of the hilt and swung
> the blade in an arc, a resolute blow
> that bit deep into her neck-bone
> and severed it entirely, toppling the doomed
> house of her flesh, she fell to the floor.
> The sword dripped blood, the swordsman was elated.

But Beowulf was not yet finished:

> Now the weapon was to prove its worth.
> The warrior determined to take revenge
> for every gross act Grendel had committed—
> and not only for that one occasion
> when he'd come to slaughter the sleeping troops,
> fifteen of Hrothgar's house-guards
> surprised on their benches and ruthlessly devoured,
> and as many again carried away,
> a brutal plunder. Beowulf in his fury
> now settled that score: he saw the monster
> in his resting-place, war-weary and wrecked,
> a lifeless corpse, a casualty
> of the battle in Heorot. The body gaped
> at the stroke dealt to it after death:
> Beowulf cut the corpse's head off.

Meanwhile those waiting for Beowulf on the shore feared he would never return:

> The ninth hour of the day arrived.
> The brave Shieldings abandoned the cliff-top
> and the king went home; but sick at heart,
> staring at the mere, the strangers held on.
> They wished, without hope, to behold their lord,
> Beowulf himself.

While they were waiting, Beowulf swam to the surface, carrying the head of Grendel and the hilt of the great sword (the blade had melted, corroded by the blood of Grendel's mother).

> The seafarers' leader made for land,
> resolutely swimming, delighted with his prize,
> the mighty load he was lugging to the surface.

His thanes advanced in a troop to meet him,
thanking God and taking great delight
in seeing their prince back safe and sound.
Quickly the hero's helmet and mail-shirt
were loosened and unlaced. The lake settled,
clouds darkened above the bloodshot depths.
With high hearts they headed away
along footpaths and trails through the fields,
roads that they knew, each of them wrestling
with the head they were carrying from the lakeside cliff,
men kingly in their courage and capable
of difficult work. It was a task for four
to hoist Grendel's head on a spear
and bear it under strain to the bright hall.

Once he reached Heorot, Beowulf presented the hilt to Hrothgar:

Hrothgar spoke; he examined the hilt,
that relic of old times. It was engraved all over
and showed how war first came into the world
and flood destroyed the tribe of giants.
They suffered a terrible severance from the Lord;
the Almighty made the waters rise,
drowned them in the deluge for retribution.
In pure gold inlay on the sword-guards
there were rune-markings correctly incised,
stating and recording for whom the sword
had been first made and ornamented
with its scroll-work hilt.

Beowulf returned to the land of the Geats, and in time he succeeded Hygelac as king. But after fifty years he was again confronted with the forces of darkness:

He ruled it well
for fifty winters, grew old and wise
as warden of the land until one began
to dominate the dark, a dragon on the prowl
from the steep vaults of a stone-roofed barrow
where he guarded a hoard; there was a hidden passage,
unknown to men, but someone managed
to enter by it and interfere
with the heathen trove. He had handled and removed
a gem-studded goblet; it gained him nothing,
though with a thief's wiles he had outwitted
the sleeping dragon and driven him to a fury,
as the people of that country would soon discover.

The dragon was furious and "hurtled forth/ in a fiery blaze."

> The first to suffer
> were the people on the land, but before long
> it was their treasure-giver who would come to grief.
> The dragon began to belch out flames
> and burn bright homesteads; there was a hot glow
> that scared everyone, for the vile sky-winger
> would leave nothing alive in his wake.
> Everywhere the havoc he wrought was in evidence.

Even Beowulf was affected:

> Then Beowulf was given bad news,
> a hard truth: his own home,
> the best of buildings, had been burnt to a cinder,
> the throne-room of the Geats. It threw the hero
> into deep anguish and darkened his mood:
> the wise man thought he must have thwarted
> ancient ordinance of the eternal Lord,
> broken His commandment. His mind was in turmoil,
> unaccustomed anxiety and gloom
> confused his brain; the fire-dragon
> had rased the coastal region and reduced
> forts and earthworks to dust and ashes,
> so the war-king planned and plotted his revenge.

So Beowulf decided to fight the dragon, and forced the man who stole the dragon's goblet to guide him to the barrow where the dragon lived:

> Against his will
> he led them to the earth-vault he alone knew,
> an underground barrow near the billowing sea
> and the heave of the waves, heaped inside
> with exquisite metalwork. The one who stood guard
> was dangerous and watchful, warden of that trove
> buried under earth: no easy bargain
> would be made in that place by any man.
> The veteran king sat down on the cliff-top.
> He wished good luck to the Geats who had shared
> his hearth and his gold. He was sad at heart,
> unsettled yet ready, sensing his death.
> His fate hovered near, unknowable but certain:
> it would soon claim his coffered soul,
> part life from limb. Before long
> the prince's spirit would spin free from his body.

Beowulf then addressed his men:

> "I would rather not
> use a weapon if I knew another way
> to grapple with the dragon and make good my boast

as I did against Grendel in days gone by.
But I shall be meeting molten venom
in the fire he breathes, so I go forth
in mail-shirt and shield. I won't shift a foot
when I meet the cave-guard: what occurs on the wall
between the two of us will turn out as fate,
overseer of men, decides. I am resolved."

Finally, Beowulf called out to the dragon, and battle was joined:

Unyielding, the lord of his people loomed
by his tall shield, sure of his ground,
while the serpent looped and unleashed itself.
Swaddled in flames, it came gliding and flexing
and racing towards its fate. Yet his shield defended
the renowned leader's life and limb
for a shorter time than he meant it to:
that final day was the first time
when Beowulf fought and fate denied him
glory in battle. So the king of the Geats
raised his hand and struck hard
at the enamelled scales, but scarcely cut through:
the blade flashed and slashed yet the blow
was far less powerful than the hard-pressed king
had need of at that moment. The mound-keeper
went into spasm and spouted deadly flames:
when he felt the stroke, battle-fire
billowed and spewed. Beowulf was foiled
of a glorious victory. The glittering sword,
infallible before that day,
failed when he unsheathed it, as it never should have.
For the son of Ecgtheow, it was no easy thing
to have to give ground like that and go
unwillingly to inhabit another home
in a place beyond; so every man must yield
the leasehold of his days. Before long
the fierce contenders clashed again.
The hoard-guard took heart, inhaled and swelled up
and got a new wind; he who had once ruled
was furled in fire and had to face the worst.

All Beowulf's companions then fled except for Wiglaf, son of Weohstan, who stood by Beowulf and encouraged him to fight:

After these words, a wildness rose
in the dragon again and drove it to attack,
heaving up fire, hunting for enemies,
the humans it loathed. Flames lapped the shield,
charred it to the boss, and the body-armour

on the young warrior was useless to him.
But Wiglaf did well under the wide rim
Beowulf shared with him once his own had shattered
in sparks and ashes. Inspired again
by the thought of glory, the war-king threw
his whole strength behind a sword-stroke
and connected with the skull. And Naegeling snapped.
Beowulf's ancient iron-grey sword
let him down in the fight.

Soon the dragon struck again:

Then the bane of that people, the fire-breathing dragon
was mad to attack for a third time.
When a chance came, he caught the hero
in a rush of flame and clamped sharp fangs
into his neck. Beowulf's body
ran wet with his life-blood: it came welling out.
Next thing, they say, the noble son of Weohstan
saw the king in danger at his side
and displayed his inborn bravery and strength.
He left the head alone, but his fighting hand
was burned when he came to his kinsman's aid.
He lunged at the enemy lower down
so that his decorated sword sank into its belly
and the flames grew weaker. Once more the king
gathered his strength and drew a stabbing knife
he carried on his belt, sharpened for battle.
He stuck it deep into the dragon's flank.
Beowulf dealt it a deadly wound.
They had killed the enemy, courage quelled his life;
that pair of kinsmen, partners in nobility,
had destroyed the foe.

But Beowulf was also badly wounded:

Then the wound
dealt by the ground-burner earlier began
to scald and swell; Beowulf discovered
deadly poison suppurating inside him,
surges of nausea, and so, in his wisdom
the prince realized his state and proceeded
towards a seat on the rampart. He steadied his gaze
on those gigantic stones, saw how the earthwork
was braced with arches built over columns.

Before he dies, Beowulf gives Wiglaf instructions about his funeral:

"Order my troops to construct a barrow
on a headland on the coast, after my pyre has cooled.

> It will loom on the horizon at Hronesness
> and be a reminder among my people—
> so that in coming times crews under sail
> will call it Beowulf's Barrow, as they steer
> ships across the wide and shrouded waters."

Finally, the time came for Beowulf's funeral:

> The Geat people built a pyre for Beowulf,
> stacked and decked until it stood foursquare,
> hung with helmets, heavy war-shields
> and shining armour, just as he had ordered.
> Then his warriors laid him in the middle of it,
> mourning a lord far-famed and beloved.
> On a height they kindled the hugest of all
> funeral fires; fumes of woodsmoke
> billowed darkly up, the blaze roared
> and drowned out their weeping, wind died down
> and flames wrought havoc in the hot bone-house,
> burning it to the core. They were disconsolate
> and wailed aloud for their lord's decease.
> A Geat woman too sang out in grief;
> with hair bound up, she unburdened herself
> of her worst fears, a wild litany
> of nightmare and lament: her nation invaded,
> enemies on the rampage, bodies in piles,
> slavery and abasement. Heaven swallowed the smoke.
> Then the Geat people began to construct
> a mound on a headland, high and imposing,
> a marker that sailors could see from afar,
> and in ten days they had done the work.
> It was their hero's memorial; what remained from the fire
> they housed inside it, behind a wall
> as worthy of him as their workmanship could make it.
> And they buried torques in the barrow, and jewels
> and a trove of such things as trespassing men
> had once dared to drag from the hoard.

Beowulf appears to be set in the 6th century. Late in the poem, Beowulf tells how his king, Hygelac, died while attacking the land of the Franks. The *History of the Franks* by Gregory of Tours mentions that in 521 there was an attack on the Rhine River by a northern leader named *Chlochilaichus*— a Latin version of Hygelac.[3] Two other kings are mentioned in *Beowulf*, Ohthere and Eadgils. In Vendel parish, Uppland province, Sweden, there is a barrow known as Ohthere's barrow, which was excavated between 1914 and 1916 and found to contain a gold coin dated 477.[4] According to the Icelandic historian, poet and politician Snorri Sturluson (1179–1241), Eadgils was buried in one of the royal mounds of Gamla Uppsala (Old Uppsala), in the mound known as *Adil's Mound*. An excavation in this mound showed that a man was buried there around 575 on a bear skin with two dogs and rich grave offerings. There were luxurious weapons and other objects, both domestic and imported, show that the buried man was very powerful. These remains include a Frankish sword adorned with gold and garnets and a board game with Roman pawns of ivory. He was dressed in a costly suit made of Frankish cloth with golden threads, and he wore a belt with a costly buckle. There were four cameos from the Middle East which were probably part of a casket.[5]

The Place and Date of Beowulf

As I said, nobody knows when *Beowulf* was written, but there are clues. The *Liber Monstrorum* ("Book of Monsters") was probably composed in the 7th or 8th century by a student or colleague of Aldhelm, abbot of Malmesbury (Wiltshire) and later Bishop of Sherborne (Dorset), and contains a reference to Hygelac[6]:

> And there are monsters of an amazing size, like King Hygelac, who ruled the Geats and was killed by the Franks, whom no horse could carry from the age of twelve. His bones are preserved on an island in the river Rhine, where it breaks into the Ocean, and they are shown as a wonder to travellers from afar.

The *Liber Monstrorum* probably preceded *Beowulf*, and it is possible that Hygelac's qualities were transferred to Beowulf—when Beowulf is first introduced the poet says of him: "There was no one else like him alive./ In his day, he was the mightiest man on earth,/ high-born and powerful." And when Beowulf fights Grendel, he literally crushes the monster to death in his vice-like grip.

The West Saxon royal genealogies of the late 9th century preserve, as alleged ancestors of the West Saxon kings, a number of legendary names which also figure in *Beowulf*: Sceaf, Scyld, Heremod and Beaw. Sceaf is a ruler of the Lombards and the distant ancestor of Skyld, Heremod is the father of Skyld, Skyld is the father of Beaw, and all of them are ancestors of Hrothgar. There are two principal sources for this genealogy: the Parker, or Winchester, version of the *Anglo-Saxon Chronicle*, in the entry for 855 which gives a genealogy of Alfred's father Æthelwulf; and the first chapter of Asser's late 9th century *Life of Alfred*.[7]

The mention of Hygelac in the *Liber Monstrorum* and the names in the West Saxon genealogy suggest that *Beowulf* was composed some time between about 700 and 900. Michael Swanton in his *Beowulf: Revised Edition* remarks that the Anglian dialect elements suggest an Anglian origin for the poem, but give no clues as to the date. However, Swanton goes on to say[8]:

> one or two archaic forms, surviving the process of transmission like linguistic fossils embedded in the text, suggest that the original, at several stages removed from our manuscript, may have been written at least two centuries earlier than the surviving copy.... Other textual details suggest that at least one copy was made at the time of King Alfred, and that at some stage after the middle of the ninth century a Kentish scribe probably had a hand in its transmission.
>
> A date of composition during the eighth century might be supported on other than linguistic grounds. The common use of phrases such as *wuldur cyning, sigora waldend* "King of glory, ruler of victories" to describe the Almighty shows that the author was familiar with poetry of the Cædmonian school, which is presumed to have flourished during the last decades of the seventh century and the opening of the eighth. And it might be supposed that the lay of creation which Hrothgar's minstrel is described singing during the inaugural ceremonies at Heorot, was a direct imitation of Cædmon's creation hymn, which the historian Bede reliably states to have been the first vernacular Christian poem.

An 8th century date is given some support by a letter from the Northumbrian scholar Alcuin, who was trained at the York school and became a teacher there in the 750s. Alcuin joined Charlemagne's Palace school at Aachen (Germany) around 781, and wrote a famous letter in 797 to Bishop Hygebald of Lindisfarne, in which he said[9]:

> let the word of God be read at priestly repast. There should the reader be heard, not the harpist; the sermons of the Fathers, not the songs of pagans. What has Ingeld to do with Christ? The House is narrow, it cannot hold both. The King of Heaven wished to have no fellowship with so-called kings who are pagan and lost; for the eternal King reigns in Heaven, the lost pagan laments in Hell.

Ingeld is mentioned in *Beowulf* as a leader of the Heathobards (possibly a branch of the Langobards or Lombards) involved in a feud with Hrothgar. After Beowulf returns to Hygelac's court he reports[10]:

> Sometimes Hrothgar's daughter distributed
> ale to older ranks, in order on the benches:
> I heard the company call her Freawaru
> as she made her rounds, presenting men
> with the gem-studded bowl, young bride-to-be
> to the gracious Ingeld, in her gold-trimmed attire.
> The friend of the Shieldings favours her betrothal:
> the guardian of the kingdom sees good in it
> and hopes this woman will heal old wounds
> and grievous feuds. But generally the spear
> is prompt to retaliate when a prince is killed,
> no matter how admirable the bride may be.
> Think how the Heathobards will be bound to feel,

> their lord, Ingeld, and his loyal thanes,
> when he walks in with that woman to the feast.

Beowulf goes on to warn that no good will come of the marriage between Hrothgar's daughter and Ingeld. The fact that Alcuin mentions the "songs of the pagans" suggests that poems like *Beowulf* were current in monastic circles.

As I said, it is not known where *Beowulf* was composed, but the historian Dr. Sam Newton has argued plausibly, in *The Origins of Beowulf and the Pre-Viking Kingdom of East Anglia*, that it was composed some time during the reign of King Ælfwald of East Anglia (713–749), who commissioned the 8th century *Life of Guthlac*. Ælfwald was member of the Wuffingas dynasty and a descendant of Rædwald, who may have been buried in a ship at Sutton Hoo, in a type of burial celebrated in the funeral of Scyld in *Beowulf*. Before the end of his rule, East Anglia contained a group of ecclesiastical centers, all of which had strong associations with the Wuffingas dynasty. These included the episcopal sees at *Dommoc* (Dunwich in Suffolk) established by King Sigeberht, and *Helmham* (either North Elmham in Norfolk or South Elmham in Suffolk) established by Ealdwulf (663–713); St. Botulph's monastery at *Icanho* (Iken in Suffolk); the religious foundations at Ely (Cambridgeshire), which was established by Æthelthryth, daughter of King Anna, and Dereham, Norfolk, established by Withburga, another possible daughter of King Anna; and the minster at Blythburgh (Suffolk), where King Anna was believed to have been buried[11] (the *Liber Eliensis*, or *Book of Ely* claims that the body of King Anna was still being venerated at Blythburgh in the 12th century).[12] *Beowulf* could well have been produced at one of these religious centers on the instruction of King Ælfwald. A number of East Anglian monasteries were destroyed in Danish raids in the late 9th century, and a manuscript of *Beowulf* could well have made its way to Wessex at this time.

On the other hand, Mercia was the most powerful kingdom in the 8th century, and its most powerful king was Offa (757–796). A certain Offa, is mentioned in *Beowulf* as the wife of Modthryth,[13] who

> perpetrated terrible wrongs.
> If any retainer ever made so bold
> to look her in the face, if an eye not her lord's
> stared at her directly during daylight,
> the outcome was sealed; he was kept bound
> in hand-tightened shackles, racked, tortured
> until doom was pronounced—death by the sword,
> slash of blade, blood-gush and death qualms
> in an evil display.

But after she married Offa, she changed:

> she was less of a bane to people's lives,
> less cruel-minded, after she was married
> to the brave Offa, a bride arrayed
> in her gold finery, given away
> by a caring father, ferried to her young prince
> over dim seas. In days to come
> she would grace the throne and grow famous
> for her good deeds and conduct of life,
> her high devotion to the hero king
> who was the best king, it has been said,
> between the two seas or anywhere else
> on the face of the earth. Offa was honoured
> far and wide for his generous ways,
> his fighting spirit and his far-seeing
> defence of his homeland.

This Offa may be the same as the legendary Offa, the king of Angeln (now part of the German state of Schleswig-Holstein), who killed a Saxon prince in single combat. This legendary Offa is mentioned briefly in the Anglo-Saxon poem *Widsith*, which may date from the 8th or 9th century, and may have originally been composed in Mercia. Interestingly, the Mercian kings traced their origins to the legendary Offa of Angeln.

Beowulf *in Anglo-Saxon England*

At least one of the anonymous writers of the late 10th century *Blickling Homilies*, named after Blickling Hall in Norfolk where the manuscript was kept until 1932, was familiar with *Beowulf*. It has been recognized since the late 19th century that the description of Hell in *Blickling Homily XVI* closely matches the passage in *Beowulf* that describes Grendel's Mother's mere. Here is the passage from *Blickling Homily XVI* as translated by Richard Morris, who first recognized the resemblance between this and the description of Grendel's Mother's mere[14]:

> As St. Paul was looking towards the northern region of the earth, from whence all waters pass down, he saw above the water a hoary stone; and north of the stone had grown woods very rimy. And there were dark mists; and under the stone was the dwelling place of monsters and execrable creatures. And he saw that on the cliff there hung on the icy woods many black souls with their hands bound ; and the devils in likeness of monsters were seizing them like greedy wolves; and the water under the cliff beneath was black. And between the cliff and the water there were about twelve miles, and when the twigs broke, then down went the souls who hung on the twigs and the monsters seized them.

And here is the corresponding passage from *Beowulf*, in which *They* refers to Grendel and his mother:

They are fatherless creatures,
and their whole ancestry is hidden in a past
of demons and ghosts. They dwell apart
among wolves on the hills, on windswept crags
and treacherous keshes [causeways], where cold streams
pour down the mountain and disappear
under mist and moorland. A few miles from here
a frost-stiffened wood waits and keeps watch
above a mere; the overhanging bank
in a maze of tree-roots mirrored on its surface.
At night there, something uncanny happens:
the water burns. And the mere-bottom
has never been sounded by the sons of men.

In both texts the waters tumble down, there are mists, frosty groves, and trees on the cliff that overhangs the mere. In the *Blickling Homily*, the water contains water monsters, and we know that the mere in *Beowulf* contains Grendel's Mother.

It is difficult to know how popular *Beowulf* was in the Anglo-Saxon period, since the Normans after 1066 effectively destroyed Anglo-Saxon culture, killing or driving out Anglo-Saxon aristocrats and churchmen and replacing Old English with French as the language of the elite. But the West Saxon genealogies and the description of Hell in *Blickling Homily XVI* suggests that *Beowulf* was well-known, and we also have evidence from Anglo-Saxon charters. The bounds of a number of Anglo-Saxon charters refer to local topographical features—usually pits, meres or bogs—by names containing the element *grendel*. The earliest dated charter containing bounds referred to as Grendel's Pit is a grant dated 708 by King Cenred of Mercia to Bishop Ecgwine and his foundation at Evesham (Worcestershire). This charter is preserved only in a 12th century copy in Evesham cartulary, and is almost certainly a forgery. The name of Grendel's Pit near Abbots Morton (Worcestershire) is no doubt genuine, but there is no proof it existed before the 12th century.[15]

There is also a reference to a Grendel's Pit, this time in the bounds of a charter relating to land at Crediton (Devon). This charter is a grant by King Æthelheard of Wessex in favor of Crediton, and is dated 739. The main body of the charter and its witness-list appear to be genuine, although it is not preserved in a contemporary copy. However, charters do not normally include detailed descriptions of bounds before the second half of the 8th century; and since the bounds of this charter have been transmitted separately in a 10th century copy, there is reason for thinking for thinking the bounds were drawn up as late as the 10th century.[16]

In 931 there was a grant of land at Ham in east Wiltshire by Æthelstan to his thane Wulfgar: "from there north over the hill westwards to the mossy bank; then down to the escarpment to the fence of *Beowa's place*, then eastwards to the blackberry copse; then to the black cave; then north by the unploughed headland to the short ditch except for one acre; then to the bird-mere to the road; along the road to Otter's ford; thence to the wood-mere; then to the hedge of row [trees]; then to the long meadow; then to *Grendel's mere* ; then to the hidden gate...." Here we have not only *Grendel's mere*, but also *Beowa's place*.[17]

It may also be significant that Grendel's association with low-lying, watery places seems to be echoed in the cognate East Anglian dialect word *grindle*, "drain" or "ditch." This word is preserved in the names of several Suffolk watercourses, such as the Grundles of Wattisfield and Stanton, or Grindle Lane, Sproughton.[18]

Beowulf as "Bee-Wolf," or Bear

There seems little to link the Welsh Arthur and the Anglo-Saxon Beowulf, but in fact both of them are somehow connected to bears. Arthur of course is the "Bear-Man," but Beowulf's bear-ancestry is less obvious. The name *Beowulf* is thought to mean "wolf, or foe, of the bee," that is "bear." As the literary scholar R.W. Chambers says,[19] "bear" is "an excellent name for a hero of story":

> The O.E. *beorn*, "warrior, hero, prince" seems originally to have meant simply "bear" The bear, says Grimm, "is regarded, in the belief of the Old Norse, Slavonic, Finnish and Lapp peoples, as an exalted and holy being, endowed with human understanding and the strength of twelve men. He is called 'forest-king,' 'gold-foot,' 'sweet-foot,' 'honey-hand,' 'honey-paw,' 'honey-eater,' but also 'the great,' 'the old,' 'the old grandsire.'"

Chambers argues that there are two reasons for considering Beowulf as "Bear"[20]: "The first is that it agrees excellently with Beowulf's bear-like habit of hugging his adversaries to death—a feature which surely belongs to the original kernel of our story, since it is incompatible with the chivalrous weapon-loving trappings in which that story has been dressed." The second is Beowulf's connection with the hero Bothvar Bjarki, whose story has some similarities with the story of Beowulf[21]:

> Bjarki, bent on adventure, leaves the land of the Gautar (Götar), where his brother is king, and reaches Leire, where Rolf, the king of the Danes, holds his court. But despite the fame and splendour of the Danish court, it has long been subject to the attacks of a strange monster, a winged beast. Bjarki is scornful at the inability of the Danes to defend their own home: "if one beast can lay waste the kingdom and the cattle of the king." He goes out to fight with the monster by night. He tries to draw his sword, but the sword is fast in its sheath: he tugs, the sword comes out, and he slays the beast with it.

Bjarki means "Little-Bear," and in the *Saga of Hrolf Kraki* (14th or 15th century) we are told at length how the father of Bjarki was a prince who had been turned by enchantment into a bear.[22]

So Arthur and Beowulf were probably both inspired by bears in Germanic folklore. Arthur probably emerged some time in the Roman period, but soon lost all his bear characteristics; while Beowulf emerged several centuries later and still retained one particular characteristic of the bear—the ability to hug his adversaries to death. Interestingly there is one scene in *Culhwch and Olwen* which we can compare to *Beowulf*. When Arthur attacks the Very Black Witch in her cave at the head of the Valley of Grief in the uplands of Hell and cuts her in two, he is in a way replicating the incident in which Beowulf dives to the bottom of the lake and decapitates Grendel's Mother and mutilates the corpse of Grendel. Both Arthur and Beowulf symbolically descend into Hell, both mutilate their victims, and both carry off trophies (the blood of the Very Black Witch, the head of Grendel).

Arthur Becomes a National Hero

As I implied earlier, the Normans invaded England in 1066 and put an end to five centuries of Anglo-Saxon rule. Anglo-Saxon aristocrats and churchmen were replaced by Norman aristocrats and churchmen, and French became the language of the elite. English virtually disappeared as a literary language for 150 years, with only the Peterborough version of the *Anglo-Saxon Chronicle*, which continued until 1154, still speaking for the English.

In this long period of virtual silence, the only people who could speak for the conquered English were the Normans, and in the 12th century the Norman cleric Geoffrey of Monmouth set about creating a new British national hero in his Latin work *The History of the Kings of Britain*. Geoffrey drew on a variety of sources—Arthur's battles in the 9th century *History of the Kings of Britain*, and a variety of unknown Welsh sources for Uther Pendragon, Arthur's father in the *History*, Arthur's wife Guinevere, the treachery of Guinevere and Mordred, and Arthur's final resting place on the island of Avalon—to create a might warrior and king who forged an empire stretching from Ireland to Gaul. Geoffrey's influence was enormous: his court became the center of knights such as Lancelot and Perceval in the late 12th century romances of the French poet Chrétien de Troyes, which in turn inspired the five-volume 13th century prose romance known as the *Lancelot-Grail*. Geoffrey's *History* also inspired, directly or indirectly, a number of 13th–14th century works—Layamon's *Brut*, the *Alliterative Morte Arthure* and *Sir Gawain and the Green Knight*—in which we can see the influence of *Beowulf* and poems of exile like *The Wanderer*.

7

The Arthur of the Normans

Geoffrey of Monmouth's History of the Kings of Britain

The Norman Conquest and Wales

In 1066 the Anglo-Saxon king Edward the Confessor died childless and William, Duke of Normandy, who was related to Edward through Edward's mother, Emma of Normandy, invaded England. Edward named as his successor Harold Godwinson, but William killed Harold at the Battle of Hastings, and was crowned king in Westminster Abbey.

By the time William the Conqueror died in 1087, most of the Anglo-Saxon aristocrats and senior churchmen had been replaced by Normans, and Norman French was the language of the elite. Wales had never been part of the Anglo-Saxon kingdom, but the new ruler had different ideas. Shortly after the Conquest, William installed three of his most trusted confidants, Hugh d'Avranches, Roger de Montgomerie, and William FitzOsbern as earls of Chester, Shrewsbury and Hereford respectively, with responsibilities for containing and subduing the Welsh. Between 1067 and 1071, William FitzOsbern built a castle at Monmouth, and Withenoc, a Breton, who became lord of Monmouth in 1075, founded a Benedictine priory there. By the early 12th century the Normans had established a string of castles in south Wales, including Chepstow, Cardiff, Swansea and Pembroke. Meanwhile, William gave most of the land in Cornwall to Robert, Count of Mortain, who administered his holdings from his castle in Launceston, Cornwall.

One of the first fruits of the Norman interest in Wales was the *History of the Kings of Britain* (AD 1136), written in Latin by a Norman priest known as Geoffrey of Monmouth, who was probably born in Wales or the Welsh Marches, possibly to a family that originally came from Brittany. Geoffrey of Monmouth's *History* is not only about Arthur, but Arthur is certainly at the center of the story, fighting the Saxons and creating an empire that included

103

Britain, France and Ireland, very like the empire that the Normans had acquired or wished to acquire. It was obviously designed to extol the virtues of the British at the expense of the conquered Anglo-Saxons. We don't know what sources Geoffrey used, but he clearly drew on the account of Arthur's battles in the 9th century *History of the Britons* (Geoffrey probably didn't know Welsh, but he obviously knew Latin).

Geoffrey of Monmouth's History of the Kings of Britain

The Birth of Arthur

The story of Arthur in Geoffrey's *History* really begins with Uther Pendragon. He is first mentioned in *Pa gur?*, which lists among Arthur's retinue Mabon, son of Modron, described as "servant of Uthir Pendragon." He is also the subject of a poem, *The Death-song of Uther Pendragon* (9th–11th century): in the poem the deceased Uther claims that his "champion's feats partook in a ninth part of Arthur's valour."[1] Geoffrey's Uther becomes king after his brother, Aurelius (Gildas' Ambrosius Aurelianus), is poisoned by a Saxon disguised as a priest. Uther then wins a great victory over the Saxons and holds a celebration in London, attended by, among others, Gorlois, Duke of Cornwall and his wife Igerna, the greatest beauty in all Britain. As the Celtic scholar John Koch points out,[2] Uther, in *The Death-song of Uther Pendragon*, says that "he is the one called *gorlassar*, possibly connected with Geoffrey's Duke Gorlois" (*gorlassar* is derived from Welsh *gorlas*, which means "bright blue").

As soon as Uther saw Igerna, he "fell passionately in love with her." She was "the only lady that he continually served with fresh dishes, and to whom he sent golden cups by his confidants; on her he bestowed all his smiles, and to her he addressed all his discourse." Gorlois noticed this and "fell into a great rage, and retired from the court without taking leave."[3] Incensed by this, Uther ordered him to return to court, but Gorlois refused, whereupon Uther marched into Cornwall and set fire to the main cities and towns. Gorlois then put Igerna in the town of Tintagel, which "he looked upon as a place of great safety," while he himself went to his castle at *Dimilioc* (probably the hillfort close to Domellick Farm, St. Dennis).[4] Tintagel in Cornwall was a stronghold of the British kingdom of Dumnonia (Devon and Cornwall): large quantities of Mediterranean pottery and glass dating from the 5th and 6th centuries have been found there, as well as a large and elaborate building, making it clear that this was a high-status site, presumably the center of the kings of Dumnonia.[5] Near the parish church of Tintagel is an earthwork enclosure, and excavations in 1991 showed that the enclosure is an early Christian churchyard dating back to the 6th century. Many of the graves in the inhumation cemetery were cist graves.[6]

Uther sent for Merlin who, with the help of his "medicines," transformed Uther into the exact likeness of Gorlois.[7] Uther then proceeded to Tintagel in the guise of Gorlois, was admitted without any problems, and "stayed the night with Igerna and had the full enjoyment of her, for she was deceived with the false disguise which he had put on, and the artful and amorous discourses wherewith he entertained her." That same night Igerna "conceived of the most renowned Arthur."

Merlin, Myrddin and Lailoken

Merlin is the character in Welsh mythology known as *Myrddin Wyllt* ("Myrddin the Wild"). In a number of medieval Welsh poems, he is portrayed as a Wild Man of the Woods living in the Caledonian Forest, where he has fled after losing his reason at the battle of Arfderydd (Arthuret in Cumbria); with this lapse into madness Myrddin is said to have acquired the gift of prophecy.[8]

Two of the Welsh Myrddin poems, *Cyvoesi Myrddin a Gwenddydd ei Chwaer* ("Dialogue Between Myrddin and His Sister Gwenddydd") and *Ymddiddan Myrddin a Thaliesin* ("The Dialogue of Myrddin and Taliesin") were certainly composed before 1100. According to Rachel Bromwich, Geoffrey of Monmouth's *Vita Merlini* "must be in part based upon the Welsh poems, rather than that the influence was in the opposite direction." The Myrddin story closely resembles traditions concerning a certain Lailoken, whose story is preserved in early records of St. Kentigern, the patron saint of Glasgow. Indeed, the authority on Welsh literature, A.O.H. Jarman, has argued that "Lailoken (W. *Llallawg, Llallogan*) was the prophet's name in the original north-British saga." The word *llallawg* ("friend, lord") and its diminutive *llallogan* are used by Gwenddydd as terms of address to her brother in the *Cyvoesi*.[9]

The *Life of St. Kentigern* was written in the late 12th century by Jocelyn of Furness, and was partly based on the *Fragmentary Life of St. Kentigern*, written at the request of Herbert, Bishop of Glasgow (1147–1164). The *Life* includes a reference to Lailoken, who may be the inspiration for Myrddin/Merlin[10]:

> In the same year that Saint Kentigern was released from the affairs of men and departed into heaven, King Rederech, who has been named often, stayed for a longer time than usual in a royal village which is called Pertnech. A certain foolish man, who was called Laleocen, lived at his court, and he received his necessary sustenance and garments from the bountifulness of the king. For it is customary for the

chief men of the earth and for sons of kings to be given to vain things and to retain with them men of the sort who are able to excite these lords and their households to jests and loud laughter by foolish words and gestures. But after the burial of Saint Kentigern, this man was himself afflicted with the most severe mourning, and he would not receive any comfort from anyone.

When they sought why he grieved so inconsolably, he answered that his lord King Rederech and another of the first men of the land, named Morthec, would not be long in this life after the death of the holy bishop, but that they would succumb to fate in that present year and die. The deaths of those whom he mentioned that followed in that year clearly proved that the words of the fool were not spoken foolishly, but rather they were spoken prophetically.

King Rederech is Rhydderch Hael, King of Alt Clut (580–614) and Pertnech is Partick, an area of Glasgow on the north bank of the Clyde.

Lailoken also appears in a 15th century version of the story, portrayed as a naked, hairy madman whom Kentigern met while praying in a lonely wood. On being questioned by Kentigern, Lailoken accepted responsibility for his sad condition, stating that he had been "the cause of the slaughter of all the dead who fell in the battle … which took place in the plain lying between Lidel and Carwannock."[11] Lidel may refer to Liddel Water (a river) or Liddel Strength (a 12th century castle), both on the border between Cumbria and Scotland, while Carwannock (presumably a *caer*, or fort) has not been identified.

Arthur Becomes King and Triumphs Over the Saxons

When Arthur was 15 years old, Uther died, poisoned, like his brother Aurelius, by the Saxons, and a meeting was held at Silchester at which it was agreed that Arthur should be crowned king. Silchester in Hampshire is the Roman town of Calleva Atrebatum, the capital of the Atrebates; the name Calleva is probably related to Welsh *celli*, Irish *caille* "wood, grove," meaning perhaps "the town in the wood." Silchester is indeed a Roman town where Arthur could have been crowned. After the Roman legions left Britain, Calleva continued to function. The archaeologist Ken Dark believes that Calleva may also have been occupied into the 5th and even 6th centuries, and that dykes to the north of the town, on the roads to Dorchester-on-Thames and Cirencester, may have been built as a defense against the Saxons.[12] An inscription written on a Roman column in ogham (an ancient Irish form of writing) was discovered in a well during excavations in the 19th century. The well was deliberately filled in to prevent its re-use, and wood discovered in the filling of the well was carbon-dated to the 5th century.[13] The archaeologists Fulford and Clarke "have estimated, based on the pattern of infilling of wells, a case can be made for between a half and two thirds of the level of the fourth century population surviving into the late sixth century-early seventh century."[14]

Once Arthur was crowned, he marched to York (the old Roman town of *Eboracum*) and joined battle with Colgrin and a huge army of Saxons, Scots and Picts near the River Duglas (this is the *Dubglas* mentioned by Nennius as the scene of one of Arthur's battles). Arthur was victorious and pursued Colgrin to York, where he besieged him. Colgrin's brother Baldulph went with 6,000 men to relieve the siege, but Arthur, hearing of this, sent Cador, Duke of Cornwall, who ambushed the Saxons and put them to flight. Colgrin or Colgrim is a Danish name associated with Lincoln in the 11th century, when Lincoln was one of the Five Boroughs of the Danelaw; Badulph, or Beadwulf, was the name of the last Anglo-Saxon bishop of Whithorn (791–803).

Cador is probably based on an early Welsh figure called Cato. The *Life of St. Carantoc*, written around 1100[15] mentions Cato; in this passage Carantoc has just returned from Ireland[16]:

> And afterwards he came again to his own country, Ceredigion, to his cave, with many clergymen, and there performed many miracles [...] And Christ gave him an honourable altar from on high, the colour of which no person could comprehend; and afterwards when he came to the Severn to sail over it, he cast the altar into the sea, and it went before him where God wished him to go. In those times, Cato and Arthur lived in that country, dwelling in Dindrarthou.

At the time a terrible dragon was laying waste the countryside, and Arthur was trying to catch this dragon. When Carantoc arrived, he asked Arthur if he knew where his altar had landed, and Arthur replied: "If I shall be paid for it, I will tell thee," and asked the saint to catch the dragon for him. Carantoc prayed, and the dragon "came with a great noise, running as a calf to its dam." He then brought the dragon to Cato in his castle in *Carrum*, where people tried to kill the dragon—but the saint set the dragon free, "which injured none as God had commanded." By now Carantoc had recovered his altar—"Arthur intended to make it a table, but whatsoever was put thereon, was thrown off to some distance. And the king requested that he would receive Carrum for ever by a written deed, and afterwards he built there a church." *Carrum* is thought to be Carhampton in the west of Somerset, and excavations there have revealed "an occupation site dating from the fifth to eighth century AD."[17] Imported 5th to 7th century Mediterranean pottery has been found in the area, the churchyard is curvilinear, and a church, first recorded in 1189, was dedicated to the Welsh holy man St. Carantoc.[18] The old church of St. Carantoc may have continued in use as a private chapel, as the antiquary Leland mentions it in the 1540s.

Meanwhile, the Saxons were reinforced by the arrival of 600 ships laden with soldiers under the control of Duke Cheldric (Childeric is the name of several Frankish kings). Arthur returned to London, and held a meeting with the clergy and nobility, at which it was decided to enlist the aid of Arthur's relative, King Hoel of Brittany (also seen as Hywel, which is the name of several Welsh kings). Arthur, Hoel and their forces then went to Lincoln, which the Saxons were besieging, and killed large numbers of them. The remaining Saxons retreated to the "wood of Celidon"—presumably the Caledonian Forest in Scotland—and took a stand against the British forces. Eventually they surrendered and set sail for Germany, but changed their mind and landed at Totnes in Devon.

From Totnes the Saxons laid waste the country as far as the River Severn and besieged Bath. Arthur and his forces made for Bath—Hoel lay sick in Alclud—and after a long and bloody struggle were victorious, with Colgrin and Baldulph being killed. Cador pursued the remaining Saxons as far as the Isle of Thanet, while Arthur meanwhile headed for Alclud (Alt Clut, or Dumbarton Rock), which the Scots and Picts were besieging.

After lifting the siege of Alclud and subduing the Scots and Picts, Arthur went to York to celebrate Christmas. The city was in ruins, so Arthur ordered the rebuilding of the churches, and restored the rights of three brothers: he restored to Augusel (Angusel) sovereignty over the Scots; he honored Urian (Urien) with the scepter of Mureif; and he re-established Lot in the consulship of Londonensia (Lothian).

According to Rachel Bromwich,[19] Augusel is Geoffrey's version of Arawn, son of Cynfarch, the brother of Urian in Triad 70. Urian is Urien Rheged, the late 6th century king of Rheged—*Mureif* is usually translated as Moray, but Bromwich suggests that it could be Monreith near Whithorn in Dumfries and Galloway. Lot of Londonensia/Lothian was Arthur's brother-in-law: in the time of Aurelius Ambrosius, says Geoffrey, Lot had married Arthur's sister Anna and had two sons by her, Walgan (Gawain) and Modred (Mordred).

Lot of Lothian is derived from Leudonus, king of Leudonia, who appears in the *Fragmentary Life of St. Kentigern*. According to the *Fragmentary Life*, Ewen, son of Queen Erwegende and King Ulien (in other words, Owein, son of Urien), seduces Thaney, daughter of King Leudonus of Leudonia. Ewen courted Thaney, but she refused to marry him. In punishment, her father made her work as a swineherd's servant. Ewen sent a female intermediary to persuade Thaney to love him, but when persuasion did not achieve his ends, he disguised himself as a girl and approached Thaney near a fountain. He tricked her into accompanying him to an isolated place, where he raped her. Thaney then conceived the son who would become St. Kentigern. In punishment for her pregnancy, her father had her thrown from a mountaintop, but she miraculously survived.[20]

Arthur and Guinevere

Then, when everything was back to normal, Arthur married Guinevere (Guanhumara, Gwenhwyvar), "descended from a noble family of Romans, who was educated under duke Cador, and in beauty surpassed all the women of the island." Guinevere was mentioned as Arthur's wife in *Culhwch and Olwen*. She also appears in the *Triads of the Island of Britain*, Triad 56, "Arthur's Three Great Queens"[21]:

> Gwennhwyfar daughter of (Cywryd) Gwent,
> and Gwenhwyfar daughter of (Gwythyr) son of Greidiawl,
> and Gwenhwyfar daughter of (G)ogfran the Giant.

Little is known of (Cywryd) Gwent and (G)ogfran the Giant, but (Gwythyr) son of Greidawl, was the character in *Culhwch and Olwen* who must fight Gwyn, son of Nudd, every May Day for the maiden Creiddylad.

Gwenhwyfar appears to be a triple goddess, reminiscent of the *Matres* or *Matronae* ("Mothers" or "Matrons"), who always appear in groups of three, and were venerated in eastern Gaul and Germania (Germany), but also in Britain. One of the most important sculptures from Ancaster, a Roman town in the south of Lincolnshire, was an image of the mother-goddesses. It was discovered in 1831 while a grave was being dug in the southeastern corner of the churchyard of the parish church of St. Martin. The sculpture, which is 1 foot, 7 inches long and 1 foot, 4 inches high,

> shows three seated goddesses and represents the Romano-Celtic Mother-Goddess in triple form. When it was found the sculpture was still standing upright, facing south and had been placed on top of a rough stone block at one end of a massive 6 feet × 4 feet stone slab. At the southern end of the slab was a small, elaborately carved stone altar 1 foot high and 5 inches wide, which had been set on a stone disc 9 inches in diameter placed on top of a stone column 1 foot 8 inches high. The column itself stood on a stone block 5 inches × 15 inches × 15 inches. This somewhat curious arrangement gave the discoverers the impression that both the altar on the column, and the sculpture of the Mother-Goddesses were in their original positions and it seems possible that what the gravedigger had accidentally stumbled on was in fact the remains of a shrine or temple dedicated to the worship of the Mother-Goddess.[22]

A Roman altar dedicated to the three Mother Goddesses has been used as a font in Lund Church near Kirkham, Lancashire, since 1688. The altar may have come from the Roman fort at Ribchester, some 12 miles away.[23] At Benwell Roman Temple (Newcastle upon Tyne), an altar from the subterranean level of the temple, reddened by fire, bears an inscription *Lamiis Tribus* ("To the three Witches"). Although the Latin name is used, "the concept is Celtic, and it is noteworthy that Cormac glosses Mache, the war goddess, as *lamia*."[24] Mache or Macha, along with Badb, "Crow," and Nemain, "Panic," make up the three sisters called the Morrigan, who are perhaps another aspect of the three mother-goddesses.

In Roman times, much of the north of England was inhabited by a tribe called the *Brigantes*, who worshipped a goddess called *Brigantia*. Brigantia is related to the Irish goddess Brigit, who was a triple goddess. *Cormac's Glossary* says of Brigit[25]:

> poetess, daughter of the Dagda. This is Brigit the female sage, or woman of wisdom, i.e., Brigit the goddess whom poets adored, because very great and very famous was her protecting care. It is therefore they call her goddess of poets by this name. Whose sisters were Brigit the female physician [woman of leechcraft], Brigit the female smith [woman of smithwork] …

Brigantia is represented in a sculpture from the Roman fort of Birrens in Dumfries and Galloway, not far from the English border. Brigantia is shown in the guise of Minerva, patron goddess of engineers and of war. She is crowned and winged, holding a spear and a globe. The inscription reads: "Sacred to Brigantia: Amandus, the engineer, fulfilled the order by command."[26]

Arthur at War with the Romans

After his marriage to Guinevere, Arthur conquered Ireland, Iceland, Norway, Dacia (Denmark), Aquitaine and Gaul. To celebrate his victories he held a great assembly at the City of Legions. The City of Legions is Caerleon near Newport in south Wales, which in Roman times was known as *Isca*[27]:

> Underlying the modern town of Caerleon are the remains of a vast and magnificent Roman legionary fortress. This was ISCA, named for the Usk or Wsyg, established in about 75 AD as the base for the Second Augustan Legion—LEGIO II AUGUSTA. The fortress lay at the centre of an extensive settlement fringed by cemeteries, covering in all an area of perhaps 100ha [hectares]. It was occupied throughout the Roman period and its ruins dominated the town well into the middle ages.

At the end of the assembly at the City of Legions, Arthur received a letter from the (fictional) Roman general Lucius Tiberius, demanding that he pay tribute to Rome. Arthur consulted his advisers, and it was agreed they should go to war with Rome. Before setting out for Rome, he entrusted the government of the kingdom to his nephew Mordred (Modred). Geoffrey has borrowed this name from earlier Welsh tradition: Mordred appears in the *Annales Cambriae* ("Annals of Wales"), which probably date from the mid–10th century, in this entry: "The Battle of Camlann, in which Arthur and Medraut fell." The Arthurian scholar Caitlin R. Green says[28]: "Geoffrey's form of the name, *Mordredus*, was derived from a Cornish or Breton source and the name is known from Cornish *Domesday* returns and the Bodmin manumissions of AD 960–1000." Green is presumably referring to Tre-Modret (Tremodrett) near Roche in Cornwall, and Carveddras (Carvedras) near Truro in Cornwall, which is derived from *Kaervodred* "Fortress of Mordred." The Celtic scholar Kenneth Jackson[29] believes that *Camlann* is *Camboglanna*, or Castlesteads, a Roman fort on Hadrian's Wall in Cumbria, which has virtually been destroyed by the gardens of Castlesteads House (late 18th century). The fort was situated on a high bluff commanding the valley of the River Cam Beck, a tributary of the River Irthing.

Before his departure for continental Europe, Arthur had a dream[30]:

> it happened that about midnight he fell into a very sound sleep, and in a dream saw a bear flying in the air, at the noise of which all the shores trembled; also a terrible dragon flying from the west, which enlightened the country with the brightness of its eyes. When these two met, they began a dreadful fight; but the dragon with its fiery breath burned the bear which often assaulted him, and threw him down scorched to the ground. Arthur upon this awaking, related his dream to those that stood about him, who took upon them to interpret it, and told him that the dragon signified himself, but the bear, some giant that should encounter with him; and that the fight portended the duel that would be between them, and the dragon's victory the same that would happen to himself. But Arthur conjectured it portended something else, and that the vision was applicable to himself and the emperor.

Superficially, the dragon stands for Arthur, while the bear stands for a giant or Lucius. However, "the name Arthur = 'bear,' which was evidently common knowledge at the time, acts as a signal that the dream refers to Arthur's victories over the giant and Lucius only on a surface level. Its true meaning lies in its function as a portent of Arthur downfall."[31]

Arthur then set out for France, and did indeed kill a giant who had abducted Helena, the niece of Duke Hoel, and taken her to the top of St. Michael's Mount (Mont Saint-Michel in Normandy).[32] After this interlude, Arthur and his men headed for Augustodunum (Autun, in the Burgundy region of eastern France), where he expected Lucius Tiberius to be. The British forces joined battle with the Romans, and inflicted losses on the Romans. Lucius decided to return to Augustodunum and on the way entered Lengriae (perhaps Langres, in the Champagne-Ardennes region of France). Arthur, hearing of this, entered a certain valley called Suesia (perhaps the valley of the Suize, not far from Langres), where Lucius would pass. A fierce battle ensued, Lucius was killed, and the Romans either fled or surrendered.

Mordred's Treachery

Arthur was on his way to Rome and beginning to pass the Alps, when he received news[33] that "his nephew Modred, to whose care he had entrusted Britain, had by tyrannical and treasonable practices set the crown upon his own head; and that queen Guinevere, in violation of her first marriage, had wickedly married him."

Geoffrey did not invent this particular story, in the sense that there was a tradition involving Guinevere and another man. Thomas Green[34] discusses the *Dialogue of Melwas and Gwenhwyfar*, which dates from the early to mid–12th century. In this extract, Guinevere is talking:

> "Who is the man who sits in the common part of the feast,
> without for him either its beginning or end,
> sitting down there below the dais?"

> "The Melwas from Ynys Wydrin (Isle of Glass);
> you, with the golden, gilded vessels,
> I have drunk none of your wine."

> "Wait a little …
> I do not pour out my wine
> for a man who cannot hold out and would not stand in battle
> [and] would not stand up to Cai in his wine."

In the following verses Gwenhwyfar continues to taunt Melwas, while he proclaims his valor versus that of Cai. In the poem

> there is a reference to Gwenhwyfar and Melwas having met at a court in *Dyfneint*, "Devon," but the nature of this meeting isn't clear. The background to this poem is a pre–Galfridian Welsh story concerned with the rescue of Gwenhwyfar ("white fairy/ enchantress") by Arthur from an Otherworld Island of Glass controlled by Melwas ("honey youth")—who appears in other works as a magician who was a "thief that by magic and enchantment took a girl [presumably Gwenhwyfar] to the end of the world."

The story of Arthur's rescue of Guinevere is told in Caradoc of Llancarfan's *Life of Gildas*,[35] which dates from the 1120s or 1130s. In this story, the saint went to *Glastonia* (Glastonbury in Somerset) "at the time when king Melwas was reigning in the summer country." Caradoc goes on to say:

> Glastonia, that is, the glassy city, which took its name from glass, is a city that had its name originally in the British tongue. It was besieged by the tyrant Arthur with a countless multitude on account of his wife Gwenhwyfar, whom the aforesaid wicked king had violated and carried off, and brought there for protection, owing to the asylum afforded by the invulnerable position due to the fortifications of thickets of reed, river, and marsh. The rebellious king had searched for the queen throughout the course of one year, and at last heard that she remained there. When he saw this, the abbot of Glastonia, attended by the clergy and Gildas the Wise, stepped in between the contending armies, and in a peaceable manner advised his king, Melvas, to restore the ravished lady. Accordingly, she who was to be restored, was restored in peace and good will.

Having heard about Mordred and Guinevere's treachery, Arthur returned to Britain. Mordred with a large army met Arthur at Rutupi (Richborough in Kent) and slaughtered many of Arthur's men, but Arthur's army managed to regroup and put Mordred's army to flight. Mordred entered Winchester and Guinevere fled from York to the City of Legions, where she entered a nunnery. Arthur besieged Mordred in Winchester, and he fled to Cornwall. Arthur pursued him to the river Cambula (possibly the River Camel, which flows near to Castle Killibury, an Iron Age fort which may have been occupied in the 5th/6th century). In the battle that followed, Mordred was killed, and Arthur was mortally wounded. He was taken to the island of Avalon to be cured of his wounds, and gave up his crown to his kinsman Constantine, son of Cador, Duke of Cornwall.

The Island of Avalon

Geoffrey of Monmouth's *Life of Merlin*

Geoffrey does not describe Avalon is his *History*, but he does in a subsequent work, the *Life of Merlin*[36]:

> The island of apples which men call "The Fortunate Isle" gets its name from the fact that it produces all things of itself; the fields there have no need of the ploughs of the farmers and all cultivation is lacking except what nature provides. Of its own accord it produces grain and grapes, and apple trees grow in its woods from the close-clipped grass. The ground of its own accord produces everything instead of merely grass, and people live there a hundred years or more. There nine sisters rule by a pleasing set of laws those who come to them from our country. She who is first of them is more skilled in the healing art, and excels her sisters in the beauty of her person. Morgen is her name, and she has learned what useful properties all the herbs contain, so that she can cure sick bodies. She also knows an art by which to change her shape, and to cleave the air on new wings like Daedalus.... Thither after the battle of Camlan we took the wounded Arthur.

Avalon is probably based on the Irish *Emain Ablach* ("Emain of the Apples"), a poetic name used for the Isle of Man when seen as the blessed and otherworldly domain of Manannan mac Lir. The name *Morgen* may be derived from Welsh *mor*, "sea," and mean "sea-born"; *Morgen* is related to Irish *Muirgen*, the baptismal name given to a mermaid called Liban fished out of Lough Neagh (Northern Ireland) by a saint.[37]

The "Isle of the Strong Door" in *The Spoils of Annwn*

Avalon may be a creation of Geoffrey of Monmouth, but Arthur was already associated with an island inhabited by nine maidens in the enigmatic poem *The Spoils of Annwn*. This poem is attributed to the 6th century bard Taliesin, and is thought to have been composed between AD 800 and 1000, though as John Koch argues, some of the grammatical forms indicate that it may have been composed before AD 800.[38] *The Spoils of Annwn* concerns a voyage to Annwn, the Welsh Otherworld, in Arthur's ship *Prydwen*. Annwn seems to consist of a series of fortresses, and the island fortress is the second fortress (lines 11–24) (the *I* in the poem appears to be Taliesin himself)[39]:

> I am honored in praise. Song was heard
> in the Four-Peaked Fortress, four its revolutions.
> My poetry, from the cauldron it was uttered.
> From the breath of nine maidens it was kindled.
> The cauldron of the chief of Annwfyn: what is its fashion?
> A dark ridge around its border and pearls.
> It does not boil the food of a coward; it has not been destined.
> The flashing sword of Lleawch has been lifted to it.
> And in the hand of Lleminawc it was left.
> And before the door of hell lamps burned.
> And when we went with Arthur, brilliant difficulty,
> except seven none rose up from the Fortress of Mead-Drunkenness.
> I am honored in praise; song is heard
> in the Fortress of Four-Peaks, isle of the strong door.

The Four-Peaked Fortress contains a cauldron, and the most famous cauldron in Welsh mythology is the cauldron that Bran the Blessed gives to Matholwch, king of Ireland, in the Second Branch of the *Mabinogion*: "'I will give you this cauldron, and the peculiarity of the cauldron is this: a man who is killed today and thrown in the cauldron, by the next day he will be as good as he was at his best, except he will not be able to talk.'" The "isle of the strong door" is also to be found in the Second Branch. Bran the Blessed is forced to go to war with the Irish, and during battle, Bran was wounded in the foot with a poisoned spear. Then, because of his poisoned foot, Bran ordered the survivors to sever his head[40]:

> "Take the head" said he "and bring it to the White Hill in London, and bury it with its face towards France. And you will be on the road a long time. In Harlech you will be seven years in feasting, the birds of Rhiannon singing to you. The head will be as good company to you as it was at its best when it was ever on me. And you will be at Gwales in Penfro for eighty years. Until you open the door facing Aber Henvelen on the side facing Cornwall, you will be able to abide there, along with the head with you uncorrupted. But when you open that door, you will not be able to remain there. You will make for London and bury the head."

The seven survivors duly cut off Bran's head, and set off with it, landing at Aber Alaw in Anglesey. There Branwen died of a broken heart and was buried in a "four-sided grave," popularly believed to be the Bronze Age funerary mound known as Bedd Branwen. The men then set off for Harlech, and learned that Caswallwn, son of Beli, had overrun the island and was now the crowned king in London. They reached Harlech and

> began a feast, and the indulgence in food and drink was begun. And [as soon as] they began to eat and drink there came three birds, which began to sing a kind of song to them; and when they heard that song, every other [tune] seemed unlovely beside it. It seemed a distant sight, what they could see far above the ocean yet it was as clear as if they had been right next to them. And they were at that feast for seven years.

At the end of the seven years they moved to Gwales in Penfro (possibly the island of Grassholm, off the coast of Pembrokeshire) and a "beautiful kingly place high above the ocean," with two open door and one closed one, the one they must not open. There they "were completely free of care. Of all the grief that they had witnessed or experienced themselves—there was no longer any memory, or any of the sorrow in the world." At the end of eighty years, one of the seven survivors, Heilyn, son of Gwyn, became curious:

> "Shame on my beard," said he "if I don't open the door and find out whether it is true what is said about it." [So] he opened the door, and looked out to Cornwall and over Aber Henvelen. And when he looked, suddenly everything they had ever lost—loved ones and companions, and all the bad things that had ever happened to them; and most of all the loss of their king—became as clear as if it had been rushing in towards them.

Gwales/Grassholm with its door that must not be opened is almost certainly the "isle of the strong door" in *The Spoils of Annwn*.

The cauldron of the Four-Peaked Fortress is tended by nine maidens who sound like the Muses but may well have originated in Brittany rather than in classical Greece. The Roman geographer Pomponius Mela, writing around AD 43, says in his *Description of the World*[41]:

> In the Britannic Sea, opposite the coast of the Osismii, the isle of Sena [Sein] belongs to a Gallic divinity and is famous for its oracle, whose priestesses, sanctified by their perpetual divinity, are reportedly nine in number. They call the priestesses Gallizenae and think that because they have been endowed with unique powers, they stir up the seas and winds by their magic charms, that they turn into whatever animals they want, that they cure what it incurable among other peoples, that they know and predict the future, but that it is not revealed except to sea-voyagers and then only to those traveling to consult them.

The Osismii lived in the northwest of Brittany, and Sena is thought to be the Île de Sein, five miles from the Pointe du Raz in western Brittany.

Sacred Islands

The concept of a sacred island goes back to at least the Iron Age. The Greek historian, biographer and essayist Plutarch, in his work *On the Decline of Oracles*, written perhaps in AD 83 or 84, quotes a friend, Demetrius of Tarsus, lately returned from Britain after taking part in Agricola's educational drive or "cultural conquest" (his attempt to Romanize Britain) in the late 1st century AD[42]:

> Demetrius said that among the islands lying near Britain were many isolated, having few or no inhabitants, some of which bore the names of divinities or heroes. He himself, by the emperor's order, had made a voyage for inquiry and observation to the nearest of these islands which had only a few inhabitants, holy men who were all held inviolate by the Britons. Shortly after his arrival there occurred a great tumult in the air and many portents; violent winds suddenly swept down and lightning-flashes darted to earth. When these abated, the people of the island said that the passing of someone of the mightier souls had befallen. "For," said they, "as a lamp when it is being lighted has no terrors, but when it goes out is distressing to many, so the great souls have a kindling into life that is gentle and inoffensive, but their passing and dissolution often, as at the present moment, fosters tempests and storms, and often infects the air with pestilential properties." Moreover, they said that in this part of the world there is one island where Cronus is confined, guarded while he sleeps by Briareus; for his sleep has been devised as a bondage for him, and round about him are many demigods as attendants and servants.

Demetrius does not seem to be a figure that Plutarch invented. He has been identified with the Demetrius who offered two votive plaques in Greek at *Eboracum* (York): one to the gods of the governor's headquarters, the other "to [the Titans] Oceanus and Tethys, the god and goddess of the outer seas." Demetrius is a common name in Greek, but Greek inscriptions are very rare in Britain; and the gods to whom the vow is paid are highly appropriate for someone who has just travelled to distant islands, perhaps the Inner Hebrides.

In Greek mythology Cronus was a Titan, the son of Gaia ("Earth") and Uranus ("Sky"), known among the Romans as Saturn. He overthrew his father and ruled during the mythological Golden Age until he was overthrown by his own son Zeus and imprisoned in Tartarus (the underworld). Briareus was another son of Gaia and Uranus, who helped Zeus to overthrow Cronus. The classicist A.R. Burn, in a discussion of "holy islands" in pre–Christian Britain, cannot find any equivalent to Cronus in Welsh or Irish mythology, but suggests that this "Saturn-like figure does resemble the Earth-Father (Dis Pater, not Dyaus Pater, the Sky-Father) from whom, according to Caesar the Gauls claimed to be descended."[43] Clearly Cronus could also refer to Arthur, especially the wilderness Arthur of *Pa gur?* and *Culhwch and Olwen*.

There is no evidence that Grassholm was a sacred island, but in the 5th or 6th century, a monastery was established on Caldey Island off the south coast of Pembrokeshire, an island with a very long history of human habitation, and many caves. In the cave known as Daylight Rock, excavators found a "prolific assemblage of flint and flaked stone" dating to the Early Mesolithic, as well as the bones of a child and an adult together with a perforated bead. In Potter's Cave, excavation of the east entrance uncovered Late Bronze Age-Iron Age pottery, early Bronze Age (Beaker) pottery and Neolithic pottery in mixed upper layers, whilst some small Mesolithic implements were recovered from the basal layer. Cemented within and beneath stalagmite were flint and human bone. Later excavations of the cave interior recovered the bones of two individuals, many animal bones, four pieces of copper or bronze wire and flat pot sherds without markings, which may be of a Romano-British date. Continued excavations in the west entrance and passageway recovered forty-eight blue glass beads of an Iron Age (1st or 2nd century BC) date and two human burials. In Nanna's Cave, excavators found "the imperfect skull of an adult female and various bones of two individuals, the whole cemented together by stalagmite." Round-bottomed Neolithic bowls were also recovered together with pottery from the Bronze Age and Bronze Age/Iron Age tradition. The Romano-British period was also represented by pottery of the 3rd–4th centuries AD, and two spindle whorls.[44] Excavation of the cave Ogof yr Ychen found the remains of three human adults, and a child's bones from a much later date (they were found in Romano-British deposits).[45] In all probability Caldey was a sacred place in the prehistoric period, particularly suitable for burial.

Arthur, the Once and Future King

What happened to Arthur after he was taken to Avalon divided opinion in the Middle Ages. In 1191 the supposed tomb of Arthur and Guinevere was discovered near the site of the Old Church (a probable 7th century church) at Glastonbury in Somerset, which had been destroyed by fire in 1184. This discovery was witnessed by the Norman-Welsh priest and historian Gerald of Wales, who writes in his work *On the Instruction of Princes*[46]:

> Although legends had fabricated something fantastical about his demise (that he had not suffered death, and was conveyed, as if by a spirit, to a distant place), his body was discovered at Glastonbury, in our own times, hidden very deep in the earth in an oak-hollow, between two stone pyramids that were erected long ago in that holy place. The tomb was sealed up with astonishing tokens, like some sort of miracle. The body was then conveyed into the church with honor, and properly committed to a marble tomb. A lead cross was placed under the stone, not above as is usual in our times, but instead fastened to the underside. I have seen this cross, and have traced the engraved letters—not visible and facing outward, but rather

turned inwardly toward the stone. It read: "Here lies entombed King Arthur, with Guenevere his second wife, on the Isle of Avalon."

However, not everyone was convinced that Arthur was dead. For example, William of Malmesbury, in his Latin *Chronicle of the Kings of England*, published in 1125, says this[47]:

> At this time was found in the province of Wales called R(h)os the tomb of Walwen, who was the not degenerate nephew of Arthur by his sister. He reigned in that part of Britain which is still called Walweitha. A warrior most renowned for his valour, he was expelled fron his kingdom by the brother and nephew of Hengist, of whom I spoke in the first book, but not until he was compensated for his exile by much damage wrought upon them, worthily sharing in the praise of his uncle, in that they deferred for many years the ruin of their falling country. But the tomb of Arthur is nowhere to be beheld, whence ancient ditties fable that he is yet to come. The tomb of the other, however, as I have said, was found in the time of king William upon the sea-shore, fourteen feet in length; and here some say that he was wounded by his foes and cast out in a shipwreck, but according to others he was killed by his fellow citizens at a public banquet. Knowledge of the truth therefore remains doubtful, although neither story would be inconsistent with the defence of his fame.

William is here referring to Arthur's nephew Gawain, who is said to be buried in the cantref (hundred) of Rhos in Pembrokeshire, which is centered on the town of Haverfordwest. *Walweitha* is Galloway in southwest Scotland, and Rachel Bromwich comments[48]: "the significance of William's statement that Walwen 'reigned' in Galloway should not be overlooked. Any phonetic association between the two names may be set aside, yet the importance of the statement that Walwen belonged originally to north Britain still stands.... Geoffrey of Monmouth tacitly recognizes this association by giving his *Gualguanus* as father of the northern ruler Lot of Lothian."

According to William of Malmesbury, "ancient ditties fable that he is yet to come," and it was this version of Arthur's fate that survived into the late Middle Ages. Sir Thomas Malory, in *Le Morte d'Arthur*, first published in 1485, says in Book 21, Chapter 7[49]:

> Yet some men say in many parts of England that king Arthur is not dead, but had by the will of Our Lord Jesu in to another place; and men say that he shall come again, and he shall win the Holy Cross. Yet I will not say that it shall be so; but rather I would say, here in this world he changed his life. But many men say that there is written upon his tomb this:
> Hic iacet Arthurus Rex quondam Rexque futurus.

Hic iacet Arthurus, rex quondam, rexque futurus is "Here lies Arthur, king once, and king to be," in English, which of course provided T.H. White with the title of his Arthurian fantasy novel *The Once and Future King*.

William of Malmesbury was not the first to report such beliefs about

Arthur. In 1112 the city of Laon in northeastern France was burnt in a popular insurrection against the bishop. The clerks of the cathedral set out on a pilgrimage with the shrine of the Blessed Virgin to collect money for rebuilding. In the following year they crossed the Channel, and visited Canterbury and many other places in the south of England. According to Herman of Tournai, in his *Miracles of St. Mary of Laon*, on their way from Exeter in Devon to Bodmin in Cornwall, they were shown the Seat and Oven of King Arthur[50]; and at Bodmin a man with a withered hand, who was hoping to be cured by the shrine

> began to contend with one of our attendants named Haganel ... saying that Arthur was still alive. Whence no small tumult arose, many rushed into the church with arms, and unless the aforesaid clerk Algardus had intervened the matter would have almost come to the shedding of blood.

The Oven of King Arthur is probably the King's Oven, an ancient tin-smelting furnace used as a marker in the bounds of the royal forest of Dartmoor in 1240. This is not the only early Arthurian place-name: Lambert of St. Omer, in his *Liber Floridus* of 1120 refers to an "Arthur's Palace" in Pictland (Scotland), thought to be an old Roman temple on the Antonine Wall at Stenhousemuir near Falkirk now known as Arthur's O'on (Oven), which was demolished in 1743. There is also an Arthur's Bower ("bed-chamber") in Carlisle documented in the 1170s.[51]

Perhaps the earliest work to imply that Arthur was still alive was a Welsh work called the *Stanzas of the Graves*, which may date to the 9th century. According to stanza 44[52]:

> [There is] a grave for March, a grave for Gwythur,
> a grave for Gwgawn Red-sword;
> the world's wonder (*anoeth*) [is] a grave for Arthur.

The Arthurian scholar Thomas Green notes: "The poet's implication is that the graves of these Arthurian heroes are known but that of Arthur himself is *anoeth*, impossible to find/achieve, probably because he was rumoured not to be dead."

Geoffrey of Monmouth's Arthur

Geoffrey's Arthur tends to be associated with southwest England or southeast Wales: he is conceived at Tintagel in Cornwall; his court is at Caerleon near Newport in south Wales; Guinevere's original abduction story ends at Glastonbury in Somerset; and Arthur's final battle with Mordred takes place at the River Cambula, or Camel, in Cornwall. However, elements of the northern Arthur remain: battles take place in Lincolnshire and around York; the Saxons take refuge in the "wood of Celidon"; Hoel lies sick in Alclud; two of Arthur's closest friends are Urien Rheged and Lot of Lothian; and it is possible that Guinevere's father was originally Gwythyr, son of Greidawl, who, according to *Culhwch and Olwen*, lived in the North. And although early Arthur place-names like the Oven of King Arthur are in Devon, others like Arthur's O'on (Scotland), and Arthur's Bower (Carlisle), are in the North.

There are also vestiges of the wilderness Arthur of earlier Welsh tales. After Arthur and Hoel lifted the siege of Alclud and before they went to York, they headed for Loch Lomond, to the north of Dumbarton, where the Scots and Picts had sought refuge on the islands in the lake[53]:

> This lake contains sixty islands, and receives sixty rivers into it, which empty themselves into the sea by more than one mouth. There is also an equal number of rocks in these islands, as also of eagles' nests in these rocks, which flocked together there every year, and by the loud and general noise which they now made, foreboded some remarkable event that should happen to the kingdom.

This passage is borrowed from the "Wonders of Britain" section in Nennius' *History of the Britons*[54]:

> The first wonder is the lake Lumonoy. In there are sixty islands, and men dwell there, and sixty rocks encircle it, with an eagle's nest on each rock. There are also sixty rivers flowing into that place, and nothing goes out of there to the sea except one river, which is called Lenm/Lenin.

Lumonoy is likely to be Loch Lomond which drains south via the River Leven into the mouth of the River Clyde and is famous for its many islands. Nennius may well have got his information through ecclesiastical sources. Luss is on the west bank of Loch Lomond, and the first reference to a church there is in the 14th century. However, in the churchyard are two cross-slabs, probably of 7th to 9th century date, and a hogback of 11th century date, which suggest that there was a church on the site considerably before this.[55] The church is dedicated to the 6th century Irish missionary St. Kessog, who is believed to have had a monastery on Inchtavannach ("Island of the Monk's House"), an island in Loch Lomond.

Arthur Moves to England

Tales of Arthur were originally told in Welsh (apart from the Latin *History of the Britons*), and Geoffrey of Monmouth wrote in Latin. Both of these languages were not accessible to the average English person, but eventually Geoffrey's work was translated into Middle English, and Arthur became known in the land of his Anglo-Saxon foes. Layamon's *Brut* is a Middle English retelling of Geoffrey's *History*, but with wilderness scenes and battle violence more typical of Anglo-Saxon literature. The *Alliterative Morte Arthure* is also based on Geoffrey's *History*, but it depicts Arthur as a flawed character brought down by overweening ambition. There are some graphic scenes of violence in this work that are far removed from the tone of Geoffrey's *History* and closer perhaps to the Anglo-Saxon tradition.

King Arthur in Medieval England
Layamon's Brut
and the Alliterative Morte Arthure

The English Version of the History of the Kings of England: Layamon's Brut

The Birth and Coronation of Arthur

After the Norman Conquest in 1066, the writing of literature in English virtually ceased, with the exception of the Peterborough version of the *Anglo-Saxon Chronicle*, which continued to be produced until 1154. Apart from the *Peterborough Chronicle*, one of the earliest works in Middle English was Layamon's *Brut*, which was probably composed between 1185 and 1216,[1] and was based on Wace's *Roman de Brut*, a Norman French version of Geoffrey on Monmouth *History of the Kings of Britain*. Both works are named after Brutus, the legendary founder of Britain in Geoffrey's *History*.

Layamon (also known as Lawman) describes himself in his poem as a priest at Areley Kings (Worcestershire), at "a noble church on the River Severn." Although written in Middle English, it follows the conventions of Old English alliterative poetry like *Beowulf*. Like Wace, he follows Geoffrey's *History*, but on occasions Layamon enlarges on the original narrative. (I'll just provide a selection of extracts from the poem, starting with the birth and coronation of Arthur.[2])

Layamon gives a rather lyrical account of the birth of Arthur:

> Uther made Ygerne at once his consort.
> With child was Ygerne, and the child was King Uther's,
> Because of Merlin's magic before the marriage.
> Arrived the term for the birth, and Arthur was born.

> Into the world forth he came, and fairies then fetched him,
> With charms of great strength they strove to enchant him.
> Wondrous might would be his, worthiest of warriors.
> And more, he'd reign as the richest of rulers.
> The gift they gave last, his life to be long.
> From them he got great virtue and goodness,
> And was the mildest of men who draw breath.
> Such were the gifts they gave, with them the child thrived.

As in Geoffrey's *History*, Arthur was crowned at Silchester:

> And the British in bold bands assembled.
> That host was quite happy when Arthur arrived;
> Trumpets sounded high, the soldiers took heart.
> then to be ruler, young Arthur they raised up.
> Now when Arthur was king (an amazing event),
> To all the folk he made known his free hand,
> Bestowed much on his knights, this man in his bounty,
> To the children a father, to the aged a comfort,
> And the unruly found him exceptionally stern.
> Injustice he loathed, but loved men of loyalty.
> The staff of his servants, helpers of his household,
> Good men in his chambers, all these got gold coin,
> Were clad in fine clothes, dear drapes for their couches,
> No cook did he keep who did not bear arms,
> No squire not proven bold in battle,
> In high esteem holding his household knights,
> And with such soldiers ruined other rulers,
> With his fierceness of force, and the gifts that he gave.

Arthur at War with the Saxons

The new king then set off for York:

> The king advanced with the most awesome of armies,
> A force of fine splendor, to the city of York,
> Remained there one night, at dawn made his way
> To where Colgrim lay camped, his lords at his side.
> After Octa was brought down bereft of his life,
> (Who was Hengest's son, a hero from Saxony).
> Colgrim was highest in rank of those from that country
> After Hengest, and Horsa his brother,
> And Octa, Ossa, and their companion Ebissa.
> For the Saxons Colgrim set down the statutes,
> Ruled over and managed them, judged them with rigor.
> An army immense, the warriors that went with Colgrim.

Then Colgrim heard that Arthur was on the move:

> Colgrim moved forth, his fighters among him,
> Rushed off with his troops, came to a river;
> Douglas its name—deadly to warriors!
> Arthur fought him there, his men in formation.
> At a ford that was broad, he offered him battle.
> Men struck at each other, speeding their strokes,
> The doomed falling dead, right down to the dirt.
> Gore rushing everywhere, corpses in clumps.

Arthur's troops then fell back, and the Saxons pursued them:

> High to his head, Arthur hefted his shield,
> At their warriors he rushed, like a ravenous wolf,
> When, bristling with snow, he bursts from the woods,
> Bent on mangling every man whom he meets.
> He summoned his soldiers, this Arthur their sovereign:
> "Make fast for those men, my fighters most keen.
> All massed as they are, they shall be mowed down.
> And to the earth they'll tumble, like trees in the forest,
> When the wind in its wildness strikes with great strength."
> Over the hill hastened this host in their thousands,
> Slew Colgrim's soldiers, the doomed sought the dirt.
> Broad spears were broken, shields shaken and shivered.
> Saxons sank to the ground, covering the grass.
> Colgrim witnessed all, and thought it great woe,
> This high-born hero, who'd sailed there from Saxony.
> As fast as a fiend, Colgrim then took flight,
> With brute strength, his steed bore him off
> Over that deep-running stream, saved him from death.
> To the sand sank the Saxons, fated at the ford,
> Arthur's spear showed they would not be spared,
> Seven thousand Saxons drank death at that shore.
> Some wandered off, like the wild crane
> In the marshy moors, when in that fen his flock scatters,
> With hawks to harry them, who hunt in their swiftness,
> When raging hounds through the reeds ruthlessly pursue,
> But no safety to seek, neither the shore nor the stream.
> Hawks swoop with talons, dogs tear with their teeth.
> Regal but wretched, these birds destined for death.

Colgrim then fled to his fortress in York, and Arthur's forces besieged York. However, when Arthur heard that the "emperor Childric" had landed in Scotland, he decided to return to London. Childric then occupied land from the Humber to London: "All England was afflicted, mired in misery." Arthur then sent for Howel of Brittany, who arrived in Southampton with thirty thousand troops. Howel and Arthur then marched to Lincoln, which was besieged by Childric, and attacked Childric's army:

The Saxons were struck, could not flee for the forest,
Doomed to die there, no safety to seek, slaughter found them.
In no book of the British is another such battle recorded,
So many cut down, killed in their multitudes,
No army fated so ill, its fighters felled to earth.
Blood blotted the field, bodies bloated with gore.
Death roamed wide, a din from woe welled up.
Childric the king had constructed a castle,
A fort in the field, close to Lincoln it lay,
Built to withstand what battle might bring it,
There the king camped, with Colgrim and Badolf,
Witnessed the war then wating their army.
Arrayed themselves in arms, and with a coward's courage
Abandoned the fort, no fight would they offer,
Fled the field for the forest men call Calidon.

Arthur then besieged Childric in the forest of Calidon, and Childric finally promised to leave Britain and never return. However, Childric and his forces set sail and headed for Dartmouth in Devon. From there they laid waste the country and headed for Bath. When Arthur, who was in Scotland, heard this, he set off for Bath. There they joined battle with the enemy:

Arthur stepped forward, struck a Saxon with a sword,
In the man's mouth the blade lodged, stuck tight in his teeth.
Then brought it down on that man's brother,
Hewed into the man's helmet, to the dirt threw him down.
Yet another man came upon him, with his blade cut him in half,
Such deeds, done with courage, emboldened the Britons,
Who struck at the Saxons, with sword strokes they slew them,
Spiked them on their spears, pierced them with sword points.
Their foes fell down to earth, these enemies fated to die.
In their hundreds they were hewed down, the dead were in heaps.
A massacre that mounted to thousands and thousands,
Toward Colgrim Arthur advanced, and that king caught sight of him,
Encompassed by corpses, Colgrim could not escape,
But Badolf his brother bravely stood there beside him.
With a brash cry, Arthur bravely called out:
"Here I come, Colgrim, contest now the kingdom.
This land we'll divide, but the deal won't delight you."
Speaking his speech, Arthur raised up his sword arm,
Down went the blade for a blow, it cut Colgrim through,
His helmet was hewn, the sword split him in half,
Did not halt in his hauberk, but broke into his breast.
Then at Badolf he struck, the stroke beheading the man.

This and other battle descriptions in the *Brut* are much more graphic than those in Geoffrey's *History*, and are reminiscent of *Beowulf*. For example, after Grendel's death

> The bloodshot water wallowed and surged,
> there were loathsome upthrows and overturnings
> of waves and gore and wound-slurry.

And when Beowulf killed Grendel's mother, he

> took a firm hold of the hilt and swung
> the blade in an arc, a resolute blow
> that bit deep into her neck-bone
> and severed it entirely, toppling the doomed
> house of her flesh, she fell to the floor.
> The sword dripped blood, the swordsman was elated.

After his victory, Arthur went to Alclud (Dumbarton Rock), which the Scots and Picts were besieging; he defeated them and they fled to Loch Lomond, just to the north of Dumbarton, where Arthur pursued them. Layamon describes Loch Lomond in an passage which evokes the loch much more effectively than the rather bland description given by Geoffrey[3]:

> This is an uncanny mere set upon middle earth,
> With marshland and reeds and the water is very broad,
> With fish and with water-fowl, with fiendish creatures!
> The water cannot be measured; vast sea-monsters swim around within it;
> There are elvish creatures playing in the terrible pool;
> There are sixty islands stretching down the long water:
> On each of the islands is a rock both high and strong
> Where eagles make their nests and other huge birds;
> The eagles have a certain custom in the reign of every king
> Whenever any invading force comes flocking to the country:
> Then all the birds fly far up into the air,
> Many hundred thousand of them and create a huge contention;
> Then the people know without doubt that a great trial is to come to them
> From some kind of people who propose to visit that land.
> For two or three days this sign occurs in this way
> Until unknown men journey to that land.
> There is still one more marvel to mention concerning that water:
> There flow into that mere on many a side
> From dales and from downlands and from deep valleys
> Sixty different streams, all gathered together,
> Yet out of that mere no man has ever found one
> Which flows outwards there, except at one end
> A normal sized brook which discharges from the mere
> And trickles very tranquilly down to the sea.

The fact that Loch Lomond has been placed *mid fenne* ("in a fenland"), and the specific mention of *nikeres* ("sea-monsters") have been interpreted by Dorothy Everett and Roger Sherman Loomis as possible echoes of Grendel's mere in *Beowulf*.[4] Here is a description of the mere in *Beowulf*[5]:

A few miles from here
a frost-stiffened wood waits and keeps watch
above a mere; the overhanging bank
in a maze of tree-roots mirrored on its surface.
At night there, something uncanny happens:
the water burns. And the mere-bottom
has never been sounded by the sons of men.
On its bank, the heather-steppe halts:
the hart in flight from pursuing hounds
will turn to face them with firm-set horns
and die in wood rather than dive
beneath its surface. That is no good place.
When wind blows up and stormy weather
makes clouds scud and the skies weep,
out of its depths a dirty surge
is pitched towards the heavens.

And a further description:

The water was infested
with all kinds of reptiles. There were writhing sea-dragons
and monsters slouching on slopes by the cliff,
serpents and wild things such as those that often
surface at dawn to roam the sail-road
and doom the voyage.

The description of Loch Lomond also evokes the vision of St. Paul in the *Blickling Homilies.*[6]

Thus St. Paul was looking into the north of this middle earth, where all waters depart downwards, and there he saw over the water a certain hoary stone. And north of the stone were growing very frosty groves, and there were dark mists, and under the stone was the dwelling of monsters and water monsters.

Arthur Sets Off to Wage War with the Romans

Before Arthur set off to wage war with the Roman emperor he had a dream[7]:

"It seemed to me that in the sky a mysterious beast appeared,
In the clouds to the east, ugly in appearance,
With lightning and thunder, menacingly it advanced;
There is no bear so hideous in any land on earth;
Then there came from the west, whisking through the clouds,
A dragon all burning which engulfed boroughs;
With its fire it set alight all this land's realm:
It seemed to me as I stared that the very sea caught alight
With lightning and the fire which the dragon carried by.
This dragon and bear, both from opposite directions,

With intense speed were approaching each other,
They crashed into each other with furious impact:
Their eyes were flaring as if they were firebrands;
Time and again the dragon was winning, and then again it was losing,
But all the same eventually it managed to fly up
And flew down instantly with a furious assault
And struck at the bear which then tumbled to the earth,
And there he killed the bear and tore it limb from limb.
When the battle was finished the dragon flew away.
This was the dream I had when I was lying there asleep!"
The bishops listened to this, and men who'd learned from books;
Earls listened to it; barons listened to it;
Each from his understanding spoke intelligently:
They interpreted this dream [as they thought appropriate];
No knight there had the courage to interpret it unfavourably
Lest he would be made to lose those parts he specially loved!

This dream also appears in Geoffrey's *History*, where it is interpreted as Arthur's victory over a giant. However, Layamon seems to imply that the dream may not be a good omen when he remarks: "No knight there had the courage to interpret it unfavourably."

Arthur's Second Dream ... and the Death of Arthur

On occasions Layamon even introduces new material. After Arthur's defeat of the Roman emperor, he has another dream[8]:

I dreamed someone had lifted me right on top of some hall
And I was sitting on the hall, astride, as if I was going riding;
All the lands which I possess, all of them I was surveying,
And Gawain sat in front of me, holding in his hand my sword.
Then Modred came marching there with a countless host of men,
Carrying in his hand a massive battle-axe.
He started to hew, with horrible force,
And hacked down all the posts which were holding up the hall.
I saw Guinevere there as well, the woman I love best of all:
The whole roof of that enormous hall with her hands she was pulling down;
The hall started tottering, and I tumbled to the ground,
And broke my right arm, at which Modred said 'Take that!'
Down then fell the hall and Gawain fell as well,
Falling on the ground where both his arms were broken,
So with my left hand I clutched my beloved sword
And struck off Modred's head and it went rolling over the ground,
And I sliced the queen in pieces with my beloved sword,
And after that I dropped her in a dingy pit.
And all my fine subjects set of in flight,

And what in Christendom became of them I had no idea.
Except that I was standing by myself in a vast plain,
And then I started roaming all around the moors;
There I could see griffins and really gruesome birds.
Then a golden lioness came gliding over the downs,
As really lovely a beast as any Our Lord has made.
The lioness ran up to me and put her jaws around my waist,
And off she set, moving away towards the sea,
And I could see the waves, tossing in the sea;
And taking me with her, the lioness plunged into the water.
When we two were in the sea, the waves swept her away from me;
Then a fish came swimming by and ferried me ashore.
Then I was all wet and weary, and I was sick with sorrow.
And upon waking, I started quaking,
And then I started to shudder as if burning up with fire,
And so all night I've been preoccupied with my disturbing dream,
For I know of a certainty this is the end of my felicity,
And all the rest of my life I must suffer grief.

Arthur's plunge into the sea with the lioness seems to foreshadow his death and his trip to Avalon[9]:

Arthur was mortally wounded, grievously badly;
To him there came a young lad who was from his clan,
He was Cador the Earl of Cornwall's son;
The boy was called Constantine; the king loved him very much.
Arthur gazed up at him, as he lay there on the ground,
And uttered these words with a sorrowing heart:
"Welcome, Constantine; you were Cador's son;
Here I bequeath to you all of my kingdom,
And guard well my Britons all the days of your life
And retain for them all the laws which have been extant in my days
And all the good laws which there were in Uther's days.
And I shall voyage to Avalon, to the fairest of all maidens,
to the Queen Argante, a very radiant elf,
And she will make quite sound every one of my wounds,
Will make me completely whole with her health-giving potions.
and then I shall come back to my own kingdom
And dwell among the Britons with surpassing delight."
After these words there came gliding from the sea
What seemed a short boat, moving, propelled along by the tide
And in it were two maidens in remarkable attire,
Who took Arthur up at once and immediately carried him
And gently laid him down and began to move off.
And so it had happened, as Merlin said before:
That the grief would be incalculable at the passing of King Arthur.
The Britons even now believe that he is alive
And living in Avalon with the fairest of the elf-folk,

> And the Britons are still always looking for when Arthur comes returning.
> The man has not been born of any favoured lady,
> Who knows how to say any more about the truth concerning Arthur.
> Yet once there was a prophet and his name was Merlin:
> He spoke his predictions, and his sayings were the truth,
> Of how an Arthur once again would come to aid the English.

Significantly, in the last line of his poem, Layamon, who was almost certainly of Anglo-Saxon descent, refers to Arthur coming to the aid of the English (*not* the Britons), no doubt referring to an England dominated by another foreign invader (the Normans) for the past century.

Probably the main difference between Geoffrey's *History* and Layamon's *Brut* is that Layamon draws on images of the wilderness such as we see in Anglo-Saxon poetry (but not in Norman literature). So after the battle of the River Douglas, Layamon says of the Saxons[10]:

> Some wandered off, like the wild crane
> In the marshy moors, when in that fen his flock scatters,
> With hawks to harry them, who hunt in their swiftness,
> When raging hounds through the reeds ruthlessly pursue,
> But no safety to seek, neither the shore nor the stream.

Later Layamon says of Arthur when he is slaughtering Saxons:

> Wracked with rage, battle-minded as the boar,
> When wild in the woods he spies huge herds of swine.

And when Arthur describes Loch Lomond he says:

> This is an uncanny mere set upon middle earth,
> With marshland and reeds and the water is very broad,
> With fish and with water-fowl, with fiendish creatures!
> The water cannot be measured; vast sea-monsters swim around within it;
> There are elvish creatures playing in the terrible pool.

Clearly Layamon is much more aware of the wilderness than Geoffrey, and in a way he anticipates later Arthurian works like *Sir Gawain and the Green Knight*, and a set of 14th/15th century Arthurian romances set in Inglewood Forest in Cumbria.

The Alliterative Morte Arthure

The *Alliterative Morte Arthure* is one of the principal works of a school of anonymous narrative poetry that flourished in the Midlands and north of England during the second half of the 14th century, and that derives in some way from the Old English alliterative tradition, embodied in a poem like

Beowulf. It paints a rather different portrait of Arthur from that of the just and righteous king in Layamon's *Brut*, brought down by the treachery of Guinevere and Mordred.

The poem begins late in the story of Arthur, when Arthur is at Caerleon celebrating his victories and receives messengers from the Roman Emperor "Lucius Iberius" demanding that the King do homage and pay tribute as a vassal of Rome. Arthur refuses and sets sail from Britain, leaving Mordred as regent. On the sea, Arthur has a dream which is based on Geoffrey's *History* but is subtly different[11] (lines 760–803):

> He dreamed of a dragon, dreadful to see,
> Who came driving over the deeps, to drown [*drenchen*] all his people,
> Winging straight out of the western wastes,
> Wandering wickedly over the wide waves;
> His head and his neck all over the surface
> Were rippled with azure, enameled most fair;
> His shoulders were scaled in the same pure silver
> Spread over all the beast's body in sparkling points;
> His belly and his wings of wondrous colours,
> In his glittering mail he mounted most high,
> And all whome he smote were forfeit forever.
> His feet were blazoned a beautiful black,
> And such a deadly flare darted from his lips,
> That the sea from the flecks of fire seemed all aflame.
> Then out of the east directly towards him
> Up in the clouds came a savage black bear,
> With each shank like a pillar and paws most enormous,
> Their talons so deadly—all jagged they looked;
> With legs all crooked and filthily matted,
> Most vilely snarled, and foaming lips,
> Rough and repulsive he looked, and worse,
> His form the foulest that ever was framed.
> He stomped, he sneered, then swaggered about;
> He bounds to battle with brutal claws;
> He bellowed, he roared, so that all the earth rocked,
> So lustily he smote it for his own sheer delight.
> Then from afar the dragon charged toward him,
> And with his thrusts drove him far off toward the heavens.
> He moved like a falcon, fiercely he struck;
> He fought all at once with both fire and claw.
> Still, the bear seemed the stronger in battle,
> And savagely slashed him with venomous fangs;
> He gave him such blows with his great paws
> That his breast and his belly were all bathed in blood.
> The bear raged so wildly he rent all the earth,
> Which ran with red blood like rain from the heavens.
> He would have brought down that serpent by sheer brute force,

> Were it not for the fierce fire with which he fought back.
> Then soared the serpent away toward his zenith,
> Swooped down from the sky and struck full straight:
> Smote the bear with his talons, tore open his back,
> Which was ten feet in length from the top to the tail.
> Thus the dragon crushed the bear and drove him from life;
> May he fall in the flood and float off to his fate!

Arthur summoned the "cleverest of clerics in all Christendom" (line 809) and asked them to interpret his dream (lines 810–828):

> He told them of his torment during the time he slept:
> "Wracked by a dragon, and such a dread beast,
> He has made me most weary—so help me dear God,
> Interpret my dream, or I die at once!"
> "Sire," said they presently, these sage men of knowledge,
> "The dragon you dreamed of, so dreadful to see,
> Who came driving over the deeps to drench—not drown [*drenchen*]—your folk,
> Truly and for certain symbolizes you yourself,
> Who here sail over the sea with your steadfast knights;
> The colors that were painted upon his brilliant wings
> Must be all the kingdoms that you have justly conquered;
> And the tentacled tail with tongues so huge
> Signifies these fair folk who in your fleet go forth;
> The bear that was vanquished high up in the clouds
> Betokens the tyrants who torment your people,
> Or that a day of battle must be braved by you alone,
> In single-hand combat with some kind of giant,
> And you shall gain victory through the grace of our Lord,
> As you in your vision were vividly shown.
> Be not troubled, Sir Conqueror, but hearten yourself,
> As well as these who sail the sea with your steadfast knights."

The dream of the dragon and bear occurs in Geoffrey's *History* and Layamon's *Brut*, but in the *Alliterative Morte Arthure*, the dream is slightly different. In contrast to all earlier versions, the description of the dragon precedes that of the bear. The author describes the dragon as a magnificent animal shining in silver and brilliant colors; nearly all his features are positive ones. The bear, however, is a wild monster; all the epithets applied to him are negative. The dragon comes over the ocean from the west in order to destroy Arthur's people: "drown [*drenchen*] all his people." This statement is repeated by the clerics when they explain Arthur's dream, and they stress specifically that the dragon coming to drown Arthur's people is Arthur himself (Krishna translates the clerics' interpretation as "drench—not drown," but the original Middle English simply says *drenchen*, "drown"). The clerics are predicting, quite correctly, that Arthur will destroy his own people and the only comfort they can offer is "Be not troubled, Sir Conqueror, but hearten yourself,/ As well as these who sail the sea with your steadfast knights."[12]

Upon landing in Brittany, Arthur fights and slays the giant of St. Michael's Mount, who has carried off and devoured many people of that land, including the young Duchess of Brittany. After a number of battles in which Arthur and his knights are victorious, they finally join battle with the Emperor. Lucius is slain and Arthur is victorious, but Kay, Bedevere and many other British knights fall in battle. The violent scene in which Kay is mortally wounded is described in graphic detail (lines 2165–2178):

> Then Sir Kay the keen levels his lance,
> Gives chase on a courser and charges a king;
> With a spear of Lithuania he rips through his ribs,
> So both liver and lungs are impaled on the lance;
> The shaft shivered and sailed toward the great lord,
> Ripped clear through the shield and came to rest in the man.
> But on entry Sir Kay was ignobly attacked
> By a coward knight from that great land;
> Just as he turned the traitor struck,
> Right through the flesh and into the flank,
> So the brutal lance ripped open the bowel,
> And burst on impact and broke in the center!
> Sir Kay knew full well by that infamous wound
> He was doomed by that stroke and done out of his life.

Arthur's response to the death of Kay was equally violent (2197–2209):

> Then the great king cries out with grief in his heart,
> And rides into the rout to avenge Sir Kay's death,
> Pushes into the press and encounters a prince,
> Known as heir of Egypt in those eastern lands,
> And with Caliburn cleaves him cleanly asunder;
> Slices right through the man, splits the saddle in two,
> And right there on the steed's back burst open the bowel.
> In his fury he fiercely takes on another,
> And the middle of that mighty man, who maddened him mightily,
> Through the mail he slits it asunder at center,
> So that half of the man falls on the hill,
> And the other half, haunch down, is left on the horse
> —Of that hurt, I vow, he will never be healed.

Once Arthur is victorious, he sends the bodies of his enemies back to Rome with a scornful message, calling them the "tribute" which Rome had demanded, and finally buries his men with great honor. These and other passages seem to be particularly violent, but it is worth remembering that when the *Alliterative Mort Arthure* was written the Hundred Years' War (1337–1453) between England and France was in full swing, and it is perfectly possible that the writer of the work had first-hand experience the kind of violence he describes.

After his victory over Lucius, Arthur decides to make war on the Duke of Lorraine, claiming that he was a disloyal vassal. He settles down to a siege of the city of Metz, sending Gawain and other knights out on a foraging expedition. Gawain, looking for adventure, encounters and fights Priamus, a Saracen knight, in a joust that ends with the two knights becoming friends and Priamus converting to Christianity. A battle against the duke's forces and the siege of the city both end in victory for Arthur, Arthur then marches down through Italy, conquering city after city in a campaign that ends with the Romans offering Arthur the Imperial crown. Arthur is usually depicted as a heroic figure, but his Italian campaign seems the opposite of heroic (lines 3150–3161):

> He turns into Tuscany, when the time seems ripe,
> Swiftly takes over towns, with their towers so tall,
> Battered down walls and wounded knights,
> Overturned towers, put people to torment,
> Made worthy widows wail of woe,
> Curse and weep one and all and wring their hands,
> And lays waste by war wherever he rides,
> Their wealth and their dwellings, and wreaked wretchedness.
> Thus they spread and dispersed and spared but little,
> Robbed without pity and ravaged their vines,
> Lavishly spent what had been long in saving,
> Then sped to Soleto with spears by the score.

Just at this moment of greatest triumph, Arthur has a second dream, unlike any dream in Geoffrey's *History* or Layamon's *Brut*, which he recounts to his sages (3230–3287):

> It seemed I was in a wood, lost and alone,
> And knew not at all which way I should go,
> For wolves, wild boars, and bloodthirsty beasts
> Stalked that wasteland, searching for prey;
> There hideous lions were licking their fangs,
> In their lust to lap the blood of my royal knights.
> Through that forest I fled to where flowers grew high,
> To hide me, in fear of those foul things.
> I came on a meadow surrounded by mountains,
> Most delightful on earth that men might behold;
> The valley all round was covered all about
> And clad clear over with clover and blooms;
> The vale was circled with vineyards of silver,
> All hung with gold grapes, there never were grander,
> Trimmed with arbors and all types of trees,
> Fine, fair groves, with flocks grazing beneath.
> There were furnished all fruits that flourish on earth,

Nicely fenced in upon those fair boughs;
With no dropping of damp that could damage the blooms,
In the warmth of the day all dry were the flowers.
Down from the clouds descended into that dale
A lady dressed richly in damasked robes,
In a surcoat of silk of such a rare hue,
All fretted with fur full to the hem,
And with elegant lappets as long as a yard,
All lovingly lined with layers of gold;
Jewels, gold coins, and other bright gems
On her back and her breast were embroidered all over;
With head-dress and coronal richly arrayed,
Another so fair of face could never be found.
With her white hands she whirled round a wheel
As if she might suddenly upset it completely;
The rim was red gold set with rare royal stones,
Arrayed with richness and rubies aplenty;
The spokes were all plated with splints of pure silver,
And splendidly spread out a full spear's span.
At the summit was a seat of snow-white silver,
Fretted with rubies, flashing with fire.
Round the rim there clung kings, one after another,
With crowns of pure gold, all cracking apart.
Six from that seat had been struck down abruptly,
Each one in turn, and they cried out these words:
"That I reigned on this wheel I shall rue it forever!
Never monarch mighty as me had ruled on this earth.
When I rode with my retinue I recked [cared] nothing more
But to hunt and revel and ravage the people;
And thus I drew out my days, as long as I could endure,
And for that I am ruthlessly damned for ever."
The lowest was a little man, who had been thrown beneath;
His loins lay there all lean and loathsome to look at,
His locks grey and long, the length of a yard,
His flesh and his form full foully disfigured;
And one of his eyes was brighter than silver,
And the other was yellower than the yolk of an egg!
"I was lord," cried that man, "of lands beyond measure,
And all men bowed before me who drew breath on this earth!
Now not a rag is left me to lay on my body,
And I am suddenly forsaken—let all men see the truth!"

The four other kings had much the same message for Arthur, and when they had finished speaking, Arthur approached the lady (lines 3338–3361):

Then I went toward that fair one and greeted her warmly,
And she said, "Welcome indeed, it is well you are come;
If you were wise, you would worship my will,

Of all the worthy men there ever were in this world;
For all your glory in war through me you have won;
I have been friendly to you, Sir, and hostile to others,
Whom you have fought, in faith, and many of your folk;
For I felled Sir Frollo, for all his fierce knights,
And thus the fruits of France are all freely yours.
You shall achieve this chair, I choose you myself,
Above all other chieftains honored on earth."
She lifted me smoothly in her slim hands,
And set me gently in the seat and presented me the scepter;
And with a comb deftly she dressed my hair,
So the waving locks curled up round my crown,
Put on me a diadem, dazzling fair bedecked,
Then offered me an orb, all studded with fair stones,
And enameled with azure, earth blazoned thereon,
Encircled with the salt sea on every side,
As a symbol that I truly was supreme on all the earth.
Then she brought me a sword with a most splendid hilt,
And bade me "Brandish the blade; this sword is my own;
Many a man by its stroke has shed his life's blood,
And while you work with this weapon it will fail you never."

The lady then went to the orchard and "bade the boughs bow down and yield
to my hands/The best that they bore on their branches so high" (lines 3366–7),
and then (lines 3370–3421)

She bade me spare not the fruit but sample at will:
"Taste of the finest, you worthy man;
Reach for the ripest and revel yourself;
Rest, royal King, for Rome is your own.
And I shall willingly whirl the well-wheel straightway,
And reach you rich wine in clear-rinsed cups."
Then she went to the well at the edge of the wood,
That welled up with wine and wondrously flowed,
Dipped a cupful and drew it up deftly,
Then bade me draw deeply and drink it to her.
And thus she led me about the space of an hour,
With all the fondness and love any man could desire;
But exactly at midday her mood changed completely,
And she turned on me with terrible words.
When I entreated her she drew down her brows:
"King, you cry to no use, by Christ who created me!
You must lose this game and later your life;
You have lived with delight and lands long enough!"
Round she spun the wheel and whirled me under,
So all my limbs then and there were pounded to pieces,
And with the chair my spine was broken asunder.
Then I wakened, truly all worn down with these dreams;

And now you know my woe, speak out as you wish."
"Sire," said the sage, "your good fortune is passed:
You shall find her your foe—test her out as you wish;
You are now at your zenith, I tell you in truth;
Take what challenge you wish, you will achieve nothing more.
You have spilled much blood and destroyed many men,
All sinless, by your pride, in sundry kings' lands.
Shrive you of your sins and prepare for your end;
You have had a sign, Sir King, please you, take heed,
For you shall fall fearfully within five winters.
Found abbeys in France—her fruits are your own—
For Frollo, for Ferrant, and for all those fierce knights,
Who in France you have savagely felled on the field.
Take heed of the other kings and search in your own heart:
They were renowned conquerors, crowned on this earth.
The most ancient was Alexander, whom all earth bowed before,
The next Hector of Troy, that hardy hero,
The third Julius Caesar, renowned as a giant,
Acclaimed by knights in all battles as mighty;
The fourth was Sir Judas, a jouster most noble,
That unconquered Maccabee, mightiest of strength;
The fifth was Joshua, that gallant man-at-arms,
That much joy brought to Jerusalem's host;
The sixth, David, the peerless, deemed by kings
One of the noblest that ever was knighted;
For with a sling he slew with a stroke of his hands
Goliath the giant, most ferocious on earth,
Then composed in his day all those beloved psalms,
That in the Psalter are set down in such a strange tongue."

The night after the dream, Arthur encounters Cradok, a knight from his court garbed in humble pilgrim's clothes and traveling to Rome. Cradok informs him of Mordred's seizure of the crown and adultery with Guinevere. Arthur hastens back to Britain and engages is a sea battle with Mordred's heathen allies. After Arthur's victory, Gawain and his men go ashore and engage in battle against heavy odds, which ends with the slaying of Gawain by Mordred (lines 3840–3859):

Then [Gawain] moves in on Mordred among all his knights,
Smote him mid-shield and thrust him through,
But the traitor swerved slightly from the sharp weapon,
And he slashed him in the ribs a six-inch span.
The shaft shivered and sank into that splendid knight,
So the spurting blood streamed clear to his shank,
And gleamed on his greave, burnished so bright.
They so struggle and shove, Mordred sprawls in the dust;
With the force of the lance, he lands on his shoulders,

A furlong off, on the ground, all gruesomely wounded.
Gawain flew after him and flung himself flat;
As his grief was fixed, so followed his fortune:
He whipped out a short knife, sheathed in silver,
And would have slit his throat through, but no chink chanced;
His hand slipped and slid aslant down the mail,
And the other one slyly slung him under.
With a sharp knight the traitor struck,
Through helm and head, up into the brain.
Thus Sir Gawain is gone, that good man-in-arms,
With no rescue at all—rue is the more.

Even Mordred was moved by the death of Sir Gawain when he speaks to King Frederick of Friesland (lines 3875–3894):

"He was unmatched on earth, Sir, on my oath.
He was Gawain the good, most gracious of men,
And the greatest of knights who lived under God,
The man boldest of hand, most blessed in battle,
And the humblest in hall under all the wide heavens;
In leadership the lordliest as long as he lived,
And lauded as a lion in lands far and wide;
Had you known him, Sir King, in the country he came from,
His wisdom, his valor, his virtuous works,
His conduct, his courage, his exploits in arms,
You would weep for his death all the days of your life."
Then the traitor freely let fall his tears,
Turned away suddenly and spoke no more,
Rode off crying and cursed the hour
That ever his fate was written to work such woe.
It wrung his heart when he thought on this thing;
For the sake of his blood-ties sorrowing he rides.
When that fugitive wretch recalled to himself
The glory and the good times of the Round Table,
He railed and he rued all his ruinous works.

Arthur laments Gawain's death, realizes that his own good fortune is at an end, and vows vengeance on Mordred. In a final battle, Arthur comes face to face with Mordred (lines 4227–4251):

"Turn, untrue traitor; no more shall you thrive.
By the great God you shall die by dint of my hands!
No man shall rescue you, nor all the riches on earth!"
And the King with Caliburn heroically smites:
The corners of his shining shield shears right through,
Straight into the shoulder a six-inch span,
So the bright red blood gleamed on the mail.
Mordred shivered and shuddered, but shrank only a little;
Then bounded back boldly in his bright garb;

The felon with that fine sword fiercely struck,
And the flesh on the far flank he slashes asunder.
Straight through surcoat and hauberk of splendid mail
He flaps open the flesh a half-foot span.
That dread blow was Arthur's deathwound—dole is the more
That ever the gallant have to die except at God's will.
Still with his sword Caliburn bravely he strikes,
Thrusts forth shining shield and shelters him well,
And swipes off Mordred's sword hand as he sweeps by!
An inch from the elbow he cleft it clean off
So Mordred sprawls on the sod and sinks into a faint—
Through armplate of bright steel and shining chain mail,
So both hilt and hand lie on the heath.
Then in a flash he heaves that fiend to his feet,
Runs him through with his blade right to the bright hilt,
So he sprawls on the sword and sinks down to his death.

Arthur then addresses his men (lines 4303–4331):

"Let us go to Glastonbury—nothing else will do now—
Where we may peacefully rest and care for our wounds.
For this lofty day's labour, praise be the Lord,
Though he has destined and doomed me to die alone."
Then at once they wholeheartedly heed his behest,
And proceed toward Glastonbury by the readiest route,
Reach the Isle of Avalon, and Arthur alights,
And goes to a manor there—he could move no further.
A surgeon of Salerno searches his wounds,
And the King sees from this he will never be sound,
And soon to his steadfast men he speaks these words:
"Do call me a confessor with Christ in his hands;
I must have the Host quickly, whatever else chance.
My kinsman, Constantine, shall wear the crown,
In keeping with his kinship, if Christ allows it.
Sir, if you prize my blessing, bury these lords
Who in that struggle with swords were sundered from life;
And then sternly mark that Mordred's children
Be secretly slain and slung into the seas:
Let no wicked weed in this world take root and thrive –
I warn you, by your worth, work as I bid.
I forgive all offenses, for Christ's love in heaven:
If Guinevere has fared well, fair fortune be with her."
With all his strength he said "*In manus*" on the ground where he lay,
And gave up his spirit and spoke nevermore.
The royal blood of Britain then, bishops and all,
Proceed toward Glastonbury, with hearts full of grief,
To bury the brave king and bring him back to the earth,
With all the honour and majesty that any man could have.

The Arthur of the *Alliterative Morte Arthure* is very different from Geoffrey's Arthur, Layamon's Arthur, and the Arthur of the French romances. As Valerie Krishna says in the Introduction to her translation[13]:

> this Arthur is more than a simple heroic warrior-king; he is an ambiguous and not wholly laudable figure, perhaps the most complex Arthur in all Arthurian literature. In recent years critics have begun to see the King as a tragic hero—flawed and guilty of hubris—and to consider the poem a medieval tragedy with affinities not to the drama but to the "Fall of Princes" literature, moral stories which recount the fickleness of fortune and the fall of the great in the manner of Chaucer's *Monk's Tale.*

The Monk's Tale by Chaucer is a collection of seventeen short stories which recount the tragic end of historical figures, including Alexander and Julius Caesar, two of the kings on the wheel in Arthur's dream.

It's worth pointing out too that the *Alliterative Morte Arthure* is more violent even than Layamon's *Brut*, and aligns the poem with the Anglo-Saxon tradition rather than with Geoffrey of Monmouth's *History*. The wilderness does not play much of a role in the poem, but it does appear at the beginning of Arthur's second dream:

> It seemed I was in a wood, lost and alone,
> And knew not at all which way I should go,
> For wolves, wild boars, and bloodthirsty beasts
> Stalked that wasteland, searching for prey;
> There hideous lions were licking their fangs,
> In their lust to lap the blood of my royal knights.

The Return to Anglo-Saxon Roots

The *Alliterative Morte Arthure* was probably the last work to draw solely on the Arthur created by Geoffrey of Monmouth. The 14th century produced another work in the alliterative tradition, *Sir Gawain and the Green Knight*, which took Arthurian romance in a very different direction. This poem draws on French works, particularly the *Lancelot-Grail*, to create characters like Bertilak de Hautdesert (the real-life identity of the Green Knight) and his guest Morgan le Fay, but also returns to Anglo-Saxon heroic poetry like *Beowulf* and poems of exile like *The Wanderer* for some of its episodes—the Green Knight's arrival at Camelot, and Gawain's journey through the "wilds of the Wirral."

9

An Arthurian Hero
in the Wilderness
Sir Gawain and the Green Knight

French Arthurian Romances

In the second half of the 12th century, the story of Arthur was taken up by the French poet Chrétien de Troyes, whose most influential works were *Lancelot, the Knight of the Cart*, and *Perceval, the Story of the Grail*. Chrétien created Lancelot, who became one of Arthur's most popular knights, and introduced the theme of Lancelot's adultery with Guinevere, which became a staple of medieval romances.

Chrétien also introduced the quest for the Grail, although in *Perceval* it was simply "a grail," not the Holy Grail. Chrétien saw the Grail as a serving dish, but in Robert de Boron's *Joseph of Arimathea* (late 12th/early 13th century), the Grail became the Holy Grail, the cup used by Jesus at the Last Supper. The works of Chrétien and Robert de Boron were very popular, and led to the most definitive work on the quest for the Holy Grail, the *Lancelot-Grail*, also known as the *Prose Lancelot* or the *Vulgate Cycle*, which dates to between 1220 and 1240. The *Lancelot-Grail* consists of five parts: the *Estoire del Saint Graal* ("History of the Holy Grail"), the *Estoire de Merlin* ("History of Merlin"), the *Lancelot propre* ("Lancelot Proper"), the *Queste del Saint Graal* ("Quest for the Holy Grail"), and the *Mort Artu* ("Death of Arthur").

In England the French Arthurian tradition produced one notable work, the 14th century *Stanzaic Morte Arthur*, which is a condensed version of the French *Mort Artu*; and it underlies a second work of the 14th century, *Sir Gawain and the Green Knight*.

The Return of the Wilderness

In early Arthurian tales like *Pa gur?* and *Culhwch and Olwen*, Arthur and his companions Cai and Bedwyr were associated with wild places and with monstrous beings like Dog-heads and giants. The wild places largely disappeared in *Geoffrey's History*, made fleeting appearances in Layamon's *Brut*, and were virtually absent in the *Alliterative Morte Arthure*. However, they returned once more in *Sir Gawain and the Green Knight*, a late 14th century romance written in the North West Midland dialect of Middle English, somewhere in the area where southeast Cheshire meets northwest Staffordshire. This poem, like the *Alliterative Morte Arthur*, was part of the alliterative revival of the 14th century, and is reckoned to be one of the greatest works of medieval English literature. The poem is clearly familiar with French Arthurian literature, but also draws on Anglo-Saxon heroic tales like *Beowulf*, and poems of exile like *The Seafarer* and *The Wanderer*.

The Early History of Gawain

Gawain was popular in the French romances, but in fact Gawain as a character pre-dates the French romances and even Geoffrey's *History*. He appears in *Culhwch and Olwen* as Gwalchmei, who "never returned home without achieving the adventure of which he went in quest. He was the best of footsoldiers and the best of knights." In Triad 4 of the *Triads of the Island of Britain*, Gwalchmai, son of Gwyar, is said to be one of the "Three Well-Endowed Men of the Island of Britain" (the other two are Llachau, son of Arthur, and the obscure Rhiwallawn Broom-Hair). The name *Gwalchmei* may mean something like "Hawk of the Plain."

As I said earlier, Gawain is referred to by William of Malmesbury as Walwen, and is said to be buried in the cantref (hundred) of Rhos in Pembrokeshire. In Geoffrey's *History*, he is called Walgan, and is said to be the son of Lot and Arthur's sister, and brother of Mordred. He takes part in Arthur's campaign against Lucius Tiberius, and eventually dies when Arthur returns to Britain to fight Mordred. There is an episode in Geoffrey's *History*, repeated in Layamon's *Brut*, that seems to anticipate *Sir Gawain and the Green Knight*. Arthur and his men are about to confront the Roman forces at the River Aube in France, and Arthur sends a delegation to Lucius:

> They went to Lucius, and commanded him to retire out of Gaul, or hazard a battle the next day. But while he was answering them, that he was not come to retire, but to govern the country, there was present Caius Quintilianus, his nephew, who said that the Britons were better at boasting and threatening, than they were at fighting. Walgan immediately took fire at this, and ran upon him with his drawn sword,

wherewith he cut off his head, and then retreated speedily with his companions to their horses.[1]

Sir Gawain and the Green Knight

The Green Knight at Camelot

As *Sir Gawain and the Green Knight* opens, Arthur is holding a feast at Camelot[2]:

> It was Christmas at Camelot—King Arthur's court,
> where the great and good of the land had gathered,
> all the righteous lords of the ranks of the Round Table
> quite properly carousing and revelling in pleasure.

Gawain was seated next to Guinevere, and as the guests were starting to eat

> a fearful frame appeared, framed in the door:
> a mountain of a man, immeasurably high,
> a hulk of human from head to hips,
> so long and thick in his loins and his limbs
> I should genuinely judge him to be a half-giant,
> or a most massive man, the mightiest of mortals.
> But handsome too, like any horseman worth his horse,
> for despite the bulk and brawn of his body
> his stomach and waist were slender and sleek.
> In fact in all features he was finely formed
> it seemed.
> Amazement seized their minds,
> no soul had ever seen
> a knight of such a kind—
> entirely emerald green.

All the knight's garments were green, the horse and horse-gear were green, the knight's hair and beard were green:

> No waking man had witnessed such a warrior
> or weird war-horse—otherworldly, yet flesh
> and bone.
> A look of lightning flashed
> from somewhere in his soul.
> The force of that man's fist
> would be a thunderbolt.

> Yet he wore no helmet and no hauberk either,
> no armoured apparel or plate was apparent,
> and he swung no sword nor sported any shield,

but held in one hand a sprig of holly—
of all the evergreens the greenest ever—
and in the other hand held the mother of all axes,
a cruel piece of kit I kid you not:
the head was an ell in length at least
and forged in green steel with a gilt finish;
the skull-busting blade was so stropped and buffed
it could shear a man's scalp and shave him to boot.
The handle which fitted that fiend's great fist
was inlaid with iron, end to end,
with green pigment picking out impressive designs.
From stock to neck, where it stopped with a knot,
a lace was looped the length of the haft,
trimmed with tassels and tails of string
fastened firmly in place by forest-green buttons.

The green knight then addressed the assembled guests:

"And who," he bellows, without breaking breath,
"is governor of this gaggle? I'll be glad to know.
It's with him and him alone that I'll have
my say."
The green man steered his gaze
deep into every eye,
explored each person's face
to probe for a reply.

Finally King Arthur did reply and asked the knight what he wanted, to which the knight responded:

"at Christmas in this court I lay down a challenge:
if a person here present, within these premises,
is big or bold or red-blooded enough
to strike me one stroke and be struck in return,
I shall give him as a gift this gigantic cleaver
and the axe shall be his to handle how he likes.
I'll kneel, bare my neck and take the first knock.
so who has the gall/ The gumption? The guts?
Who'll spring from his seat and snatch this weapon/
I offer the axe—who'll have it as his own?
I'll afford one free hit from which I won't flinch,
and promise that twelve months will pass in peace,
then claim
the duty I deserve
in one year and one day.
Does no one have the nerve
to wager in this way?"

At first there was silence, but finally Arthur addressed the knight:

"Your request," he countered, "is quite insane,
and folly finds the man who flirts with the fool.
No warrior worth his salt would be worried by your words,
so in heaven's good name hand over the axe
and I'll happily fulfil the favour you ask."
He strides to him swiftly and seizes his arm;
the man-mountain dismounts in one mighty leap.
Then Arthur grips the axe, grabs it by its haft
and takes it above him, intending to attack.
Yet the stranger before him stands up straight,
highest in the house by at least a head.
Quite simply he stands there stroking his beard,
fiddling with his coat, his face without fear,
about to be bludgeoned, but no more bothered
than a guest at the table being given a goblet
of wine.
By Guinevere, Gawain
now to his king inclines
and says, "I stake my claim,
This moment must be mine."

Arthur and the whole court agreed that Gawain should wield the axe:

Gawain, with the weapon, walked toward the warrior.
and they stand face to face, not one man afraid.
Then the green knight spoke, growled at Gawain,
"Before we compete, repeat what we've promised.
And start by saying your name to me, sir,
and tell me the truth so I can take it on trust."
"In good faith, it's Gawain," said the God-fearing knight,
"I heave this axe, and whatever happens after,
in twelvemonth's time I'll be struck in return
with any weapon you wish, and by you and you
alone."
The other answers, says
"Well, by my living bones,
I welcome you, Gawain,
To bring the blade-head home."

But before Gawain could strike, the knight made another condition:

"you must solemnly swear
that you'll seek me yourself; that you'll search me out
to the ends of the earth to earn the same blow
as you'll dole out today in this decorous hall."

Finally the time came for the green knight to take the blow:

In the standing position he prepared to be struck,
bent forward, revealing a flash of green flesh

as he heaped his hair to the crown of his head,
the nape of his neck now naked and ready.
Gawain grips the axe and heaves it heavenwards,
plants his left foot firmly on the floor in front,
then swings it swiftly towards the bare skin.
The cleanness of the strike cleaved the spinal cord
and parted the fat and flesh so far
that that bright steel blade took a bite from the floor.
The handsome head tumbles onto the earth
and the king's men kick it as it clatters past.
Blood gutters brightly against his green gown,
yet the man doesn't shudder of stagger or sink
but trudges towards them on those tree-trunk legs
and rummages around, reaches at their feet
and cops hold of his head and hoists it high,
and strides to his steed, snatches the bridle,
steps into the stirrup and swings into the saddle
still gripping his head by a handful of hair.
Then he settles himself in his seat with the ease
of a man unmarked, never mind being minus
his head!
And when he wheeled about
his bloody neck still bled.
His point was proved. The court
was deadened now with dread.

For that scalp and skull now swung from his fist;
towards the top table he turned the face
and it opened its eyelids, stared straight ahead
and spoke this speech, which you'll hear for yourselves:
"Sir Gawain, be wise enough to keep your word
and faithfully follow me until I'm found
as you vowed in this hall within hearing of these horsemen.
You're charged with getting to the green chapel,
to reap what you've sown. You'll rightfully receive
the justice you are due just as January dawns.
Men know my name as the green chapel knight
and even a fool couldn't fail to find me.
So come, or be called a coward for ever."

Gawain Goes in Search of the Green Knight

When almost a year had passed, Gawain set off in search of the Green
Knight, traveling along the north coast of Wales and crossing the estuary of
the River Dee into "the wilds of the Wirral" in northwest England:

And he constantly enquires of those he encounters
if they know, or not, in this neck of the woods,

> of a great green man or a green chapel.
> No, they say, never. Never in their lives.
> They know of neither a knight nor a chapel so strange.
> He trails through bleak terrain.
> His mood and manner change
> at every twist and turn
> towards that chosen church.
> In a strange region he scales steep slopes;
> far from his friends he cuts a lonely figure.

He has a number of adventures:

> Here he scraps with serpents and snarling wolves,
> here he tangles with wodwos causing trouble in the crags,
> or with bulls and bears and the odd wild boar.

And the winter was severe:

> clouds shed their cargo of crystallized rain
> which froze as it fell to the frost-glazed earth.
> With nerves frozen numb he napped in his armour,
> bivouacked in the blackness among bare rocks
> where melt-water streamed from the snow-capped summits
> and high overhead hung chandeliers of ice.

On Christmas Day he was close to despair:

> He prayed with heavy heart: "Father, hear me,
> and Lady Mary, our mother most mild,
> let me happen on some house where mass might be heard,
> and matins in the morning; meekly I ask –
> and here I utter my pater, ave
> and creed."
> He rides the path and prays,
> dismayed by his misdeeds,
> and signs Christ's cross and says,
> "Be near me in my need."

> No sooner had he signed himself three times
> than he became aware, in those woods, of high walls
> in a moat, on a mound, bordered by the boughs
> of thick-trunked timber which trimmed the water.
> The most commanding castle a knight ever kept,
> positioned on a site of sweeping parkland
> with a palisade of pikes pitched in the earth
> in the midst of tall trees for two miles or more.

He called out to a watchman on the wall, and was warmly welcomed to the castle. After eating, he attended evensong with his hosts:

> The lord goes alone, then his lady arrives,
> concealing herself in a private pew.

Gawain attends too; tugged by his sleeve
he is steered to a seat, led by the lord
who greets Gawain by name as his guest.
No man in the world is more welcome, are his words.
For that he is thanked. And they hug there and then
and sit as a pair through the service in prayer.
Then she who desired to see this stranger
came from her closet with her sisterly crew.
She was fairest among them—her face, her flesh,
her complexion, her quality, her bearing, her body,
more glorious than Guinevere, or so Gawain thought,
and in the chancel of the church they exchanged courtesies.
She was hand in hand with a lady to her left,
someone altered by age, an ancient dame,
well respected, it seemed, by the servants at her side,
These ladies were not the least bit alike:
one woman was young, one withered by years.
The body of the beauty seemed to bloom with blood,
the cheeks of the crone were wattled and slack.

The next day was Christmas Day, and after three days of feasting, Gawain
told his host he must leave. The lord then asked him why he had left Camelot
in the middle of winter just before Christmas:

"A most pressing matter prised me from that place:
I myself am summoned to seek out a site
and I have not the faintest idea where to find it.
But find it I must by the first of the year, and not fail
for all the acres in England, so help me Lord.
And in speaking of my quest, I respectfully request
that you tell me, in truth, if you have heard the tale
of a green chapel, or the grounds where a green chapel stands,
or the guardian of those grounds who is coloured green.
For I am bound by a bond agreed by us both
to link with him there, should I live that long.
As dawn on New Year's Day draws near,
if God sees fit, I shall face that freak
more happily than I would the most wondrous wealth!
With your blessing, therefore, I must follow my feet.
In three short days my destiny is due,
and I would rather drop dead than default from duty."
Then laughing out loud the lord said, "Relax!
I'll direct you to your rendezvous when the time is right,
you'll get to the green chapel, so give up your grieving.
You can bask in your bed, bide your time,
save your fond farewells till the first of the year
and still meet him by mid-morning to do as you may.
So stay.

A guide will get you there
at dawn on New Year's Day.
The place you need is near,
two miles at most away."

Hunting and Temptation

So Gawain agreed to stay with the lord until New Year's Day. The lord
then told Gawain he would go hunting next day:

"Furthermore," said the master, "let's make a pact.
Here's a wager: what I win in the woods will be yours,
and what you gain while I'm gone you will give to me.
Young sir, let's swap, and strike a bond,
let a bargain be a bargain, for worse or for better."
"By God," said Gawain, "I agree to the terms
and I find it pleasing that you favour such fun."

While the lord was out hunting, his lady came to Gawain's room while he
was in bed snoozing, and tried to seduce him. But Gawain was unmoved,
and the lady finally said to him:

"A good man like Gawain, so greatly regarded,
the embodiment of courtliness to the bones of his being,
could never have lingered so long with a lady
without craving a kiss as politeness requires,
or coaxing a kiss with his closing words."
"Very well," said Gawain, "let's do a you wish.
If a kiss is your request I shall keep my promise
faithfully to fulfil you, so ask no further."
The lady comes close, cradles him in her arms,
leans nearer and nearer, then kisses the knight.
They courteously commend one another to Christ,
and without one more word the woman is away.

After a day's hunting, the lord returned home and showed Gawain the animals
that had been killed:

"And I give it all to you, Gawain," said the master,
"for according to our contract it is yours to claim."
"Just so," said Gawain, "and I'll say the same,
for whatever I've won within these walls
such gains will be graciously given to you."
So he held out his arms and hugged the lord
and kissed him in the kindliest way he could.
"You're welcome to my winnings—to my one profit,
though I'd gladly have given you any greater prize."
"I'm grateful," said the lord, "and Gawain, this gift

would carry more weight if you cared to confess
by what wit you won it. And when. And where."
"That wasn't our pact," he replied. "So don't pry.
You'll be given nothing greater, the agreement we have
holds good!"
They laugh aloud and trade
wise words which match their mood.
When supper's meal is made
they dine on dainty food.

The next day the lord went hunting again, the lady again tried to seduce Gawain, and this time kissed him twice. When the lord returned, he showed Gawain what he had killed, and Gawain kissed him as before, but twice. The next day, New Year's Eve, the lord went out hunting again, the lady tried once more to seduce Gawain, again kissed him and gave him her green silk girdle trimmed with gold, begging him not to tell her husband. The girdle, she said, had magical powers:

For the body which is bound within this green belt,
as long as it is buckled robustly about him,
will be safe against those who seek to strike him,
and all the slyness on earth wouldn't see him slain.

When the lord returned, Gawain kissed him three times, but did not mention the girdle.

Gawain Meets the Knight at the Green Chapel

The next day, New Year's Day, Gawain got dressed:

And he did not leave off the lady's lace girdle;
For his own good, Gawain won't forget that gift.

A servant showed Gawain the way to the green chapel, but at a certain point refused to go any further:

"the place you head for holds a hidden peril.
In that wilderness lives a wildman, the worst in the world,
he is brooding and brutal and loves bludgeoning humans."

So the servant gave Gawain directions to the green chapel, and Gawain went on alone. He followed the servant's directions:

He stalls and halts, holds the horse still,
glances side to side to glimpse the green chapel
but sees no such thing, which the thinks is strange,
except at mid-distance what might be a mound,
a sort of bald knoll on the bank of a brook
where fell-water surged with frenzied force,

bursting with bubbles as if it had boiled.
He heels the horse, heads for that mound,
grounds himself gracefully and tethers Gringolet,
looping the reins to the limb of a lime.
Then he strides forward and circles the feature,
baffled as to what that bizarre hill could be:
it had a hole at one end and at either side,
and its walls, matted with weeds and moss,
enclosed a cavity, like a kind of old cave
or crevice in the crag—it was all too unclear to
declare.
"Green church?" chunters the knight.
"More like the devil's lair
where at the nub of night,
he makes his morning prayer."

"For certain," he says, "this is a soulless spot,
a ghostly cathedral overgrown with grass,
the kind of kirk where that camouflaged man
might deal in devilment and all things dark.
My five senses inform me that Satan himself
has tricked me in this tryst, intending to destroy me.
This is a haunted house—may it go to hell.
I never came across and church so cursed."

Then the Green Knight appeared:

Then out of the crags he comes through the cave-mouth,
whirling into view with a wondrous weapon,
A Danish-style axe for doling out death,
with a brute of a blade curving back to the haft
filed on a stone, a four-footer at least
by the look of the length at its shining lace.
And again he was green, like a year ago,
with green hair and flesh and a fully green face,
and firmly on green feet he came stomping forward,
the handle of that axe like a staff in his hand.

The Green Knight asked Gawain to remove his helmet and to not resist his fate:

"No," said good Gawain, "by my life-giving God,
I won't gripe or begrudge the grimness to come,
so keep to one stroke and I'll stand stock still,
won't whisper a word of unwillingness or one
complaint."
He bowed to take the blade
and bared his neck and nape,
but loath to look afraid,
he feigned a fearless state.

The Green Knight then raised his axe, and began to bring it down; Gawain flinched, and the Green Knight stopped and "reproached the young prince with piercing words." The Green Knight raised his axe once more and began to bring it down, then stopped:

> And Gawain was motionless, never moved a muscle,
> but stood stone-still, or as still as a tree-stump
> anchored in the earth by a hundred roots.
> Then the warrior in green mocked Gawain again:
> "Now you've plucked up your courage I'll dispatch you properly.
> May the honourable knighthood heaped on you by Arthur—
> if it proves to be powerful—protect your pretty neck."
> That insulting slur drew a spirited response:
> "Get hacking, then, head-banger, your threats are hollow.
> Such huffing and fussing—you'll frighten your own heart."
> "By God," said the green man, "since you speak so grandly
> there'll be no more shilly-shallying, I shall shatter you
> right now."
> He stands to strike, a sneer
> from bottom lip to brow.
> Who'd fault Gawain if fear
> took hold? All hope is down.
>
> Hoisted and aimed, the axe hurtled downwards,
> the blade bearing down on the knight's bare neck,
> a ferocious blow, but far from being fatal
> it skewed to one side, just skimming the skin
> and finely snicking the fat of the flesh
> so that bright red blood shot from body to earth.

Immediately Gawain put on his helmet and grabbed his shield and sword, challenging the Green Knight to fight him. To which the Green Knight replied:

> "Be a mite less feisty, fearless young fellow,
> no insulting or heinous incident has happened
> beyond the game we agreed on in the court of your king.
> One strike was promised—consider it served!
> From any lingering loyalties you are hereby released.
> Had I mustered all my muscles into one mega-blow
> my axe would have dealt you your death, without doubt.
> But my first strike fooled you—a feint, no less—
> not fracturing your flesh, which was only fair
> in keeping with the contract we declared that first night,
> for with truthful behaviour you honoured my trust
> and gave up your gains as a good man should.
> Then I missed you once more, and this for the morning
> when you kissed my pretty wife then kindly kissed me.
> So twice you were truthful, therefore twice I left
> no scar.

> the person who repays
> will live to feel no fear.
> The third time, though, you strayed
> and felt my blade therefore."

> "Because the belt you are bound with belongs to me;
> it was woven by my wife so I know it very well.
> And I know of your courtesies, and conduct and kisses,
> and wooing of my wife—for it was all my work!
> I sent her to test you—and in truth it turns out
> you're by far the most faultless fellow on earth."

Ashamed that he had not told the lord about the belt, Gawain grabbed the girdle and flung it at the Green Knight. The Green Knight told Gawain that he forgave him and presented him with the girdle. Gawain then asked the Green Knight for his name:

> "Here in my homelands they call me Bertilak de Hautdesert.
> And in my manor lives the mighty Morgan le Fay,
> so adept and adroit in the dark arts,
> who learned magic from Merlin—the master of mystery—
> for in earlier times she was intimately entwined
> with that knowledgeable man, as all you knights know
> back home.
> Yes, 'Morgan the Goddess'—
> I will announce her name.
> There is no nobleness
> she cannot take and tame."

> "She guided me in this guise to your great hall
> to put pride on trial, and to test with this trick
> what distinction and trust the Round Table deserves.
> She imagined this mischief would muddle your minds
> and that grieving Guinevere would go to her grave
> at the sight of a spectre making ghostly speeches
> with his head in his hands before the high table.
> So that ancient woman who inhabits my home
> is also your aunt—Arthur's half-sister,
> the daughter of the duchess of Tintagel; the duchess
> who through Uther, was mother to Arthur, your king."

French Influences on Sir Gawain *and the* Green Knight

The "Beheading Game"

The so-called "beheading game" was popular in literature of the Middle Ages, and featured in a number of works. The author of *Sir Gawain and the*

Green Knight may have been inspired by the early 13th century French Arthurian romance *Perlesvaus*, which concerns the quest for the Holy Grail. In the course of this tale, Lancelot comes to a waste land[3]:

> Lancelot looked into the distance and a city appeared to view; he rode on towards it at a swift pace, and saw that the city was so huge that it seemed to fill an entire country. But he could see its wall crumbling round about, and the gates leaning with age. He rode inside to find the city quite empty of inhabitants, its great palaces derelict and waste, its markets and exchanges empty, its vast graveyards full of tombs, its churches ruined.

He rode through the city and came to a huge palace which seemed to be less ruined than the others:

> He drew rein before it, to hear knights and ladies lamenting bitterly and saying to a knight:
> "Oh God! What a great shame and sorrow it is that you must go and die thus, and your death cannot be delayed. Well may we hate the one who condemned you!"
> And the knights and ladies swooned as he left. Lancelot heard all this and was amazed, but could see no-one. But just then a knight came down from the hall: he was dressed in a red coat with a rich belt of silk and gold, and a beautiful brooch was pinned at his neck clustered with precious stones, and a golden hat he wore on his head, and in his hands he clutched a huge axe.

The young knight asked Lancelot to dismount, and Lancelot asked him what he wanted:

> "Sir," came the reply, "you must cut off my head with this axe, for I am con-demned to death with this weapon; if not, I shall cut off yours."
> "By my life!" cried Lancelot. "What are you saying?"
> "What you hear, sir," said the knight. "This you must do since you've come to this city."
> "Sir," said Lancelot, "only a fool would fail to see how to get the better in this game, but it would be to my discredit to kill you without cause."
> "Truly," said the knight, "you cannot leave otherwise."
> "Good sir," said Lancelot, "you look so fine and trim: how can you go so calmly to your death? You surely know I'd sooner kill you than have you kill me, since that's the choice."
> "I'm well aware of that," said the knight, "but you must swear to me before I die that you'll return to the city in a year's time and offer your head freely, without con-test, as I offer mine."

So the knight gave Lancelot the axe[4]:

> he raised the axe and smote off the knight's head with such a terrible blow that he sent it flying seven feet from the body. The knight crashed to the ground when his head was cut off, and as Lancelot threw down the axe he thought it would be a bad idea to linger there, and he returned to his horse, took up his arms and mounted. When he looked back he could see neither the body of the knight nor his head, and

he could not think what had become of them; but he heard a great mourning and crying of knights and ladies far off in the city: they were bewailing the good knight, and saying that he would be avenged, God willing, at the agreed time or sooner.

Lancelot returned to the Waste City at the appointed time and came across a knight carrying the axe with which Lancelot had beheaded the other knight, Lancelot then said[5]:

> "Good sir, what are you going to do with that axe?"
> "Truly," said the knight, "you'll find out just as my brother did."
> "What?" cried Lancelot. "Are you going to kill me then?"
> "You'll find out," the knight replied, "before you leave here. Did you not agree to put your head at stake, just like my brother whom you killed? For otherwise you could not have left here. But come forward now and knell down and stretch out your neck, and I shall cut of your head. And if you won't do so of your own free will, you'll find yourself forced to it—you would even if there were twenty of you. But I know that you've returned for no other reason than to keep your promise, and that you'll not now refuse."
> Lancelot realised he was about to die, but he wanted to be true to what he had sworn. He lay down on the ground with his arms outstretched, and prayed to God for mercy.

After crying out to his lover Guinevere, he crossed and blessed himself, rose, knelt and stretched out his neck:

> The knight raised the axe. Lancelot heard the blow coming and ducked and the axe flashed past. The knight said:
> "Sir knight, my brother whom you killed did not behave so: he kept his head and neck still. So must you."
> Just then two maidens appeared at the windows of the palace; very beautiful they were, and they recognised Lancelot at once. And just as the knight raised the axe for the second blow, one of the maidens cried:
> "If you would earn my eternal love, throw down the axe and declare the knight free. If you do not, my love you shall never have."
> The knight threw down the axe at once and fell at Lancelot's feet, begging him as the truest knight in the world to have mercy on him.
> "If you'll have mercy on me, and not kill me!" said Lancelot.

Here there is a Waste City (Bertilak's domain is Hautdesert, which probably means "High Wasteland"), and Lancelot, like Gawain, ducks when he feels the blow coming and is criticized for doing so.

Bertilak and Morgan le Fay

The name *Bertilak* may be derived from the episode of the "false Guinevere" in the French *Lancelot-Grail*, which may itself be inspired by Triad 56, "Arthur's Three Great Queens." The story of the "false Guinevere" starts in Part II, "History of Merlin," and goes as follows[6]:

On the same day two girls were born to King Leodegan; one, the true Guinevere, was the daughter of his wife; the other, the false Guinevere, was the daughter of his seneschal's wife. They looked exactly alike. Certain lords planned to substitute the false Guinevere for Artus' wife on her wedding night. Merlin arranged to defeat their plan. They bribed Guinevere's old nurse, and kidnapped Guinevere, but in the moment of success two knights whom Merlin had warned broke up the plot. The author forecasts the trouble which the false Guinevere and a knight will cause Artus. The knight was Bertolais. He hated a certain knight because the latter had slain a cousin of his. Bertolais met and killed this knight on the evening of Guinevere's abduction. Leodegan ordered the false Guinevere to be taken away. She was taken to an abbey in the realm of Carmelide, where she remained until Bertolais (whose mistress she became) found her. Bertolais was brought before Leodegan, who blamed him for killing the man without first asking his king for justice. Bertolais was tried, disinherited, and exiled. He went to the place where the false Guinevere was and there long meditated revenge.

No further mention is made of either of these characters until Part IV of the *Lancelot-Grail*, the "Lancelot Proper":

One day a beautiful damsel arrived at Artus' court with a retinue. She said that she came from Queen Guinevere, daughter of Leodegan. An old knight (Bertolais) handed the damsel a jeweled box containing a letter. The first clerk who started to read it swooned when he saw its contents. After a second had failed also, the chaplain read it aloud. The letter said that it was from the true Guinevere, who was abducted on the night of her marriage. The damsel introduced Bertolais, who was now old but very strong, as the lady's champion. He offered to defend her against Gawain or any other, but was derided by Dodinel. Artus postponed his decision until Candlemas. When the story is taken up again, the author repeats the early history of the false Guinevere, and says that the first attempt was made by counsel of Bertolais. The false Guinevere came to court at Candlemas, but by advice of Bertolais she asked for respite. Bertolais proposed a trick for capturing Artus and conveying him to Carmelide. This was done. In Carmelide the false Guinevere drugged Artus so that he became infatuated with her. He consented to recognize her as queen if the barons of Carmelide would swear that she was the true Guinevere. Led by Bertolais they did so. The true Guinevere left to become queen of Sorelois. The pope interdicted Great Britain. The false Guinevere and Bertolais became ill in a terrible and disgusting way. Bertolais sent for Artus and confessed his trickery. So did the false Guinevere. They died of their maladies.

Clearly this Bertholais was an enemy of King Arthur, and could well have become the Lord Bertilak who conspired against Arthur with the help of Morgan le Fay.

Morgan le Fay first appears in Geoffrey of Monmouth's *Life of Merlin*, then makes fleeting appearances in Chrétien de Troyes' *Éec et Énide* and *Yvain*. In both romances, the heroes are healed of their wounds through a magical potion of Morgan's. Additionally, in *Érec*, Morgan is the lover of Guingemart, lord of Avalon; in *Érec*, she dwells either in Avalon with Guingemart or in an equally mysterious realm known as the Perilous Vale.[7]

The *Lancelot-Grail,* or *Vulgate Cycle,* provides the earliest "complete story" of Morgan:

> According to the *Cycle,* she is born of Igerne, and, though her father is likely Gorlois, she is at one point referred to as a bastard (*Lancelot-Grail,* ed. Lacy, vol. 1, 207). She is fostered and sent to a nunnery where she learns healing, reading, writing, and astrology. Merlin teaches her the magic arts while Arthur is engaged in the Saxon wars, and she eventually becomes the lover of Guiomar; he is Queen Guinevere's cousin and resembles Morgan's lover mentioned in Chrétien's *Érec.* The queen, according to the *Cycle,* ends the relationship between Morgan and Guiomart, and Morgan hates Arthur and Guinevere from this point onwards. Her hatred either intensifies or inspires her love for Lancelot, who declines her affections; as a result, she attempts to expose the love affair between Lancelot and Guinevere. She also creates the Valley of No Return where she entraps various warriors; Lancelot is captured there a total of three times. Despite these attempts to undermine Arthur's court, she is, quite inexplicably, the one who takes Arthur away for healing.

Clearly Morgan le Fay, who started out as benevolent healer and friend of Arthur, had by the early 13th century become a dangerous enemy. Interestingly, Bertilak refers to Morgan as "the Goddess," which seems to link her to the Morgen of Geoffrey of Monmouth's *Life of Merlin.*

Anglo-Saxon Influences on Sir Gawain and the Green Knight

Despite the link to French romances, *Sir Gawain and the Green Knight* also recalls a number of Anglo-Saxon literary texts. Firstly, the Green Knight's sudden and threatening entry into Camelot is comparable to Grendel's invasion of Heorot in *Beowulf:*

> So, after nightfall, Grendel set out
> for the lofty house, to see how the Ring-Danes
> were settling into it after their drink,
> and there he came upon them, a company of the best
> asleep from their feasting, insensible to pain
> and human sorrow. Suddenly then
> the God-cursed brute was creating havoc:
> greedy and grim, he grabbed thirty men
> from their resting places and rushed to his lair,
> flushed up and inflamed from the raid,
> blundering back with the butchered corpses.

Both *Sir Gawain* and *Beowulf* "present monstrous beings who burst into the hall uninvited and threaten the very lives of those within."[8] The Gawain-poet refers to the Green knight as *etayn,* a word derived from the Old English *eoten*, the word used to describe Grendel's race. Both Grendel and the Green Knight have similar eyes: in the case of Grendel, "a baleful light/ flame more than light, flared from his eyes," while the Green Knight looked left and right, "his red eyes rolling/ beneath the bristles of his bushy green brows." Like Grendel, who loses an arm in the hall, the Green Knight loses his head, and Arthur mounts the Green Knight's battle axe on the wall, just as Hrothgar mounts Grendel's arm on the wall of Heorot.

When Gawain leaves Camelot he travels through the wilderness, and this recalls not *Beowulf*, but Anglo-Saxon poems like *The Wanderer* and the *Seafarer*. Here is an extract from *The Wanderer*[9]:

> So I,
> often wretched and sorrowful,
> bereft of my homeland,
> far from noble kinsmen,
> have had to bind in fetters
> my inmost thoughts,
> Since long years ago
> I hid my lord in the darkness of the earth,
> and I, wretched from there
> travelled most sorrowfully
> over the frozen waves

And here is an extract from *The Seafarer*[10]:

> how I, wretched and sorrowful,
> on the ice-cold sea
> dwelt for a winter
> in the paths of exile,
> bereft of friendly kinsmen,
> hung about with icicles

Like the characters in these Anglo-Saxon poems, Gawain is alone and far from his companions ("unloved and alone," "far from his friends he cuts a lonely figure") and almost frozen to death ("With nerves frozen numb he napped in his armour").

Most medieval romances, French and English, begin and end in the springtime, while *Sir Gawain and Green Knight*, like Anglo-Saxon poetry, focuses very much on winter. While Gawain is in the wilderness, "bedraggled birds on bare, black branches/ pipe pitifully into the piercing cold"; Gawain is "frozen numb," sleeping under "chandeliers of ice." And when Gawain leaves the castle on his way to the Green Chapel, the weather is equally wintery:

> But wild-looking weather was about in the world:
> clouds decanted their cold rain earthwards;
> the nithering [biting] north needled man's very nature;
> creatures were scattered by the stinging sleet.

But when we get back to the Green Chapel, further links with *Beowulf* emerge. In the original Middle English, Gawain tells Bertilak he has agreed to meet the Green Knight "at that mere," meaning the site of the Green Chapel. The word *mere* also occurs in *Pearl* (thought to be written by the Gawain-poet), "where it carries the more specific, Old English meaning of "pool, water," as it does in *Beowulf*."[11] Thus Beowulf sees the "boiling" water of the mere as he moves toward battle with Grendel's mother; in the same way, the "brooks boiled" as Gawain approaches the Green Chapel. Once he arrives at the Green Chapel, Gawain noticed that the stream bordering the Chapel "surged" and "boiled." When Gawain sees the Green Chapel he calls it "the devil's lair," associating it with demons, just like Grendel's mere.

Another link comes in the poet's description of the Green Chapel. The Green Chapel is described as a "mound," a "bald knoll," a "bizarre hill," using a variety of Middle English words including *lawe*, "mound, hill" and *bergh*, "mound, barrow." When Gawain first sees the Green Knight, he comes out of a hole in the mound, "suggesting the pattern of a barrow."[12] This obviously recalls Beowulf's final battle, with the dragon, which takes place outside a barrow, where the dragon is guarding his treasure. So the Green Knight and the Green Chapel are linked to Grendel, Grendel's mother and the dragon that kills Beowulf.

Bertilak seems to be a product of the French Arthurian tradition, and in some ways the encounter between Gawain and the Green Knight/Bertilak is an encounter between the Anglo-Saxons and Normans. In *Sir Gawain and the Green Knight*, Arthur's Camelot "has a decidedly Anglo-Saxon flavor."[13] The poet characterizes Arthur's dwelling exclusively as a "hall." For example, the poet says of the Green Knight: "And he kicks on, canters through that crowded hall"; and "With a tug of the reins he twisted around/ and, head still in hand, galloped out of the hall,/ so the hooves brought fire from the flame in the flint." The poet also indicates a dais, a raised platform typical of hall architecture, at one end of the hall ("banquets and buffets were beautifully cooked/ and dutifully served to diners at the dais."). Moreover, "the Green Knight's sudden entrance and exit from Camelot on horseback indicates an English-style hall, situated at ground level, as opposed to a French-style hall, which typically occupied the first floor and was accessed by a flight of steps set at a right angle to the hall."

On the other hand, Lord Bertilak lives in a Norman-style castle,[14] as described by Gawain:

> No sooner had he signed himself three times
> than he became aware, in those woods, of high walls
> in a moat, on a mound, bordered by the boughs
> of thick-trunked timber which trimmed the water.
> The most commanding castle a knight ever kept,

> positioned on a site of sweeping parkland
> with a palisade of pikes pitched in the earth
> in the midst of tall trees for two miles or more.

Later, as Gawain is approaching the castle

> In the saddle of his steed he halts on the slope
> Of the delving moat with its double ditch.
> Out of the water of wondrous depth, the walls
> Then loomed overhead to a heavenly height,
> course after course of crafted stone,
> then battlements embellished in the boldest style
> and turrets arranged around the ramparts
> with lockable loopholes set into the lookouts.

While Gawain experienced the forest as a wilderness, Bertilak's Haut-desert "features another type of forested landscape contrived by members of the French-speaking aristocracy of Norman descent and celebrated in their literature."[15] The Gawain-poet characterizes part of the forest surrounding Hautdesert as "sweeping parkland/ with a palisade of pikes pitched in the earth/ in the midst of tall trees for two miles or more," that is, a deer park, or "chase." And, of course, hunting forms a central part of Gawain's stay at Hautdesert.

I said earlier that *Sir Gawain and the Green Knight* was probably written somewhere on the Staffordshire/Cheshire border, and attempts have been made to locate the castle of Hautdesert and the Green Chapel. Hautdesert has been linked to Swythamley Grange,[16] a medieval grange (manor house) in the Staffordshire Peak District belonging to Dieulacres Abbey at nearby Leek, a Cistercian abbey founded in 1214, during the Norman period, and dissolved in 1538.[17] The Green Chapel has been linked to Lud's Church, a natural fissure in the rocks near the hamlet of Gradbach, to the northeast of where Swythamley Grange once stood.[18] As described, the green chapel could also be a Neolithic burial mound, and there are several Neolithic long barrows in the Derbyshire Peak District, not far from the site of Swythamley Grange.

The Green Knight

While Gawain was in the wilderness he batted *wodwos*, or "wild men," and this may foreshadow the Green Knight, who has many of the characteristics of a wild man. In the later medieval period the wild man differed from ordinary men mainly in his thick coat of hair, which left only his face, hands and feet bare. A variant form of the wild man, well illustrated in 15th century engravings, shows him covered with a thick growth of leafy foliage rather than hair. The universal attribute of the wild man is a large club, or occasionally an uprooted tree, which he holds in his hand, often with the end resting on his shoulder.[19] The leafy version of the wild man can be linked to the Green Man, a carved figure found in British churches mainly from the late 12th to the 16th century, with many dating from the 14th and 15th centuries. The Green Man is a representation of a face surrounded by or made from leaves. Branches or vines may sprout from the nose, mouth nostrils or other parts of the face and these shoots may bear flowers or fruit.

Like the wild man, the Green Knight was distinctly hairy:

> The hair of his head was as green as his horse,
> fine flowing locks which fanned across his back,
> plus a bushy green beard growing down to his breast,
> and his face-hair along with the hair of his head
> was lopped in a line at elbow-length
> so half his arms were gowned, in green growth,
> crimped at the collar, like a king's cape.

And he behaves like a wild man, in an uncouth way:

> Still stirruped, the knight swivelled round in his saddle
> looking left and right, his red eyes rolling
> beneath the bristles of his bushy green brows,
> his beard swishing from side to side.

Even as Bertilak, the Green Knight behaves in a rather uncouth way:

> Frequently the lord would leap to his feet
> insisting that mirth and merriment be made:
> hauling off his hood, he hoisted it on a spear—
> a prize, he promised, to the person providing
> most comfort and cheer at Christmas time.

In appearance Bertilak has some of the Green Knight's hairiness:

> Gawain gazed at the lord who greeted him so gracefully,
> the great one who governed that grand estate,
> powerful and large, in the prime of his life,
> with a bushy beard as red as a beaver's,
> steady in his stance, solid of build,
> with a fiery face but fine conversation.

Bertilak is also associated with animals, though with killing rather than protecting them. Finally, although the Green Knight does not wield a club, in both encounters with Gawain he carries a huge axe.

What inspired the Green Knight is anybody's guess, but he may have been engendered by the same beliefs that inspired carvings of wild men and green men in churches. In the cathedral at Carlisle (Cumbria), a wild man is attacking a dragon; in the cathedral at Hereford a wild man grapples with a lion; a carving in Beverley (East Yorkshire) shows the wild man trampling on dragons while standing between two docile lions. The figure of the wild man was popular in the Middle Ages: there are records showing a figure called the "woodwose" in a court masque for 1348, when Edward the III was king; and lists show costumes issued for the Christmas and Epiphany celebrations in England in 1347 and 1348, which include those for "wildmen."[20]

The Green Man is a difficult figure to interpret. In Geoffrey Chaucer's *The Friar's Tale* (late 14th century) green is the color worn by the yeoman, who is actually a demon in disguise[21]:

> It happened that he saw before him ride
> A carefree yeoman by a forest side.
> Bearing a bow, with arrows bright and keen,
> This yeoman wore a short coat, colored green,
> And had a black-fringed hat upon his head.

This demon hunter wearing a green coat may be the key to the Green Man. The Green Man is often associated with evil, as we can see from two English churches, Melbourne in Derbyshire and Kilpeck in Herefordshire. Melbourne

was begun around 1120 as a private manorial chapel for Henry I—it had an unusual west gallery that was probably the king's private pew. It is a remarkably ambitious church, with a crossing tower and two west towers, its architecture influenced by churches at Jumièges and Caen in Normandy. One of the capitals of the crossing arches depicts a grinning demon holding the branches spewing out of his or her mouth. Like the architecture, the immediate origin of the motif appears to be France. The crossing is a threshold between the sacred and secular parts of the building, the context in which the image needs to be interpreted—it uses ugliness and earthliness to represent sin and a lack of spirituality, quite different from the austere spirituality of contemporary Christian figures.

Kilpeck church was completed in 1134, "built by Hugh of Kilpeck next to Kilpeck castle. The iconography of the church's carvings is drawn to a large extent from the bestiaries (illustrated compendia of beasts), one of the earliest such instances in British churches, but some of the creatures are not found in any book. These include the green men on the south doorway and on the capitals of the west window. The south doorway has a head or a mask sprouting stylised foliage on one of the capitals." The expert in medieval art and architecture Malcolm Thurlby "has suggested that the plant represents the Biblical tree of the knowledge of good and evil, an argument strengthened by the presence of a serpent on the jamb just below it."

The link between the Green Man and evil is underlined in a series of early 16th century bench end carvings from Crowcombe in Somerset. In the best known of the bench end carvings, "the green man has a gaunt face, with leaves for hair and a mouth disgorging vines, a standard motif of local wood carvers. His bulging eyes are not level, a deliberate asymmetrical ugliness.

From his ears emerge two club-wielding mermen, representing the demons in his head. Another of the carvings has aggressive-looking fish emerging from the green man's ears and head, conveying a similar message. Crowcombe also has four bench ends where foliage emanates from a monster's mouth, and three where the foliage grows out of human hands." In one of the images two men grapple with a double-headed wyvern (a type of dragon), standing on the foliage sprouting from another monster's mouth, which is "surely a reference to the snares of the Devil and the battle with evil."[22]

So if the author of *Sir Gawain and the Green Knight* was thinking of the Green Men of church architecture when he wrote the poem, then he may well have thought of the Green Knight as demonic, and his readers may well have thought the same.

Gawain as Popular Hero

Sir Gawain and the Green Knight may have been the inspiration for three Arthurian tales set in Inglewood Forest, Cumbria—the region where Arthurian tales may have begun—in which Gawain plays a leading role. In one tale he and Guinevere confront the ghost of Guinevere's mother, who predicts the downfall of Arthur; in a second tale Arthur kills a huge boar while Gawain rescues Sir Kay; and in a third tale Gawain is forced to marry a "loathly" (ugly) lady called Dame Ragnell in order to save the life of Arthur.

10

Three Late Medieval Arthurian Romances

Arthur and Gawain in Inglewood Forest, Cumbria

Inglewood Forest in the Medieval Period

The Arthurian tales have very little sense of place, apart from *Sir Gawain and the Green Knight*, which has Gawain wander in "the wilds of the Wirral" as he searches for the Green Chapel. But in the 14th/15th century three Arthurian tales—*The Adventures of Arthur at Tarn Wadling*, *The Vows of King Arthur*, and *The Wedding of Sir Gawain and Dame Ragnell*—place Arthur and Gawain in Inglewood Forest in Cumbria, between Penrith and Carlisle. In this they may have been inspired by *Sir Gawain and the Green Knight*, since the Wirral is only a hundred miles to the south of Carlisle.

Inglewood ("wood of the English") Forest was a royal forest, created by William Rufus, the son of William the Conqueror and king from 1087 to 1100. The history of Cumbria before that is obscure. Welsh poetry of the 6th century by Taliesin suggests that Cumbria was part of Rheged—the Urien poems refer to *Lwyfenydd*, thought to be the River Lyvennet to the south of Penrith, and the *Annales Cambriae* ("Annals of Wales") mention the battle of Ardderydd, or Arthuret, to the north of Carlisle near the border with Scotland. Urien played little part in Arthurian legend, but his son Owain became Yvain in Chrétien de Troyes' *Yvain, the Knight of the Lion*, which was partly inspired by the *Fragmentary Life of St. Kentigern*.

It is impossible to know whether Carlisle was part of Rheged, but we know from Bede that there was a monastery at Carlisle in 685. There was also a monastery at Dacre near Penrith, which Bede mentions in an entry for 698. Excavations in the 1980s indicate evidence of an extensive pre–Conquest cemetery containing at least 200 inhumations, and although there are no clearly demonstrable timber buildings, there is indirect evidence that the site was that of a monastic community. A 9th century cross fragment and a 10th century cross shaft survive in the present church of St. Andrew, and a third fragment of an 8th century Anglian cross shaft found near the church is now in Dacre Castle. A stylus, a gold ring and a possible textile mount were also recovered during excavations, the copper alloy stylus dates from the 8th or 9th century.[1]

In Inglewood Forest itself, there was a Roman fort at Old Penrith in the parish of Hesket. Voreda Roman fort was occupied from the 1st to the 4th century, and an extensive settlement surrounded the fort.[2] A round cairn containing a cremation and Viking hoard comprising a sword, spears, axe, bridle bit, shield, sickle, razor, whetstone and fragment of a millstone was discovered at Hesket in 1822.[3] Not far from Hesket, at Cumwhitton to the southeast of Carlisle, a small Viking cemetery was excavated in 2004. Six burials were found, dating to the early 10th century, four male and six female. All the graves were orientated broadly east-west, although how significant this was remains unclear, as all the burials were richly furnished, and contained a wide range of artifacts, including swords, spearheads, spurs, knives, and numerous beads and other objects. Of particular note were a rare decorated drinking horn, a seax with a silver-inlaid horn handle, a locking wooden box containing implements associated with textiles, and a unique group of decorated, tinned copper-alloy buckles and strap ends.[4]

The most intriguing monument in the region is the legendary tomb of Ewen or Owen, king of Cumberland, known as the Giant's Grave, which sits in the churchyard of St. Andrew's church in Penrith. It consists of two crosses and four hogback stones (hogback stones are grave markers which probably originated with the Danes who settled in the North of England in the late 9th century). The eastern cross, which rests in a modern socket, is dated by Collingwood to around AD 1000 and the western to around 950. The hogbacks are 10th/11th century. A third Anglian cross in the churchyard is known as The Giant's Thumb, and is dated to the second quarter of the 10th century.[5] In the early part of the 10th century, Penrith was the southern capital of Strathclyde-Cumbria. When King Edmund (939–946) defeated Dunmail, the last king of Cumberland, in 945, the Cumbrian kingdom was ceded to Malcolm I, king of Scotland.[6] Dunmail may be Dyfnwal, mentioned in the *Life of Cathróe of Metz* (900–971), who may be the same as Dyfnwal, son of Owein, king of Strathclyde (died 975).[7]

The identity of Ewen, also known as Ewan Caesarius, is unknown. He may be Owein, son of Urien Rheged, but is more likely to be Owen of Strathclyde, who fought at the Battle of Brunaburh (possibly Bromborough in the Wirrral) in 934 against the English king Æthelstan, or Owen of Strathclyde who may have fought at the Battle of Carham (Northumberland) in 1018.

Whoever he may be, according to legend he hunted boar in Inglewood Forest, and is commemorated at Castle Hewen in Hesket.[8] This apparent castle was recorded as ruined by Leyland in 1553, and also recorded by Hutchinson in 1794. The foundations of Castle Hewen in 1794 were in places 8 feet thick, and one building was 233 feet by 147 feet. It was excavated in 1978–1979 by Tom Clare, but the only finds were Romano-British.[9]

After the Norman Conquest a castle was built at Carlisle in 1092. The first castle took the form of wooden buildings surrounded by a stockade upon a ringwork of earth. In 1122 Henry I (1100–1135) ordered a stone castle to be constructed on the site, including the keep, which served as the palace of David I, Prince of the Cumbrians (1113–1124) and king of Scotland (1124–1153). Over the course of the 13th century the castle fell into disrepair. However, between 1296 and 1307 the stone tower later known as Queen Mary's Tower was built. In the 1370s and 1380s, the castle's outer gatehouse was rebuilt and in 1483 the Tile Tower was constructed.[10]

In Inglewood Forest there was a nunnery in the parish of Ainstable, known as Armathwaite priory, not far from Hesket. It was first mentioned in 1200, in a charter of Roger de Beauchamp to the priory of St. Bees (Cumbria), in which it is stated that the land he gave to that monastery was near the land of the nuns of Ainstable in Seascale on the Cumbrian coast. Like other religious houses, the nuns of Armathwaite suffered heavy losses during the Scottish wars, and Edward II (1307–1327) gave them pasture for their cattle in Inglewood Forest.[11] In the mid–15th century a castle was built at Armathwaite to protect the Eden valley from Scottish raiders.[12]

The Adventures of Arthur at Tarn Wadling

The Adventures of Arthur at Tarn Wadling is a 715-line Northern poem of the late 14th or early 15th century. The Tarn Wadling of the title is a lake in Inglewood Forest, now drained, which lies near High Hesket in Cumbria. As the poem opens, Arthur and his men are hunting[13]:

> Beside Tarn Wadling, so the book states,
> In Arthur's day an adventure befell,
> When to Carlisle had come that conqueror great,
> With dukes and peers, to stay for a spell
> And hunt the herds there, hid long of late.
> One day they departed for the deep dell,
> To fell female deer shielded from fate
> Through off-season to fatten in forest and fell.
> Thus they went to the wood in their finest array,
> Both the King and Queen,
> And all their company keen.

> Sir Gawain, dressed in green,
> Led Dame Guinevere that day.

As the hunting proceeded, Gawain and Guinevere were left on their own:

> With joy they assembled, all proud and tall,
> And followed their sovereign through forests serene;
> And only Sir Gawain, most gallant of all,
> Remained with Dame Guinevere in the grove green.
> Under a leafy shelter by a laurel she lolled,
> Of barberry and boxwood, built for the Queen.
> Suddenly, before midday a wonder did fall,
> And of this great marvel to tell I am keen.
> Now of this miracle I shall speak, if I might:
> The day grew dark and drear,
> As if midnight drew near,
> And Arthur lost his cheer,
> And on foot did alight.
>
> Thus on foot they went forth, every fierce thane,
> And fled to the forest from the green dell.
> For refuge they ran from the raging rain,
> From the slicing sleet that slashed as it fell.
> Then to tell truly, from the tarn sprang a flame,
> In the likeness of Lucifer, most loathsome in hell.
> Toward Guinevere glided this ghost profane,
> Yowling and yammering a blood-chilling yell.
> It wept, it wailed, and made many a moan,
> And sorrowfully sighing swore,
> "I curse the body that me bore,
> for alas, now I sorrow sore;
> I grieve and groan."

The ghost was not a pretty sight:

> Bare was its body and black to the bone,
> In clotted clay, all hideously clad.
> It whimpered, it wailed, like a woman made moan,
> But for hide or for head no cover it had.

Gawain spoke to the ghost, which said it wished to speak to Guinevere:

> After gay Guinevere went Gawain alone;
> To the body he brought back that lady bright.
> "Welcome, Guinevere, worthy Queen and my own.
> Behold your mother's drear deathly plight!
> I was redder of cheek than roses full-blown,
> My face like a lily, lovely and white;
> Now I am a grisly ghost and gruesomely groan,
> In Lucifer's lake, banished from the earth's light.
> Yes, I am like Lucifer, take warning from me:

Your mirror can err;
For all your finery and fur,
Like king and emperor,
Death shall your end be."

Guinevere then asks the ghost of her mother how she can help
ease her suffering:

"Reveal to me what might ease your plight,
And I shall have sextons sing for your sake,
But those vile beasts that your body bite
Cause my blood to blanch and my bones to quake!"
"It was unlawful love, lust and delight
That landed and locked me in Lucifer's lake.
All the wealth of the world has now taken flight,
And only wretched worms are left in its wake.
These worms unto me great woe have wrought.
Thirty trentals [thirty times thirty masses] are the boon,
From morning unto noon:
My soul were succored soon,
And to blessedness brought."

Then Gawain asks the ghost for guidance:

"How shall we fare," asked Gawain, "who are fated to fight,
And win wealth and fame through force of our hands,
And ride over realms without reason or right,
And harry the folk in many kings' lands?"
"Your king is too covetous, I caution you, knight.
No strength will stun him while the wheel still stands;
But at his moment of majesty, matchless in might,
Struck down he shall be, along the sea strands.
Your conquering king shall fall victim to chance:
Fortune, false in fight,
That wondrous wheelwright,
Makes lords low alight,
Take witness of France.

"France with your fighting have you fully won,
And Frollo and his force to their fate left;
Brittany and Burgundy are both overrun,
And the dukes of France dazed by your dints deft.
Guyenne may grieve that this war was begun;
Not a soul alive in that land is left.
And even the staunch Romans shall your strength stun,
Of their revenues by the Round Table bereft.
But the truce by the Tiber shall turn weal to woe:
Guard yourself, Gawain.
Tuscany you shall attain;

But Britain, your domain,
Shall fall to a fierce foe.

"This foe shall completely capture the crown;
And at Carlisle this cruel one shall be crowned king.
And when this man's titles and claims are laid down,
War and wretchedness that day to Britain shall bring.
You shall be told of this treason in a Tuscany town;
And you shall turn back with these tidings.
Then shall the Round Table lose its renown,
Beside Romsey, while in battle riding.
In Dorset shall die the most dauntless of all.
Guard yourself, Gawain,
Bravest of Britain;
In sludge you shall be slain.
Such strange fates shall fall.

"A strange fate shall fall, and this is no fable:
On the Cornwall coast, through a cruel knight,
The gracious King Arthur, honest and able,
Shall suffer his death wound's dolorous bite.
And all the royal retainers of the Round Table
On that day shall die, in defense of the right,
Surprised by a subject who bears arms of sable,
With a serrated saltier of silver so bright.
He bears arms of sable, the plain truth I say.
In great Arthur's hall,
Plays a man at ball,
Who shall destroy you all,
On that darkest day.

"Now goodbye, Guinevere, and Gawain the good;
I have no more further tidings to tell.
I must wander my way through this wild wood,
To my woeful dwelling, to welter in Hell.
By Him that conquered death on the Cross of wood,
Think on the danger and dole where I dwell.
For my sake feed folk who are starving for food,
And remember me with matins and masses as well.
Masses are medicine to souls unsanctified.
To us a mass is as sweet
As any spice you eat."

The ghost's predictions follow closely the account of the downfall of Arthur and the Round Table in the *Alliterative Morte Arthure*: the ghost even makes an indirect reference to the wheel of fortune ("Fortune, false in fight,/That wondrous wheelwright"), and to Mordred's arms (the "serrated saltire" is "His engrailed saltire" in the *Alliterative Morte Arthure*).

The ghost of Guinevere's mother may be inspired by *The Three Dead*

Kings, an early 15th century Middle English poem attributed to the Shropshire priest John Audelay. In the poem the unnamed narrator describes seeing a boar hunt. Three kings are following the hunt; they lose their way in mist and are separated from their retainers. Suddenly three walking corpses appear[14]:

> And out of the grove, three men come in view:
> Shadowy phantoms, fated to show,
> With legs long and lean, and limbs all askew,
> Their liver and lights all foetid.

The kings are terrified, but show a range of reactions to the three Dead, ranging from a desire to flee to a resolve to face them. The three corpses, in response, state that they are not demons, but the three kings' forefathers:

> "Fiends? Demons? Nay! You're mistaken!
> We're your fathers—salt of the earth—soon forgotten
> As you flourish like leaves on the linden,
> Holding lordships of towns from Lorne to London.
> Those who doubt your decree, or don't do your bidding,
> You beat and bind, or defraud for a flogging.
> Look! The worms use my bowel for a womb, all writhing,
> Each ribboned like the rope my shroud is a-binding.
> With this rope I am bound
> Though the world once esteemed
> Me. My carrion was found
> Kissable once. But you—unsound
> Masters—say no mass, leave us unredeemed!"

The Vows of King Arthur

The Vows of King Arthur, Sir Gawain, Sir Kay and Baldwin of Britain is a Northern poem of 1,148 lines that is thought to have been composed in the early 15th century. The action of the poem starts when a hunter comes to see Arthur[15]:

> The King at Carlisle lodged one day;
> A hunter came to him to say
> "Sire, there steals and stalks my way
> A beast of staggering size.
>
> "The creature is a savage boar
> —The like I never saw before—
> Who has brought me sorrows by the score
> And harried my hounds.
> He has slain them savagely,
> Fighting with such ferocity,
> I have no hound left so hardy

Dares come within his bounds.
Striking him I split my spear
And splintered much of my other gear,
But that hulks hide no blow could tear,
Nor work any wound.
Massively made and great is he;
All he takes on their doom will see.
No bull so big could ever be,
That in the field is found.

"He towers taller than a horse,
That thing with body great and coarse;
No animal has greater force
When he stands fast to fight.
Moreover, black as any bear,
Most folk will fill with fear;
And that hulks hide no blow can tear,
Nor kill him outright.
When he wants to whet his tusks,
Then he rampages through the bush;
He tears up roots in his mad rush,
Mangling all in sight.
Grim and gruesome is his rush
When he tosses up his tusks;
Who dares to take a blow from such
Would be bold all right."

He said, "In Inglewood Forest is he."
And Arthur answered, "let him be;
That creature we shall surely see,
If he be there," he swore.

So Arthur, Sir Kay, Sir Gawain and Baldwin of Britain set off for Inglewood
Forest. There they encountered the boar, and Arthur made his vow:

He said, "Sirs, in your company,
A vow and pledge I take on me:
No matter how hardy he may be,
Yonder fiend to slay;
To crush that beast and bring him down,
Singlehanded and all alone,
Tomorrow before day has dawned,
On that my life I lay.
And Sirs, now I command you too
To do as I have done just now:
Each of you swear some kind of vow."
Gladly assented they.

First to the King spoke Sir Gawain
Graciously answering back again,

"I vow that by Tarn Wadling
I'll watch and wake all night."
"And I take a vow," replied Sir Kay,
"To ride this wood all night till day,
And whosoever comes in my way
To the death to fight!"
Then Baldwin spoke: "To stop this strife,
I take a vow upon my life,
Never to be jealous of my wife,
Nor any beauty bright;
Nor turn away any man from my bread,
As long as I have food to spread;
Nor fear my death for any dread
Of either king or knight."

Baldwin of Britain is a figure of Middle English romances, inspired perhaps by Bishop Bytwini, Chief Bishop in Celliwig in Triad 1 of the *Triads of the Island of Britain*; and by "Bidwini the Bishop (who blessed Arthur's meat and drink)," mentioned in the 11th century Welsh tale *Culhwch and Olwen*. Baldwin's vows are tested outside Inglewood Forest, so I'll focus on Arthur, Gawain and Kay.

First, Arthur took on the boar:

Then the King gripped fast his spear.
Down on the boar he wished to bear;
And of his force he had no fear,
So sturdy was his shield.
The great spear's shaft so stout and long
Into splinters quickly sprung;
And his great steed that was so strong
Was struck down in the field.
The cunning boar in wait had lain,
And before the King could catch his reign,
He struck him with such might and main
As ever he did wield.
His sturdy steed was struck stone dead,
And never stirred a step ahead.
Of Jesus Christ a boon he pled:
Him from harm to shield.

The King still in his saddle was set,
And swiftly to his feet he leapt,
And sent a prayer to Saint Margaret
To shield him from fear.
Then he did as a stalwart knight:
He drew and brandished his sword bright,
And shoved his shield straight upright,
For splintered was his spear.

Swiftly, without more delay,
He got ready for the fray,
To fight that fiend who stood at bay
With a hideous leer.
They came together in the field,
But, for all the weapons he did wield,
The boar struck out and shattered the shield
That the King did bear.

Then the King fell on his knee
And prayed to God in majesty"
"Grant to me the victory
Over this foe," he spoke.
Wild as wind the boar raged out,
Snorted and snarled and raised his snout;
Like a furnace or hell's mouth,
His body steamed with smoke.
The King no more could clearly see,
But he crouched down behind a tree,
So nearly overcome was he,
For the smoke made him choke.
And as the boar came round an oak,
The King jumped up and sternly smote.
And bloodied both eyes with that stroke,
And thus the boar's might broke.

The mighty one was thus made meek
By the blows the King did wreak;
Never had one so far from weak
Challenged that one so.
The King then did not hesitate,
But met the boar as he charged straight,
And to the hilt of his stout blade
Swiftly ran him through.
At the throat he thrust him through;
After that stroke no joy he knew,
But he began to stumble and swoon,
For it was his death blow.
He started to stagger and sway around;
To finish him the King was bound;
He sundered and struck to the ground
Both forelegs of his foe.

Up to this point, the boar hunt is reminiscent of the hunt for the supernatural boar Twrch Trwyth in *Culhwch and Olwen*, but what follows is not drawn from the Welsh tale:

The King was trained in venery,
And cut the boar up skilfully;

The head of him, once so hardy,
He stuck upon a stake.
Then he cut and dressed the rest,
As game is cut in the forest,
Loin and liver, lung and breast,
And hung it on an oak.

This scene may be inspired by *Sir Gawain and the Green Knight*, which describes the cutting up of animals after each hunt. For example, after the boar hunt the poet says:

then one who was wise in woodland ways
began carefully to cut up and carve the carcass.
First he hacks of its head and hoists it aloft,
then roughly rives it along the spine;
he gouges out the guts and grills them over coals,
and blended with bread they are titbits for the bloodhounds.
Next he fetches out the fillets of glimmering flesh
and retrieves the intestines in time-honoured style,
then the two sides are stitched together intact
and proudly displayed on a strong pole.

The poem then switches to Sir Kay:

As Kay rode throughout the night.
In the forest he met a knight
Leading a lady of beauty bright,
Who wept wondrous sore.
She cried, "Holy Mary, help me succeed!
Preserve my maidenhood, I plead!
And send this knight for his dire deed
Sorrow evermore!"

Thus she cried out to that knight,
Lamenting loud and clear her plight,
While Kay held back and just sat tight,
Waiting in the wood.
Then he spurred out suddenly,
And overtook them readily,
And to that knight yelled lustily,
And rebuked him good:
Loudly he shouted, "Recreant knight,
I challenge you now to a fight!
For the cause of this lady bright,
I throw down my glove."
The other spoke with grace and skill,
And said, "I am ready at your will,
That agreement to fulfil
In every way I should."

> "Now where do you come from?" shouted Kay,
> "And whither are you on your way?
> Your right name to me do say!
> How got you this made bright?"
> The other answered him with pride:
> "My proper name I will not hide;
> Sir Menalfe of the Mountain am I;
> My godfather named me right.
> And this lady, truth to tell,
> Her I captured at Lidell."

Menealfe can be interpreted as "Man-Elf," suggesting that Sir Menealfe is a supernatural knight, while Liddel may be Liddel Strength, a 12th century castle associated with the battle in which Lailoken/Myrddin went mad.[16]

So Sir Kay and Sir Menealfe fought, and Kay was quickly defeated. Kay then told Menealfe that Gawain was at Tarn Wadling, and would pay a ransom for him, to which Menealfe replied:

> "Sir Kay, your death-blow I withhold
> For one joust with that night so bold."
> Yet Menealfe, before midnight tolled,
> His rashness would regret.

Menealfe and Kay rode to Tarn Wadling, and there Gawain and Menealfe jousted. Gawain was victorious, and Gawain, Kay and Arthur went with Menealfe and the maiden to Carlisle, where Menealfe was made a knight of the Round Table.

The Wedding of Sir Gawain and Dame Ragnell

The Wedding of Sir Gawain and Dame Ragnell is a 15th-century East Midland romance of 852 lines dealing with the "loathly lady" legend best known from Geoffrey Chaucer's 14th-century *Wife of Bath's Tale*. The "loathly lady" (ugly lady) legend goes back to the 12th century, when an ugly lady appears in Chrétien de Troyes' *Perceval, the Story of the Grail*. The story also served for the plot of an interlude performed at one of Edward I's Round Tables in 1299: a loathly lady, with foot-long nose, donkey ears, neck sores, a gaping mouth, and blackened teeth, rode into the hall and demanded of Sir Perceval and Sir Gawain (Edward's knights had assumed Arthurian identities for the occasion) that they recover lost territory and end the strife between commons and lords.[17]

As the poem opens, Arthur was hunting in Inglewood Forest. He shot a deer with his bow, then gave the deer its death blow[18]:

> As King and deer were all alone,
> Out of nowhere came a strange unknown,
> A man armed well and sure:
> A knight as stout and strong as an oak,
> And grim words to the King he spoke:
> "Well met, King Arthur!
> You have done me wrong for many a year,
> And gruesomely I shall repay you here;
> Your life-days are near flown.
> You have given my lands, to make it plain,
> Unjustly unto Sir Gawain.
> What say you, King alone?"
>
> "Sir Knight, your name please tell me true."
> "Gromer Somer Jour, Sir King, to you;
> I tell it to you right."

The name *Gromer* may be derived from Middle English *grome*, "man" (Modern English *groom*), and *Somer Jour* ("summer day") may refer to Midsummer, known in medieval times as St. John's day. In the 13th century a monk from Winchcombe in Gloucestershire recorded how St. John's Eve was celebrated in his time.[19]

> the boys collect bones and certain other rubbish, and burn them, and therefrom a smoke is produced on the air. They also make brands and go about the fields with the brands. Thirdly, the wheel which they roll.

The fires, explained the monk of Winchcombe, were to drive away dragons, which were abroad on St. John's Eve, poisoning springs and wells. The wheel that was rolled downhill he gave its explicitly solstitial explanation: "The wheel is rolled to signify that the sun then rises to the highest point of its circle and at once turns back; thence it comes that the wheel is rolled.

If Sir Gromer Somer Jour is the "Midsummer man" then he may be related to the Green Knight in *Sir Gawain and the Green Knight*, and this is reinforced in what follows. Arthur pleads for his life:

> Now said the King, "So God me save,
> Spare my life, and whatever you crave
> To you I shall grant it.
> To slay me while hunting is base and mean,
> You armed and I, by God, only in green."
> "All this shall not help one bit;
> For I care not at all for gold or land.
> That you meet me again is my only command,
> On a set day and in this array."
> "Yes," said the King, "Lo, here is my hand."
> "Yea, but wait, King, and hear my demand;
> On my bright sword your vow you must lay:

"To meet me here without further request
And tell me what in the world women love best,
On this day at the year's end;
And you must swear upon my sword bright
By the Cross you will bring with you no knight,
Neither stranger nor friend.
If you bring not the answer, be sure, without fail,
Your head you shall forfeit, for all your travail,
And this shall your oath be.
What say you, King? Let us be done!"

Sir Gromer then swore Arthur to secrecy, but finally Arthur told Gawain, and they both set off looking for the answer to Sir Gromer's question, each armed with a book in which to write what they heard. They received many different answers, and Arthur was downcast:

"By God," said the King, "I am filled with dread.
Into Inglewood Forest now I will head,
A little more to quest.
I have only a month till my set day;
Some lucky tidings may come my way.
This seems to me now best."
"Do as you wish," Sir Gawain bade;
"Whatsoever you do will make me glad.
To keep seeking is always best.
Doubt you not, Lord, you shall succeed;
Some of your sayings shall answer your need,
Or things are worse than I guessed."

King Arthur rode forth on the next day;
Into Inglewood Forest his road lay,
And there a lady he saw.
She was as unlovely a being
As a man could look on without fleeing,
And King Arthur stood stock sill in awe.
Her face was beet-red, her nose was snot-smeared;
Her teeth were all yellow, her mouth wide and weird,
Her eyes like huge balls, bulging and bleared;
Her great jaw was hanging all slack.
Her long, ugly teeth lapped over her lips;
Her cheeks were as huge as most women's hips,
And she carried a lute on her back.
Her neck was all knotted and gnarled;
Her hair in a heap was all snarled.
She had shoulders a yard broad and hairy,
Dangling paps no draft horse could carry,
And was big as a barrel in size.
So hideous was he and hoary,
No tongue could relate the whole story.

For gruesomeness she took the prize!
She sat on a palfrey, all decked out,
With gold and rich gems all about;
There was a sight grotesque!
Such a creature, foul beyond measure,
Riding bedecked in such a treasure
Was hardly picturesque!

She rode to Arthur, and there she wheezed:
"God speed, Sir King, I am well pleased
That I have with you met.
Do speak to me before you fly;
It is in my hands that you live or die.
A few words you'll not regret."

"Why what do you want, lady, now with me?"
"Sir, to speak with you is all my plea,
And tell you tidings good.
Of all the answers you can yelp,
Not one shall be of any help;
Know this by the Cross of wood.
You think I know not your secret,
But I warn you, I know it every bit;
If I help not, you are dead!
Grant me, Sir King, but one thing I crave,
And I shall save you from your grave,
Or else you lose your head!"

"What mean you lady, tell me quick!
For at your words my heart grows sick.
Of you I know no need.
What is your desire, lady fair?
Your wishes quickly let me share.
What is it you plead?
Why is my life now in your hand?
Tell me, and whatever you demand
To that I will accede."

"In truth," said the lady, "no fiend I be.
A knight to wed you must give me;
His name is Sir Gawain.
And I will give this guarantee:
Unless your life be saved by me
Let my desire be vain;
And if my answer save your life,
Grant that I be Gawain's wife.
Sir King, advise you well.
For it must be so, or you are dead.
Choose now, for soon you may lose your head.
Now quickly speak and tell."

So Arthur said he would consult Gawain:

> "Good," said she, "now go home again,
> And speak fair words to Gawain,
> That your life I may save;
> For I am lusty, though I be plain.
> Through me may he your life sustain,
> Or send you to your grave."
> "Alas," he said, "this day I rue.
> That I should Gawain to wed you!
> For he is too good to say no.
> A being like you, so ugly and hoar,
> I never saw walking the earth before.
> What to do I do not know."

> "Never mind, Sir King, that I be foul;
> Choice of a mate has even an owl.
> No more shall be revealed.
> When you come back your answer to learn,
> Right to this place I shall return,
> Or else your doom is sealed!
> Yes, a bird there is men call an owl,
> But I am a lady and not a fowl."
> "Lady," said the King, "farewell.
> What is your name, I pray you tell."
> "Sir King, I am called Dame Ragnell,
> Who never on a man yet cast a spell."

The name *Ragnell* is otherwise unknown in Arthurian romance, but in *Patience*, a poetic version of the Jonah story usually attributed to the author of *Sir Gawain and the Green Knight*, the gentile sailors on whose ship the Hebrew prophet tries to escape from the Lord curse him by "Ragnel," apparently intended to be taken as the name of a pagan god or devil. In the late medieval play *Mary Magdalen* a heathen priest and his servant perform a comic exorcism in broken Latin, and then call on the gods "Ragnell and Roffyn."[20]

Arthur then leaves the lady and meets Gawain. He explains to Gawain what has just happened:

> "Gawain, I met the loathliest lady today,
> That ever I saw, the truth to say.
> She promised me my life she would save,
> If I to her as husband gave.
> And for that my spirit is heavy as stone,
> And thus in my heart I make my moan."

> "And is this all?" answered Gawain;
> "I shall marry her twice over again,
> Even if she were the Fiend!

Even had she Beelzebub's face,
Her I should wed, I swear by God's grace,
Or as your friend I were demeaned.
Since you are my lord and lawful king,
Who has honored me in everything,
I shall not hesitate.
To save your life, Lord, is my pleasure,
Or I would be weak and false beyond measure;
My glory thus will be great."

A few days later Arthur returned to Inglewood Forest:

The King had ridden but a little while,
Not much more than the space of a mile,
Before Dame Ragnell appeared.
"King Arthur, I bid you welcome fair;
I know you ride your answer to bear,
But all in vain," she sneered.

"Now," said the King, "since I see no other way,
"Tell me your answer and save me I pray,
And Gawain shall you wed.
This he has promised, my life to save;
And you shall have the pleasure you crave,
Both in chamber and bed.
Tell me now, before it's too late,
That which will save me from my fate;
Be quick, I may not tarry."
"Sir," said Dame Ragnell, "now you shall know
What women want most, both high and low;
From this I will not vary.

"Some say we desire to be fair;
To frolic freely, others will swear,
With men of every land.
Some say we love our pleasure in bed,
Or that we desire to be many times wed;
Thus you men don't understand.
We are said to desire yet another thing:
That with tricks and praises and flattering,
To be deemed ever youthful and fresh;
Thus do your wiles us women enmesh,
As you flatter us in pursuit of our flesh.

"A subtle answer, that I agree.
But one thing above all is our fantasy,
And that you now shall know.
One thing above all else is our dream:
To possess sovereignty—mastery supreme—
Over men, both the high and the low.

> For where we have sovereignty there we have power;
> And if a man be of knighthood the flower,
> Him we most wish to enslave.
> To rule the mightiest is all our lust;
> To have dominion and mastery we must.
> With cunning and craft this we crave.
> Therefore ride, Sir King, on your way,
> And tell that knight just as I say,
> What we crave at all cost.
> He will be furious and distraught,
> And curse the one who has this taught,
> For his labor now is lost.

> "Go forth, Sir King, and keep your vow.
> Your life is fully secure now;
> That I do ensure."

Arthur immediately rode to meet Sir Gromer, who said to him:

> "Come on, Sir King, now let me see
> What your answer now might be,
> For I am all prepared."

> The King his two books did display:
> "Sir, here is the answer, I dare say;
> One of these must serve my need."
> Sir Gromer looked at them every one.
> "Nay, nay, Sir King, you are dead and done.
> Therefore, now you shall bleed!"
> "Wait, Sir Gromer, now you I assure
> I have one answer that will make me secure."
> Sir Gromer then said, "Let's see;
> Or else, God help me, I now swear,
> Your death you shall meet with no time for prayer;
> That I guarantee."

> "Now," said the King, "I see and I guess,
> In you there is little courteousness,
> By God, the Keeper of all!
> Here is my answer, for what it's worth,
> To what women desire most on this earth,
> From both freeman and thrall:
> I will say no more, but above everything,
> Women want sovereignty; to that they cling,
> And that is their deepest desire.
> The mightiest men they wish to subdue;
> Then they are glad—this they tell me is true.
> They want to rule, Gromer Sire!"

> "Now am I filled with fury and ire!
> May she who told you this burn on a pyre!

> She was my sister, Dame Ragnell.
> The ugly old hag, God give her shame!
> Without her you surely would have been tamed.
> All my efforts have come to nil!
> Now go where you wish, King Arthur,
> For from my threats you are ever secure.
> Alas that I saw this day!
> Now well I know my foe you will be;
> And never again will you be caught by me.
> My song must be wellaway!"

So Gawain and Dame Ragnell were wed, and the wedding banquet was quite an occasion:

> The foul lady sat at the table's head,
> But she was gross, uncouth, and ill-bred
> —To that they all did assent.
> When the food before her was set,
> As fast as six men she ate all she could get;
> The guests watched, still as stone.
> With nails three inches long, or more,
> In an ungodly fashion her meat she tore,
> And therefore she dined alone.
> She ate up three capons and three game birds too,
> And great roasted meats she chewed her way through.
> Men were awestruck at Dame Ragnell.
> There was no food that before her was set
> That she did not gobble without a regret,
> That hideous, vile demoiselle.
>
> Everyone there who this display saw
> Bade that the Devil her bones should gnaw,
> Squire as well as knight.

The manuscript is missing one leaf, containing about seventy lines; the narrative continues at the moment of Ragnell and Gawain's wedding night:

> Ah, Sir Gawain, since we two are wed,
> Now show me your courtesy in bed,
> For it can't be rightly denied.
> Sir Gawain," she continued, "I am aware
> You would act otherwise if I were fair.
> In wedlock you take no pride.
> But grant my request and give me one kiss;
> For Arthur's sake I ask only this.
> Let's see if you can succeed."
>
> Then Sir Gawain said, "More will I do,
> I swear before God, than only kiss you."
> He turned himself to her.

He suddenly saw her fair beyond measure,
A beauteous creature, to love and to treasure;
She said, "What is your will, Sir?"
   "Ah Jesu!" he cried, "What can you be?"
"Sir, I am your wife, as you plainly see.
Why are you so unkind?"
"Ah lady, forgive me, I am to blame;
I cry you mercy, fairest dame;
But this is too much for my mind.
You are now a lady fair to my seeing,
And just today you were the ugliest being
That ever I saw with my eyes.
Glad am I, my lady, I have you like this."
He clasped her in his arms and gave her a kiss,
Rejoicing indeed in his prize.

"To this, Sir," she said then, "you must agree,
For my beauty may suddenly flee;
One way or the other it has to be:
You can choose to have me thus fair by night,
And by day just as foul to all men's sight,
Or by day I can be fair, lovely and bright,
And fouler by night than the ugliest fright;
One or the other you must choose.
Make your choice now of one of these two,
Whichever, Sir Knight, most pleases you,
Or your honor you'll lose."

"Alas!" said Gawain, "hard is this choice.
Neither course is cause to rejoice,
Whichever one that I choose.
To have you fair by night and no more
Would grieve my heart forevermore,
For all respect I should lose.
To have you fair by day I am eager,
But then at night my joy would be meager.
I very much want to choose best …
I do not know what in the world to say,
So do as you wish, my lady, I pray;
The choice is yours to request.

"To do as you wish I put in your hand;
Reward me as you will, I am at your command.
The choice I give to you now.
My body and goods, my soul and heart,
Are yours to dispose, in every part.
That to God I vow."
Cried the lady, "Gracious knight, gramercy!
Of all earthly knights, most blessed may you be;
For I am honored at last.

You shall have me fair by both day and night,
And as long as I live this lovely and bright;
Therefore be no longer downcast.

"For I was transformed through sorcery,
By my stepmother—God give her mercy—
And by a magic spell;
And this disgrace I had to stand,
Until the best knight in the land
Had wed me with good will,
And also had given me sovereignty
Over body and goods, unconditionally;
Thus was I blighted and bent.
And you, Sir Knight, gracious Gawain,
Have given men sovereignty, clear and plain;
This you shall never repent.

"Kiss me, Sir Knight, my love and my dear.
I pray you be happy and make good cheer;
You have freed me from despair."

The choice that Dame Ragnell gives Gawain "is different from the choice in the *Wife of Bath's Tale*, though no less difficult. As the choice between virtuousness and beauty underlies the theme of *gentillesse* in the *Wife of Bath's Tale*, so here the choice of public vs. private beauty underlines the theme of public shame and humiliation."[21]

From Arthur to Robin Hood

Arthur began as a hunter/warrior god and Arthur and his retinue were very much wilderness figures in the Welsh tale *Culhwch and Olwen*. In Geoffrey's *History* and the English Arthurian tales that followed in the next 200 years or so, Arthur was part of the establishment, and it his outlaw role was taken by other figures. In the next two chapter, I look at Hereward the Wake, who led a rebellion against William the Conqueror from the fens of Cambridgeshire and south Lincolnshire, and his later successor, Robin Hood, who frequented Sherwood Forest in Lincolnshire but ranged as far north as Barnsdale in West Yorkshire. In Chapter 11, I survey two early Robin Hood works, one of them—*Robin Hood and the Monk*—typical of early Robin Hood tales, the other—*Robin Hood and Guy of Gisborne*—most untypical. In Chapter 12 I analyze the most substantial Robin Hood tale, *A Gest of Robyn Hode*, and an outlaw ballad *Adam Bell, Clim of the Clough, and William of Cloudesley* which is not a Robin Hood tale but is set in Inglewood Forest, the haunt of Arthur and Gawain.

11

The Wilderness Hero
Robin Hood in the Late Middle Ages (Part I)

Hereward: The First English Outlaw

The Arthur of the Welsh tale *Culhwch and Olwen* belonged to the wilderness, and some have seen him as an outlaw like the Irish hero Fionn (or Finn) mac Cumhaill. Geoffrey of Monmouth turned Arthur into a warrior and king, and the Arthurian tales only returned to the wilderness in *Sir Gawain and the Green Knight* and the three romances set in Inglewood Forest. However, Arthur never regained the outlaw status he may have had in *Culhwch and Olwen*, and the role of the outlaw was taken by other figures, including the post–Conquest hero Hereward and his later medieval descendant Robin Hood.

Hereward is first mentioned in the Peterborough version of the *Anglo-Saxon Chronicle*, recorded by the monks of Peterborough Abbey until 1154. In its entry for 1070 the *Chronicle* says[1]:

> Here the earl Waltheof made peace with the king. And in the following spring the king allowed all the minsters which were in England to be raided. Then in the same year King Swein came from Denmark into the Humber, and the local people came to him and made peace with him—thought that he would conquer that land. Then Christian, the Danish bishop, came to Ely, and Jarl Osbern and the Danish house-carls with them. And the English people from all the Fenlands came to them—thought that they would win all that land. Then the monks of Peterborough heard say that their own men, that was Hereward and his band, wanted to raid the minster—that was because they had heard say that the king had given the abbacy to a French abbot called Turold, and that he was a very stern man and had then come into Stamford with all his French men. There was then a sacristan called Yware; he at night took all he could: that was Christ's books and chasubles and copes and robes and such little things—whatsoever he could, and straightway before dawn travelled to the abbot Turold, and told him that he sought his protection, and informed him how the outlaws were to come to Peterborough. He did that entirely on the advice of the monks. Then straightway in the morning all the outlaws came

with many ships and wanted [to get] into the minster, and the monks withstood so that they could not come in. Then they laid fire to it, and burned down all the monks' buildings and all the town, except for one building. Then, by means of fire, they came in at Bolhithe Gate. The monks came to meet them, asked them for peace, but they did not care about anything, went into the minster, climbed up to the holy rood, took the crown off our Lord's head—all of pure gold—then took the rest which was underneath his feet—that was all of red gold—climbed up to the steeple, brought down the altar-frontal that was hidden there—it was all of gold and of silver. They took there two golden shrines, and 9 silver, and they took fifteen great roods, both of gold and of silver. They took there so much gold and silver and so many treasures in money and in clothing and in books that no man can tell another—said they did it out of loyalty to this minster.

Earl Waltheof was the Anglo-Saxon Earl of Huntingdon and Northampton; Swein was the King of Demark who briefly invaded England in 1069 and captured York (he left after King William paid him off).

Hereward is again mentioned in the entry for 1071. In that year the rebels Earl Edwin of Mercia and Earl Morcar of Northumbria "ran off and travelled variously in woods and in open country. Then Earl Morcar turned on ship to Ely, and Earl Edwin was killed treacherously by his own men." And the bishop Aethelwine of Durham and Siward Bearn (a powerful land-owner before the Conquest) and many hundreds of men with them came into Ely[2]:

> And then when the king William learnt about that, he ordered out ship-army and land-army, and surrounded that land, and made a bridge and went in—and the ship-army [was] to the seaward. And then the outlaws all came into hand: that was Bishop Aethelwine and Earl Morcar and all those who were with them, except Hereward alone, and all who wanted to be with him; and he courageously led them out. And the king took ships and weapons and many monies, and dealt with the men just as he wanted; and he sent the bishop Aethelwine to Abingdon and he passed away there soon the following winter.

Hereward seems to have been a small south Lincolnshire land-owner, holding lands from the abbeys of Crowland and Peterborough. In 1070 the Danish king Sweyn II Estridsson arrived in the mouth of the Humber, and was expected to make a bid for the crown. He dispatched a body of housecarls (household troops) under Jarl Asbjorn and Bishop Christian of Aarhus to secure a base on the Isle of Ely. Ely was "admirably suited for defense; sea-going vessels could reach it via the Wash and River Ouse, but landwards it was cut off by swamps and a network of hidden waterways." Here the Danes were immediately joined by local people (many of whom were of Danish extraction), including Hereward. At Peterborough Abbey, on the western edge of the Fens two dozen miles away, the abbot Brand, perhaps Hereward's uncle, had recently died, and now the monks were warned that Hereward and his companions wanted to remove the monastery's valuables prior to the arrival of a Norman abbot, the tyrannical Turold, who was approaching with a band of 160 soldiers. The monks resisted Hereward and his men, who set fire to the town, forced the precinct gate and looted the monastery. Soon afterwards the Danes returned to Denmark, taking this loot with them.

Ely now became "a notorious refuge for anti–Norman dissidents, including, among the better known, Earl Morcar of Northumbria, Bishop Æthelwine of Durham, and Siward Bearn, a substantial Midlands landowner." Eventually William himself led an expedition against Ely. He bottled up the defenders, placing a naval blockade on the seaward side and then constructing a lengthy causeway to allow his land forces to advance through the swamps. Eventually the defenders surrendered to William who "did with them what he wanted." Florence of Worcester says that some he imprisoned, others he let go free, having cut off their hands or put out their eyes. But Hereward slipped away with some of his followers and is heard of no more in any official record.[3]

According to the traditions of both Peterborough and Crowland Abbeys, Hereward was the nephew of Abbot Brand of Peterborough. Therefore one of the Abbot's four brothers, Asketil, Siward, Siric and Godric must have been Hereward's father. The five brothers were the son of a thegn called Toki. Since Asketil owned property in Lincoln, it suggests that the rich landowner of Lincoln, Toki Autison was Asketil's father. His lands were confiscated after the Conquest and fell into the hands of a baron called Geoffrey Alselin. It is likely that Asketil was Hereward's father, since Siward, Siric and Godric were probably too young at the time of Hereward's birth, around 1045.[4]

The exploits of Hereward were soon celebrated in a Latin text, the *Gesta Herewardi* (Deeds of Hereward). This was probably written by Richard, a monk of Ely Abbey, in the first quarter of the 12th century, at a time when Hereward himself was presumably dead, but a number of former companions were still alive and capable of remembering their old campaigns.

According to the *Gesta Herewardi*, Hereward was the son of Leofric of Bourne (Lincolnshire), the nephew of Earl Ralph the Staller ("constable"), an Anglo-Saxon landowner who became Earl of East Anglia under William the Conqueror, and Eadgyth, the great-great-niece of Duke Oslac of York. If Asketil was in fact Hereward's father, this confusion may have arisen because the lord of Bourne was Earl Morcar, the grandson of Leofric of Mercia, and that estate, along with several estates belonging to Hereward, were all passed after the Conquest to the Breton called Ogier.[5]

At the age of eighteen Hereward was exiled from his homeland by his father for disruptive behavior. During his exile, Hereward was involved in various adventures. He killed a monstrous bear in Northumberland, and a braggart in Cornwall, suitor for the hand of the princess; and the leader of an invading army in Ireland. He returned to the Cornish princess and attended her wedding in disguise, rescued the girl and ensured her marriage to an Irish prince. Now determined to return home, Hereward was shipwrecked in Orkney, and again in Flanders where he was honorably detained by the count, changing his name to Harold. Hereward fought on behalf of the Count of Flanders against the neighboring Count of Guines, and his true name was revealed. During the course of his sojourn, the skilled and enterprising girl Turfrida fell in love with him, and he with her, despite the violent opposition of another knight. Hereward took the central role in two campaigns against rebellious Frisian armies. While in Frisia he acquired a particularly swift mare he names Swallow, and her colt Lightfoot.

Finally Hereward returned to England in 1069 or 1070, and discovered that his family's lands had been taken over by the Normans and his brother killed with his head then placed on a spike at the gate to his house. Hereward took revenge on the Normans who killed his brother while they were ridiculing the English at a drunken feast. He allegedly killed fifteen of them with the assistance of one helper. He then gathered followers and went to Peterborough Abbey to be knighted by his uncle Abbot Brand. He returned briefly to Flanders to allow the situation to cool down before returning to England.

After this, Frederick, the brother-in-law of William de Warenne (a Norman baron who fought at the Battle of Hastings), swore to kill Hereward, but Hereward outwitted him and killed him. Hereward then participated in the anti–Norman insurrection centered on the Isle of Ely, and later moved on to Peterborough where he captured the Norman abbot Turold[6]:

> Afterwards the aforesaid abbot of Peterborough was released from captivity by Hereward for a ransom of thirty thousand pounds. And one of Hereward's kinsmen called Siward the Blond set free the abbot's nephew and others whom they had captured, all of whom he had treated with honorable hospitality out of respect for the abbot. But remembering neither their kindness nor their agreement, they repaid Hereward by once more making war on him and his men. To this purpose, the aforesaid abbot distributed many of the estates of his church to knights on condition that they gave military assistance to subdue Hereward, on account of the trouble he had given the abbot. He arranged that they should attack Hereward as a duty in return for their lands. However, when Hereward heard reports of this, and that a punishment hung over him in return for his kindness, he did not long delay, but the same night went with his men to Peterborough to avenge themselves. And laying waste the whole town with fire, they plundered all the treasures of the church and chased the abbot, although he and his men managed to escape by hiding themselves.

But Hereward soon regretted plundering the church treasures:

> In his sleep the following night, Hereward saw standing before him a man of indescribable appearance, in old age, fearsome of countenance, and more remarkable in all his clothing than anything he had ever seen or imagined in his mind, now menacing him with a great key which he brandished in his hand, and with a fearful injunction that if he wished to ensure his safety and avoid a miserable death the next day, he should restore in their entirety all those possessions of his church which Hereward had taken the previous night. Indeed, on waking he was seized with holy

dread, and that very hour carried back everything he had taken away, and then moved on with all his men. On their journey they unexpectedly went astray, losing the right path. A marvelous thing happened to them while they were astray thus—a miracle, if such things can reasonably be said to happen to flesh and blood. For while in the stormy night and gloom they were wandering hither and thither through the forests, not knowing where they were going, a huge wolf came in front of them, fawning on them like a tame dog and walking along in front of them down the path. In the obscuring gloom they mistook it for a white dog because of its grey coat, and urged one another to follow the dog closely, declaring that it must have come from some village. This they did. And in the midst of the night, while they discovered that they had succeeded in getting out of the by-way and recognizing the road, suddenly there appeared burning lights clinging to the soldiers' lances—not very bright, but like those popularly called will-o-the-wisps. No one could get rid of them, or extinguish them, or throw them away. Whereupon, greatly marvelling amongst themselves, although they were stupefied they could see their way, and went on led by the wolf. And then with dawning day they all eventually found to their astonishment that their guide had been a wolf. And while they were at a loss to know what had happened to them, the wolf disappeared, the lights vanished, and they had got to where they wanted, beyond Stamford. And realizing that their journey had been successful, they gave thanks to God, marvelling at what had happened to them.

Eventually, Hereward attempted to negotiate with William but was provoked into a fight with a man named Ogger (probably the Ogier who took over Hereward's estates). The fight led to his capture and imprisonment. His followers, however, liberated him when he was being transferred from one castle to another. Hereward's former jailer persuaded the king to negotiate once more, and he was eventually pardoned by William and lived the rest of his life in relative peace.

However, Geoffrey Gaimar, in his *Estoire des Engleis* (History of the English), written in the 1130s, tells a different story. According to him, Hereward held out for many years against the Normans with his companions, defeating forces that outnumbered him until a lady called Alftrued sent for him to become her husband and receive her father's land. Hereward went to her under a truce from King William, and was about to fight for William in Maine, northwestern France, when a group of Frenchmen broke the truce and attacked him while he was eating. Hereward fought bravely against his attackers, killing several of them, but was eventually killed by a Breton named Ralph de Dol from Tutbury, and then beheaded by a certain Halselin.[7]

The Normans and Their Royal Forests

William the Conqueror died in 1087, and the *Peterborough Chronicle* sums up the English opinion of him in this piece of verse[8]:

He had castles built
and wretched men oppressed.
The king was so very stark
and seized from his subject men many a mark
of gold, and more hundreds of pounds of silver
that he took by weight, and with great injustice
from his land's nation with little need.
He was fallen into avarice,
and he loved greediness above all.
He set up great game-preserves, and he laid down laws for them,
that whosoever killed hart or hind
he was to be blinded.
He forbade [hunting] the harts, so also the boars;
　he loved the stags so very much,
as if he were their father;
also he decreed for the hares that they might go free.
His powerful men lamented it, and the wretched men complained of it
but he was so severe that he did not care about the enmity of all of them;
but they must wholly follow the king's will
if they wanted to live or have land –
and or property or his good favour.
Alas, woe, that any man should be so proud,
raise up and reckon himself over all men.
May the Almighty God shew mercy to his soul
and grant him forgiveness of his sins.

Clearly, what angered the Anglo-Saxon compilers of the *Peterborough Chronicle* most was the creation of vast royal forests—such as the New Forest in Hampshire, Sherwood Forest in Nottinghamshire, and Inglewood Forest in Cumbria—where only the monarch or (by invitation) the aristocracy could hunt (although Anglo-Saxon kings were keen hunters, they never set aside areas declared to be outside the law of the land). It is no coincidence that Robin Hood is most closely associated with Sherwood Forest, which was listed as *terra regis* ("Land of the King") in the Domesday book of 1086.

The Plantagenet Kings

The end of the *Peterborough Chronicle* coincided with the end of the Norman kings, and to understand Robin Hood, we need to understand the period in which he first emerged—the 14th and 15th centuries. The Norman period in England came to an end in 1154, with the accession of Henry II, the first king of the House of Plantagenet, which was descended from the counts of Anjou in western France. The Plantagenets ruled until 1485, and most famously fought against the kingdom of France in the Hundred Years

War (1337–1453). By the end of the war, the Plantagenets had lost their last French possession (Gascony in southwest France), and English had replaced French as the language of the elite. The most important king in the early years of the Hundred Years War was Edward III (1327–1377). In 1346, Edward defeated the French at the Battle of Crécy, and in the same year he captured Calais. In 1348, the Black Death struck England, killing a third of the country's population. In 1356, after the plague had passed, Edward's son, Edward, Prince of Wales, invaded France from Gascony, winning a great victory at the Battle of Poitiers, and capturing the French king John II. In 1359, Edward invaded France for the third and last time, hoping to seize the throne of France. He wanted to be crowned at Reims, and unsuccessfully besieged the city for five weeks. Edward moved on to Paris, but retreated after a few skirmishes in the suburbs. The French made contact with him and forced him to negotiate. A conference was held at Brétigny that resulted in the Treaty of Brétigny (May 8, 1360). The treaty was ratified at Calais in October. In return for increased lands in Aquitaine, Edward renounced Normandy, Touraine, Anjou and Maine and consented to reducing King John's ransom by a million crowns. Edward also abandoned his claim to the crown of France. In the next few years, the French fought back, and by 1380 the English had lost most of Gascony except for the area around Bordeaux, and all other territories except for Calais.

Edward Prince of Wales died in 1376, and Edward III died in the following year, to be succeeded by Richard II, who was a child at the time. The War was becoming increasingly unpopular due to high taxes (this was one of the factors which led to the Peasants' Revolt of 1381). The Hundred Years' War resumed in 1415 when Henry V defeated the French at the Battle of Agincourt. Henry took most of Normandy, and in 1419 Henry and Charles VI of France signed the Treaty of Troyes: Henry married Charles' daughter Catherine of Valois, and Henry's heirs would inherit the throne of France.

In 1428 the English laid siege to Orléans, but the French, inspired by Joan of Arc, forced the English to lift the siege, and took several English strongholds on the Loire. In 1430, Joan was captured by the Burgundians (allies of England) who handed her over to the English; she was burned at the stake in 1431. After her death, the French began to triumph: by 1450, the French had retaken Rouen and Caen in Normandy, and in 1453 they recaptured the last English territories in Gascony.

At the end of the Hundred Years' War, the throne of England was fought over by two rival branches of the Plantagenets, the Houses of Lancaster and York, in the War of the Roses (1455–1487). In 1461 Edward IV of the House of York deposed Henry VI of the House of Lancaster; in 1470 Edward IV was himself deposed, and replaced briefly by Henry VI, who was once more deposed by Edward IV in the following year. Edward died in 1483 and was replaced by his brother, Richard III. In 1485 Richard was defeated by the Lancastrian Henry Tudor at the Battle of Bosworth Field; he became Henry VII, the first of the Tudor monarchs, and married Elizabeth of York, daughter of Edward IV, thus uniting the Houses of Lancaster and York.

Clearly there were times during the Hundred Years' War and the War of the Roses when law and order broke down, and in these times stories of outlaws like Robin Hood must have proliferated.

Early References to Robin Hood

The earliest reference to Robin Hood comes in William Langland's *Piers Plowman*, written some time between 1370 and 1390, at a time when the war with France was becoming unpopular and Wat Tyler was leading the Peasants' Revolt. Here is the quote in Middle English, with a translation[9]:

> "I kan noght parfitly my Paternoster as the prest it syngeth,
> But I can rhymes of Robyn Hood and Randolf Erl of Chestre,
> Ac neither of Our Lorde ne of Oure Lady the leeste that evere was maked."

> ["I don't know perfectly my *Our Father* as the priest sings it;
> I know rhymes of Robin Hood and Randolf Earl of Chester,
> But neither of Our Lord nor of Our Lady the least that ever was written."]

The earliest known fragment of a Robin Hood rhyme comes from a manuscript in Lincoln Cathedral which is dated to around 1425. Here a writer, possibly a student, hastily wrote or scribbled two rhymed couplets for a Robin Hood poem, followed by a crude Latin translation[10]:

> Robyn hod in scherewod stod
> hodud and hathud hosut and schold
> ffour and thuynti arowes
> he bar in hit hondus.

> [Robin Hood in Sherwood stood
> hooded and hatted, hosed and shod
> four and twenty arrows
> he bore in his hands].

However, the first extended reference to Robin Hood comes from Andrew of Wyntoun's *Orygynale Chronicle*, composed around 1420.[11] Andrew was an Augustinian canon of St. Sers Inch, a religious house set on an island in Loch Leven (Scottish Highlands), and a daughter house of St. Andrew's priory. The chronicle is "strongly pro–Scottish in tone, especially severe on the malpractices of Edward I in his war against the Scots and his treatment of the national hero William Wallace." In the period of these wars, under the year 1283, Andrew mentions two forest outlaws (*waythmen*, or "men who lie in wait") from the long turbulent area of the borders. They operated, it seems, both just south of the border near Carlisle in Inglewood, and much further south in England in Barnsdale. Andrew's apparent approval of their efforts and his report of the common praise of them is no doubt related to the fact that they were enemies of the English crown and its officers. After the battles of Dunbar (1296) and Falkirk (1298) William Wallace and the Scots took to the forests themselves, and many later people saw resemblances between Robin Hood and the Scottish nationalist outlaw. The reference comes in four lines:

> Litil Johun and Robert Hude
> Waythmen [forest outlaws] war commendid gud [were praised];
> In Ingilwode and Bernnysdaile
> Thai oyssit [practiced] all this time thar trawale [labor].

Inglewood Forest, a royal forest in Cumbria, was never the scene of an actual Robin Hood ballad, but the ballad called *Adam Bell, Clim of the Clough, and William of Cloudesley*, which takes place in Inglewood Forest, has many of the features of a Robin Hood ballad. Barnsdale is an area to the north and northwest of Doncaster in South Yorkshire, which was the scene of several Robin Hood tales.

The next mention of Robin Hood comes from Walter Bower's Continuation of John Fordun's *Scotichronicon*.[12] In the 1440s Walter Bower, a canon of St. Andrew's priory, was reworking the chronicle written in Latin some twenty years before by John of Fordun. As well as bringing it up to date he inserted passages, including a lengthy comment on Robin Hood and Little John. Under the year 1266 he described Robin as a *famosus siccarius* (a well-known cut-throat), saying that "the foolish people are so inordinately fond of celebrating [him] in tragedy and comedy." Bower places the outlaw in the context of Simon de Montfort's rebellion against Henry III (1263–4), and refers to Robin as fighting among the "disinherited," the term given to the dissidents led by Simon. Here is an excerpt from Bower's *Scotichronicon*:

> Then arose the famous murderer, Robert Hood, as well as Little John, together with their accomplices from among the disinherited, whom the foolish populace are so inordinately fond of celebrating both in tragedies and comedies, and about whom they are delighted to hear the jesters and minstrels sing above all other ballads. About whom also certain praiseworthy things are told, as appears in this—that when once in Barnsdale, avoiding the anger of the king and the threats of the prince, he was according to his custom most devoutly hearing Mass and had no wish on any account to interrupt the service—on a certain day, when he was hearing Mass, having been discovered in that very secluded place in the woods when the Mass was taking place by a certain sheriff (*viscount*) and servant of the king, who had very often lain in wait for him previously, there came to him those who had found this out from their men to suggest that he should make every effort to flee. This, on

account of his reverence for the sacrament in which he was then devoutly involved, he completely refused to do. But, the rest of his men trembling through fear of death, Robert, trusting in the one so great whom he worshipped, with the few who then bravely remained with him, confronted his enemies and easily overcame them, and enriched by the spoils he took from them and their ransom, ever afterward singled out the servants of the church and the Masses to be held in greater respect, bearing in mind what is commonly said: "God harkens to him who hears Mass frequently."

Here Robert (Robin) Hood is again associated with Barnsdale.

The final early reference to Robin Hood comes from John Major's *History of Greater Britain*.[13] John Major was a Scottish historian and intellectual who studied at the University of Paris and taught at the University of Glasgow. In 1521 he published his *Historia Majoris Brittaniae* ("history of Greater Britain"), and relocated the story of Robin Hood to the late 12th century and the time of King Richard (1189–99) and King John (1199–1216). Here is the extract from Major:

About this time it was, as I conceive, that there flourished those most famous robbers Robert Hood, an Englishman, and Little John, who lay in wait in the woods, but spoiled of their goods those only that were wealthy. They took the life of no man, unless he either attacked them or offered resistance in defence of his property. Robert supported by his plundering one hundred bowmen, ready fighters every one, with whom four hundred of the strongest would not dare to engage in combat. The feats of this Robert are told in song all over Britain. He would allow no woman to suffer injustice, nor would he spoil the poor, but rather enriched them from the plunder taken from the abbots. The robberies of this man I condemn, but of all robbers he was the humanest and the chief.

Two things stand out in these early references: firstly, that tales of Robin Hood were circulating in the second half of the 14th century, and secondly, that Robin Hood was associated with both Sherwood Forest and Nottingham, and with Barnsdale in South Yorkshire. Why Robin Hood should be associated with Barnsdale in South Yorkshire, which was a lightly wooded area rather than a forest, is something of a mystery, but may have an historical explanation. From 1333 to 1338, the exchequer (the government department which collects taxation and other revenues) was based at York, during Edward III's Scottish campaign. During this time the sheriff of Nottinghamshire and Derbyshire was the corrupt and unpopular John de Oxenford, and he, like other sheriffs, would have had to go to York at least once a year to give an account of revenues from royal lands. The sheriff's northward journeys "would almost certainly have taken him along the main road, through Doncaster, and thence up Barnsdale, a notoriously dangerous place": we know of one highway robbery committed in 1329 at the Sayles near Pontefract in West Yorkshire, which features in *A Gest of Robyn Hode* (15th century).[14]

Robin Hood and the Monk

Robin Hood and the Monk is preserved in a Cambridge University manuscript dated to some time after 1450. The reference in line 331 to *our comely king* "has been taken as referring to the notably handsome Edward IV, which would date the ballad in this form as after 1461; this is by no means impossible, but the phrase was certainly used of his 14th century predecessor Edward III, and the error[s] in copying could well support an earlier text that has been transmitted several times." Stephen Knight and Thomas H. Ohlgren, who edited *Robin Hood and the Monk*, consider it to be "the oldest extant example of the "rymes of Robin Hood" referred to by Langland in the 1370s, implied by Andrew of Wyntoun in the 1420s, and both described and exemplified by Walter Bower in the 1440s."[15]

Robin is particularly devoted to the Virgin Mary, and when he is captured, Little John promises that he will rescue Robin from prison "With the might of mild Mary." Little John's rescue of Robin closely resembles a type of miracle known as "the knight and the Virgin," of which seven examples were printed by Wynkyn de Worde in the late 15th century *The Miracles of Our Lady*. Two of these short prose miracles "relate how two knights, captured and imprisoned by their enemies, are delivered out of prison by the intercession of the Virgin."[16]

The ballad begins on Whitsun, in late May (lines 1–28).[17] (Note than the modern English version is my own: I have tried as much as I can to keep the original rhyme scheme, by using archaic words and glossing them in square brackets, but sometimes this has not proved possible.)

In summer when the woods are bright,
And leaves are large and long,
It is very merry in the fair forest,
To hear the birds' song,

To see the deer draw to the dale,
And leave the high hills,
And shelter themselves in green leaves,
Under the green wood tree.

It befell on Whitsun,
Early in a May morning,
The sun up fair did shine,
And the merry birds did sing.

"This is a merry morning," said Little John,
"By Him that died on a tree [the Cross];
A more merry man than I am one
Lives not in Christianity.

"Pluck up thy heart, my dear master,"
Little John did say,

"And think that it is a very fair time
In a morning of May."

"Yet one thing grieves me," said Robin,
"And does my heart much woe:
That I may not on solemn days
To mass or matins go.

"It is a fortnight and more," said he,
"Since I my Savior see;
Today I will go to Nottingham," said Robyn,
"With the might of mild Mary."

Here we have two of the staples of the early Robin Hood—Nottingham and Robin's devotion to religion, in particular to the Virgin Mary.

Much the miller's son then advised Robin to take three strong men with him to Nottingham, and Robin and Little John got into an argument. Finally Robin went to Nottingham, ignoring the advice of Much the miller's son (lines 63–94):

Then Robin goes to Nottingham,
Himself grieving alone,
And Little John to merry Sherwood,
The paths he knew, every one.

When Robin came to Nottingham,
Certainly and without lie,
He prayed to God and mild Mary
To bring him out safe again.

He went into Saint Mary's church
And kneeled down before the rood [Cross];
All that were inside the church
Beheld well Robin Hood.

Beside him stood a large-headed monk,
I pray to God woe unto he!
For he recognized good Robin,
As soon as him he did see.

Out of the door he ran,
At once he did run;
All the gates of Nottingham
He made to be barred, every one.

"Rise up," he said, "thou proud sheriff,
Hurry up and make yourself ready.
I have spied the king's felon.
Forsooth, he is in this town.

I have spied the false felon
As he stands at his mass;
It is all your fault," said the monk,
"If from us he does pass.

> "This traitor's name is Robin Hood,
> Under the green wood limes;
> He robbed me once of a hundred pounds.
> It is never out of my mind."

Here we have Sherwood Forest and the Sheriff of Nottingham. Sherwood Forest had royal associations from the late 12th century. A hunting lodge, now known as King John's Palace, was built at Kings Clipstone near Mansfield in around 1164, during the reign of Henry II. It was rebuilt in stone around 1180, when it became the principal hunting lodge in Sherwood Forest, remaining popular with English kings for the next two centuries.[18] Nottingham got its first sheriff in 1449, so the sheriff in *Robin Hood and the Monk* may be the High Sheriff of Nottinghamshire and Derbyshire, perhaps even John de Oxenford.

Immediately the sheriff and his men rushed to the church (lines 99–118):

> In at the doors they strenuously pressed,
> With staves for everyone;
> "Alas, alas!" said Robin Hood,
> "Now miss I Little John."

> But Robin took out a two-hand sword,
> That hanged down to his knee;
> There where the sheriff and his men stood thickest.
> Toward them then went he.

> Thrice through at them then he ran,
> Forsooth to you I say,
> And wounded many a mother's son,
> And twelve he slew that day.

> His sword upon the sheriff's head
> Certainly he broke in two;
> "The smith that made this," said Robin,
> "I pray to God give him woe!"

> "For now am I weaponless," said Robin,
> "Alas! Against my will;
> Unless I flee these traitors now,
> I know they will me kill."

There is a gap in the narrative here because of a missing manuscript sheet; presumably the missing sheet would have told how Robin was captured and his men heard the bad news (lines 121–142):

> Some fell in swooning as if they were dead
> And lay still as any stone;
> None of them kept their heads
> Except for Little John.

> "Stop your wailing," said Little John,
> "For His love that died on a tree,

> Ye that should be doughty men;
> It is a great shame to see.
>
> "Our master has been hard beset before
> And yet escaped away;
> Pluck up your hearts and leave this lament,
> And listen to what I shall say.
>
> "He has served Our Lady many a day,
> And very well, surely;
> Therefore I trust in her especially.
> No wicked death shall he die.
>
> "Therefore be glad," said Little John,
> "And let this morning be;
> And I shall take care of the monk,
> With the might of mild Mary.
> And if I meet him," said Little John,
> "It will be him versus me."

Then Little John and Much went to stay at Much's uncle's house. From there they spied the monk riding along with a little page; they immediately went onto the road and spoke to the monk (lines 163–206):

> "From whence come ye?" said Little John.
> "Tell us tidings I you pray,
> Of a false outlaw,
> Was taken yesterday.
>
> "He robbed me and my fellows both
> Of twenty marks indeed;
> If that false outlaw be taken,
> Forsooth, we would be glad."
>
> "So did he me," said the monk,
> "Of a hundred pounds and more;
> I was the first to get my hands on him.
> You may thanks me therefore."
>
> "I pray God thank you," said Little John,
> "And we will when we may;
> We will go with you, with your leave,
> And bring you on your way.
>
> "For Robin Hood has many a wild fellow,
> I tell you for certain;
> If he knew you rode this way,
> In faith ye should be slain."
>
> As they went talking by the way,
> The monk and Little John,
> John took the monk's horse by the head,
> At once and anon.

John took the monk's horse by the head,
Forsooth to you I say;
So did Much the little page,
For he should not escape away.

By the throat-piece of the hood
John pulled the monk down;
John was not afraid of him.
He let him fall on his crown.

Little John was so aggrieved
And drew out his sword in haste;
The monk saw he should be dead,
"Lord mercy," did he cry.

"He was my master," said Little John,
"That thou has brought to bale [harm];
Shall thou never come at our king,
For to tell his tale."

John struck off the monk's head,
No longer would he dwell [wait];
So did Much the little page,
For fear lest he would tell.

Little John took the letters the monk was carrying and presented them to the king, possibly Edward III, and presumably at King John's Palace, which Edward III visited on nine occasions (lines 211–234):

Little John came unto the king.
He knelt down upon his knee:
"God save you, my liege lord.
Jesus watch over thee!

"God save you, my liege king!"
To speak John was truly bold;
He gave him the letters in his hand,
The king did them unfold.

The king read the letters immediately,
And said, "So may I thrive;
There was never yeoman in merry England
I longed so sore to see.

"Where is the monk that these should have brought?"
Our king did say.
"By the truth," said Little John,
"He died along the way."

The king gave Much and Little John
Twenty pounds for certain,
And made them yeomen of the crown,
And bade them go again.

> He gave John the seal in hand,
> The sheriff for to bear,
> To bring Robin to him,
> And no man do him harm.

After this John went to Nottingham and found all the gates shut, and called the porter (lines 243–246):

> "What is the cause," said Little John.
> "Thou shut these gates so fast?"
> "Because of Robin Hood," said the porter,
> "In deep prison he is cast."

Robin is likely to have been imprisoned in the Shire Hall and County Gaol, constructed in 1375. This is now the site of the Galleries of Justice museum, and Robin could have been imprisoned in the Sheriff's Dungeon, a cave under the museum that is accessed by an ancient staircase.[19]

Little John then went to the sheriff and showed him the king's privy seal (lines 255–266):

> When the sheriff saw the king's seal,
> He took off his hood at once.
> "Where is the monk that bore the letters?"
> He said to Little John.
>
> "He is so pleased with him," said Little John,
> "Forsooth to you I say,
> He has made him abbot of Westminster,
> A lord of that abbey."
>
> The sheriff made John good cheer,
> And gave him wine of the best;
> At night they went to their beds,
> And every man to his rest.

While the sheriff was asleep, Little John and Much went to the jail and called up the jailer (lines 275–286):

> The jailer rose at once for sure,
> As soon as he heard John call;
> Little John was ready with a sword,
> And stabbed him through the wall.
>
> "Now will I be jailer," said Little John,
> And took the keys in hand;
> He found the way to Robin Hood,
> And soon had him unbound.
>
> He gave him a good sword in his hand,
> His head therewith to keep,
> And there where the walls were lowest
> At once down did they leap.

When the day dawned and the sheriff found the jailer dead, he offered a reward for the capture of Robin Hood, but by this time Little John and Robin were in Sherwood. Of course, the king heard about Robin's escape (lines 327–354):

Then word came to our king
How Robin Hood was gone,
And how the sheriff of Nottingham,
Dared never look him upon.

Then bespake our comely [handsome] king,
In an anger high,
"Little John has beguiled [deceived] the sheriff,
In faith so has he me.

"Little John has beguiled us both,
And that full well I see;
Or else the sheriff of Nottingham
High-hanged should he be.

"I made him yeoman of the crown,
And gave him money with my hand;
I gave him security," said our king,
"Throughout all merry England,

"I gave them security," then said our king;
I say, so may I prosper,
Forsooth such a yeoman as he is one,
In all England are not three."

"He is true to his master," said our king,
"I say, by sweet Saint John,
He loves better Robin Hood
Than he does each of us.

"Robin Hood is ever obligated to him,
Both in street and stall [stable];
Speak no more of this matter," said our king,
"But John has beguiled us all."

Robin Hood and Guy of Gisborne

Robin Hood and Guy of Gisborne was probably composed in the 15th century—the two characters are referred to an early 16th century poem by the Scottish poet William Dunbar, entitled *Of Sir Thomas Norry*.[20] This ballad is very different from *Robin Hood and the Monk*, seeming to portray a more mythical version of the outlaw. The poem starts with a description of the woods, then switches abruptly to Robin narrating a dream[21] (lines 1–42). (Once again the modern English version is mine.)

When woods are bright and branches full fair,
And leaves both large and long,
It is merry walking in the fair forest,
To hear the small birds sing.

The oriole sang and would not cease,
Amongst the leaves of the lime.
"And it is by two strong yeomen,
By dear God, that I mean.

"Me thought they did me beat and bind,
And took from me my bow;
If I be Robin alive in this land,
I'll be revenged on both those two."

"Dreams are fleeting, master," quoth Little John,
"As the wind that blows over a hill,
For if it never be so loud this night,
Tomorrow it may be still."

"Prepare you, get ready, my merry men all,
For John will go with me,
For I'll go seek yon sturdy yeomen
In greenwood where they be."

They put on their gowns of green,
A shooting gone are they,
Until they came to the merry greenwood,
Where they had gladdest be;
There they were aware of a strong yeoman,
His body leaned against a tree.

A sword and dagger he wore by his side
Had been many a man's bane [killer],
And he was clad in his horse-hide,
Top, and tail, and mane.

"Stand you still, master," quoth Little John,
"Under this trysting tree,
And I will go to yon strong yeoman,
To know his meaning truly."

"Ah, John, by me you set no store,
And that's an amazing thing;
How oft send I my men before,
And tarry myself behind?

"It takes no skill to know a knave,
If a man but hear him speak;
If it were not for damaging my bow,
John, I would your head break."

Little John was angered by Robin's words, and went to Barnsdale (lines 47–70):

And when he came to Barnsdale,
Great heaviness there he had;
He found two of his own fellows
Were slain both in a glade,

And Scarlett on foot was fleeing,
Over stumps and stone,
For the sheriff with seven score men
Fast after him is gone.

"Yet one shot I'll shoot," says Little John,
"With Christ his might and main;
I'll make yon fellow that flees so fast
To be both glad and happy."

John bent up a good yew bow,
And prepared himself to shoot;
The bow was made of a tender bough,
And fell down at his foot.

"Misery come to you, wicked wood," said Little John,
"That ere you grew on a tree!
For this day you are my trouble,
When my help you should be!"

This shot it was inaccurate,
The arrow flew in vain,
And it met one of the sheriff's men;
Good William a Trent was slain.

At this point Little John was captured, and the sheriff threatened to hang him. The ballad then switches back to Robin (lines 83–138):

Let us leave talking of Little John,
For he is bound fast to a tree,
And talk of Guy and Robin Hood,
In the greenwood where they be.

How these two yeomen together they met,
Under the leaves of lime,
To see what business they made
Even at that same time.

"Good morrow, good fellow," quoth Sir Guy;
"Good morrow, good fellow," quoth he [Robin],
"Methinks by this bow you bear in your hand.
A good archer you seem to be."

"I am uncertain of my way," quoth Sir Guy;
"And of my morning tide [time]."
"I'll lead you through the wood," quoth Robin,
"Good fellow, I'll be your guide."

"I seek an outlaw," quoth Sir Guy,
"Men call him Robin Hood;

> I had rather meet with him upon a day,
> Than forty pound of gold."
>
> "If you two met, it would be seen whether were better
> You each went your separate way;
> Let us some other pastime find,
> Good fellow I thee pray.
>
> "Let us make some feats of skill,
> And we will walk in the woods even;
> We may chance meet Robin Hood,
> At some unexpected occasion."
>
> They cut them down the summer bushes
> Which grew both under a briar,
> And set them three score rods [315 yards] apart,
> To shoot the targets full near.
>
> "Lead on, good fellow," said Sir Guy,
> "Lead on, I do bid thee."
> "Nay, by my faith," quoth Robin,
> "The leader you shall be."
>
> The first good shot that Robin led
> Did not shoot an inch from the target;
> Guy was an archer good enough,
> But he could never shoot so near.
>
> The second shot Sir Guy made
> He shot within the garland [ring suspended on a stick];
> But Robin shot it better than he,
> For he split the stick that held up the ring.
>
> "God's blessings on your heart!" says Guy,
> "Good fellow your shooting is good,
> For if your heart be as good as your hands,
> You were better than Robin Hood.
>
> "Tell me your name, good fellow," quoth Guy,
> "Under the leaves of lime."
> "Nay, by my faith," quoth Robin,
> "Till you have told me thine."
>
> "I dwell by dale and down," quoth Guy,
> "And I have done many a cursed deed;
> And he that calls me by my right name
> Calls me Guy of good Gisborne."

The identity of Gisborne is unknown, but there is a Gisburn in Lancashire. Nearby is Clitheroe Castle, which was built in the 12th century and belonged to the de Lacy family of Pontefract.[22] Then the encounter between Robin and Guy continues (lines 139–178):

> "My dwelling is in the wood," says Robin,
> "And you I set at naught;

My name is Robin Hood of Barnsdale,
A fellow you have long sought."

He that had neither been kith or kin
Might have seen a full fair sight,
To see how together these yeomen went,
With blades both brown [bloodstained] and bright.

To have seen how these yeomen together fought,
Two hours of a summer day;
It was neither Guy nor Robin Hood
That was prepared to flee.

Robin was careless on a root,
And stumbled at that time,
And Guy was quick and nimble with-all,
And hit him on the left side.

"Ah, dear Lady," said Robin Hood,
"You are both mother and maid!
I think it was never man's destiny
To die before his day."

Robin thought on Our Lady dear,
And soon leapt up again,
And thus he came with a backhanded stroke;
Good Sir Guy he has slain.

He took Sir Guy's head by the hair,
And stuck it on his bow's end:
"You have been traitor all your life,
Which thing must have an end."

Robin pulled forth an Irish knife,
And knicked Sir Guy in the face,
That he was never of a woman born
Could tell who Sir Guy was.

Says, "Lie there, lie there, good Sir Guy,
And be with me not wrath [angry];
If you have had the worse strokes at my hand,
You shall have the better cloth."

Robin took of his gown of green,
On Guy's body did it throw;
And he put on that horse hide,
That clad him top to toe.

Robin's decapitation of Sir Guy, his mutilation of Sir Guy's face and his donning of the horse-hide make him a very different character from his namesake in *Robin Hood and the Monk*. Robin Hood then pretended to be Sir Guy (lines 183–218):

Robin set Guy's horn to his mouth,
A loud blast on it he did blow;

That beheard the sheriff of Nottingham,
As he stood under a hill.

"Hearken, hearken," said the sheriff,
"I heard no tidings but good,
For yonder I hear Sir Guy's horn blow,
For he has slain Robin Hood.

"For yonder I hear Sir Guy's horn blow,
It blows so well in time,
For yonder comes that sturdy yeoman,
Clad in his horse-hide.

"Come hither, you good Sir Guy,
Ask of me what you will have."
""I'll none of your gold," says Robin Hood,
"Nor I'll none of it have.

"But now I have slain the master," he said,
"Let me go strike the knave [Little John];
This is all the reward I ask,
Nor no other will I have."

"You are a madman," said the sheriff,
"You should have had a knight's fee [gift of land];
Seeing your asking be so bad,
Well granted shall it be."

But Little John heard his master speak,
Well he knew that was his voice;
"Now shall I be set loose," quoth Little John,
"With Christ's might in heaven."

But Robin he hastened towards Little John,
He thought he would loosen him at once;
The sheriff and all his company
Fast after him did drive.

"Stand aback! stand aback!" said Robin,
"Why draw you me so near?
It was never the use in our country
One's confession another should hear."

At this point, it seems, Robin is pretending to be not only Sir Guy, but a monk ready to hear Little John's confession before "Sir Guy" executes him. The story, of course, ends well for our heroes (lines 219–234):

But Robin pulled forth an Irish knife,
And loosed John hand and foot,
And gave him Sir Guy's bow in his hand,
And bade him use it well.

But John took Guy's bow in his hand
His arrows were rusty at the tip;

> The sheriff saw Little John draw a bow
> And prepare himself to shoot.

> Towards his house in Nottingham
> He fled full fast away,
> And so did all his company,
> No one behind did stay.

> But he could neither so fast go,
> Nor away so fast run,
> But Little John, with an arrow broad,
> Did cleave his heart in twain.

The most striking aspect of this ballad is the horse-hide worn by Guy of Gisborne. This "functions not at all as a type of disguise but rather as a marker for his identity"; Guy here "is a figure who is performing a bestial identity," a human who claims the traits of "wildness."[23] Following his murder, decapitation and mutilation of Guy (which "recalls the ritualistic blood-letting scenes in *Beowulf*"), Robin appropriates the horsehide for himself "along with the bestial identity that it signifies."[24] There are overtones of the "wild man" figure as described by Richard Bernheimer in his book, *Wild men in the Middle Ages*.[25] Bernheimer notes that in extreme circumstances humans are capable of losing the "unique metaphysical dignity of man" and degenerating into unreasonable instinctive behavior to protect of prolong their own existence. Like Grendel, who is referred to an ogre (*eoten*), the horsehide "marks Robin as something both more and less than human: stronger but unrestrained in his exercise of strength." The "wild man" recalls the *wodwos* that Gawain encounters in the wilderness while he is seeking the Green Chapel. The Green Knight is not a *wodwos*, but he has something of the "wild man" man about him when he turns up at Camelot:

> The hair of his head was a green as his horse,
> fine flowing locks which fanned across his back,
> plus a bushy green beard growing down to his breast,
> and his face-hair along with the hair of his head
> was lopped in a line at elbow-length
> so half his arms were gowned in green growth,
> crimped at the collar, like a king's cape.

Significantly, both the knight and his horse were green, making the Green Knight almost as much of a "horse-man" as Guy of Gisborne.

12

The Wilderness Hero
Robin Hood in the Late Middle Ages (Part II)

A Gest of Robyn Hode

The "most substantial and most ambitious" of the early Robin Hood texts was first recorded in printed form early in the first half of the 16th century, and its popularity is shown by the existence of a dozen printed editions of 16th and 17th centuries. The date of the *Gest* is not clear, but it was probably composed around 1450. While *Robin Hood and the Monk* has a clear geographical setting, the geography of the *Gest* is rather vague. The ballad is set in the Yorkshire Barnsdale, yet Little John can hurry from Nottingham, fifty miles distant, to rejoin his companions in less than a day: apparently they are in Sherwood, but that name is never used.[1]

The ballad starts with Robin in Barnsdale (lines 1–16).[2] (Again the modern English version is mine.)

> Attend and listen, gentlemen,
> That are of free born blood,
> I'll tell you of a good yeoman,
> His name was Robin Hood.
>
> Robin was a proud outlaw,
> While he walked on ground;
> So courteous an outlaw as he was
> Was never yet one found.
>
> Robin stood in Barnsdale,
> And leaned against a tree;
> And by him there stood Little John,
> A good yeoman was he.
>
> And also did good Scarlock,
> And Much, the miller's son:

There was no inch of his body
But it was worth a man.

Robin was apparently very religious (lines 29–40):

A good custom had Robin then;
In the land where that he were,
Every day ere he would dine
Three masses would he hear.

The one in worship of the Father,
Another of the Holy Ghost,
The third was of Our dear Lady
That he loved of all the most.

Robin loved Our dear Lady;
For fear of deadly sin,
Never would he harm a company
That any woman was in.

He was also very moral, in his instructions to Little John (lines 49–60):

"Never use force," then said Robin;
"We shall do well enow [enough];
But look you do no farmer harm
That tills with his plow.

"No more shall ye [rob] a good yeoman
That walks by the green wood thicket;
Neither a knight nor a squire
That would be a good companion.

"These bishops and archbishops,
Ye shall them beat and bind,
The high sheriff of Nottingham
Let him not slip your mind."

Then it was time for the outlaws to get to work (lines 65–76):

"Take your good bow in your hand," said Robin;
"Let Much go with ye;
And so shall William Scarlok
And no man stay with me.

"And walk up to the Saylis,
And so to Watling Street
And look for some unknown guest,
By chance you may them meet.

"Be he earl or any baron,
Abbot or any knight,
Bring him to lodge with me;
His dinner shall be ready."

The *Saylis* is thought to be the name of a small tenancy located on high ground to the east of Wentbridge in the medieval manor of Pontefract. The high ground which overlooks the area–120 feet above the flat terrain—was then known as Sayles Plantation. From this location it was possible to see across the whole of the Went Valley and observe the traffic that passed along the Great North Road.[3] The Watling Street that Robin mentions is actually Ermine Street (the Great North Road), that ran from Doncaster to Pontefract via Wentbridge. As I said earlier, we know of one highway robbery committed at the Sayles in 1329.

So they went up to the Sayles and looked around for a prospective guest (lines 81–92):

> But as they looked in Barnsdale,
> By a secret way,
> Then came a knight riding,
> At once they did him meet.
>
> All sad was his appearance,
> And little was his pride;
> His one foot in the stirrup stood,
> The other waved beside.
>
> His hood hung in his two eyes,
> He rode in simple array [clothing],
> A sorrier man than he was one
> Rode never in summer day.

Little John then invited the knight to dine with them (lines 101–112):

> "Who is your master?" said the knight;
> John said, "Robin Hood."
> "He is a good yeoman," said the knight,
> "Of him I have heard much good."
>
> "I agree," he said, "with you to go,
> My brothers, all in company;
> My purpose was to have dined today
> At Blythe or Doncaster."
>
> Forth then went this gentle knight,
> With a sorrowful expression;
> The tears out of his eyes ran,
> And fell down on his face.

Doncaster is south of Barnsdale on the Great North Road, and Blyth is south of Doncaster.

They took the knight to Robin, who welcomed him (lines 125–148):

> They washed together and dried their hands,
> And set to their dinner;

Bread and wine they had in plenty,
And sweetbreads of the deer.

Swans and pheasants they had full good,
And birds of the river-bank,
Not even the smallest bird they lacked,
That was ever bred on branch.

"Eat well, sir knight," said Robin;
"Thank you, sir," said he;
"Such a meal I have not had
For at least three weeks."

"If I come again, Robin,
Here by this country,
As good a dinner I shall thee make,
As you have made for me."

"Thank you, knight," then said Robin,
"My dinner when that I have,
I was never so hungry, by dear worthy God,
My dinner for to crave.

"Buy pay before you go," said Robin;
"I think it only right;
It was never the custom, by dear worthy God,
A yeoman to pay for a knight."

But the knight said he only had ten shillings, and Little John did indeed find in the knight's money chest only ten shillings. So Robin asked the knight why he was so poor, and the knight explained (lines 193–220):

"Within this two year, Robin," he said,
"My neighbors well it knew,
Four hundred pounds of good money
Full well then might I spend.

"Now I have no possessions," said the knight,
"God has shaped such an end,
But my children and my wife,
Till God it may amend."

"In what manner," said Robin,
"Have you lost your riches?"
"For my great folly," he said,
"And for my kindness.

"I had a son, forsooth, Robin,
That should have been my heir,
When he was twenty winters old,
In field would joust full fair.

"He slew a knight of Lancaster,
And a squire bold;

> For to save him in his right
> My goods are pledged and sold.

> "My lands are pledged as security, Robin,
> Until a certain day,
> To a rich abbot hereabouts
> Of Saint Mary's Abbey."

> "What is the sum?" said Robin;
> "Truth then tell to me."
> "Sir," he said, "four hundred pounds;
> The abbot counted it to me."

St. Mary's Abbey in York was founded before 1055, and re-established in 1068 as a Benedictine monastery. It was refounded in 1098 by King William Rufus (the son of William the Conqueror), and became one of the wealthiest abbeys in the Benedictine order, with a mitered abbot who sat in the House of Lords.[4] The abbot referred to could be Thomas de Multon, abbot of St. Mary's from 1332 to 1359. He had a reputation for piety and good works, but records show that he was active as a money-lender between 1332 and 1335, though less so than his contemporary, Archbishop Melton of York.[5]

The knight was about to leave when Robin offered to loan him the four hundred pounds, while asking who the knight's guarantor would be (lines 245–258):

> "Have you any friend," said Robin,
> "Your guarantor that would be?"
> "I have none." then said the knight,
> "But God that died on a tree [the Cross]."

> "Forget your jokes," then said Robin,
> "Of them I will have none;
> Think you I will have God as guarantor,
> Peter, Paul or John?

> "Nay, by Him that me made,
> And shaped both sun and moon,
> Find me a better guarantor," said Robin,
> "Or money get you none."

> "I have none other," said the knight,
> "The truth for to say,
> Unless it be Our dear Lady;
> She failed me never to this day."

> "By dear worthy God," said Robin,
> "You may search all England through,
> Yet found I never to my satisfaction,
> A security more true.

> "Come now forth, Little John
> And go to my treasury;

And bring me four hundred pound,
And see that it well counted be."

So Little John counted out four hundred pounds, and gave it to the knight. But little John said they should also give the knight a "livery" (suit of clothing), a horse, and a pair of boots. Robin also said that Little John should act as the knight's squire, and the knight said he would return in a year's time to repay his debt.

After this, the knight went to St. Mary's Abbey in York to see the abbot (lines 405–440):

Lords were seated at dinner
In that abbot's hall;
The knight went forth and kneeled down
And greeted them great and small.

"Do gladly, sir abbot," said the knight,
"I have come to hold my day."
The first word the abbot spoke,
"Have you brought my pay?"

"Not one penny," said the knight,
"By God that created me."
"You are a cursed debtor," said the abbot,
"Sir justice, drink to me.

"What are you doing here," said the abbot,
"If you have not brought your pay?"
"For God," then said the knight,
"To beg for a longer day."

"You missed your appointed day," said the justice,
"Land get you none."
"Now good sir justice, be my friend,
And defend me from my foes!"

"I am retained by the abbot," said the justice,
"Both with cloth and fee."
"Now good sir sheriff, be my friend!"
"Nay, for God," said he.

"Now good sir abbot, be my friend,
For your courtesy,
And hold my lands in your hand
Till I have paid my debt.

"And I will be your true servant,
And truly serve thee,
Till you have four hundred pounds
Of money good and free."

The abbot swore a great full oath
"By God that died on a tree,

> Get you land where you may,
> For you will get none of me."

This scene went on a little longer, with the abbot continuing to be rude to the knight, who continued to kneel before him (lines 457–484):

> Up then stood that gentle knight;
> To the abbot said he,
> "To suffer a knight to kneel so long,
> You know no courtesy.
>
> "In jousts and in tournament,
> Full far then have I been,
> And put myself in as great danger
> As any that I have seen."
>
> "What will you give more," said the justice,
> "If the knight shall his claim release?
> Otherwise dare I confidently swear
> You'll never hold your land in peace."
>
> "A hundred pound," said the abbot,
> The justice said, "Give him two."
> "Nay, by God," said the knight,
> "Yet get ye it not so.
>
> "Though you would give a thousand more,
> Yet were ye no nearer success;
> Shall there never be my heir,
> Abbot, justice or friar."
>
> He went at once to a board,
> To a table round,
> And there he shook out of a bag
> Exactly four hundred pounds.
>
> "Here have your gold, sir abbot," said the knight,
> "Which that you lent to me;
> Had you been courteous at my coming,
> Rewarded you should have been."

The knight then left York bound for home (lines 501–4):

> He went forth singing merrily,
> As men have told in tale;
> His lady met him at the gate,
> At home in Verysdale.

Verysdale is thought to be Wyresdale near Lancaster in Lancashire (recall that the knight's son killed a knight from Lancaster). After arriving home, the knight saved enough money to repay Robin, and also obtained a hundred bows, with arrows fletched with peacock feathers. As he was travelling back to Robin's base to repay him, he rode past a wrestling match at Wentbridge near Barnsdale, where he saw a yeoman who had won a fight but, because he was a stranger, was set upon by an angry crowd. So the knight stopped to save him.

The ballad then switches to Little John, who was participating in an archery contest (lines 581–616):

> Three times Little John shot about,
> And always he split the wand [a stick stuck in the ground];
> The proud sheriff of Nottingham
> By the targets did stand.
>
> The sheriff swore a full great oath,
> "By Him that died on a tree,
> This man is the best archer
> That ever yet I did see.
>
> "Tell me now, strong young man,
> What is now your name?
> In what region were you born,
> And where is your dwelling place?"
>
> "In Holderness, sir, I was born,
> Entirely from my dame [mother];
> Men call me Reynold Greenleaf,
> When I am at home."
>
> "Tell me, Reynold Greenleaf,
> Would you dwell with me?
> And every year I will you give,
> Twenty marks as your fee."
>
> "I have a master," said Little John,
> "A courteous knight is he;
> If you get leave of him,
> The better may it be."
>
> The sheriff got Little John,
> Twelve months of the knight;
> Therefore he gave him right away,
> A good horse and strong.
>
> Now Little John is the sheriff's man,
> May God grant us to succeed!
> But always thought Little John
> To pay him his just desert.
>
> "Now so God help me," said Little John,
> "And by my true loyalty,
> I shall be the worst servant to him
> That ever yet had he."

One day Little John woke up and wanted to eat, but the steward and the cook tried to stop him (lines 653–704):

"I make my pledge to God," said the cook,
"You are a cursed servant
In any house for to dwell
For to ask thus to dine."

And there he gave Little John
Good strokes three;
"I make my pledge to God," said Little John,
"These strokes well pleased me."

"You are a bold man and a hardy,
And so it seems to me;
And before I pass from this place,
Tested better shall you be."

Little John drew a full good sword,
The cook took another in hand;
They didn't think of fleeing,
But unyielding for to stand.

There they fought sore together,
For two miles and well more;
Neither could do the other harm,
The full length of an hour.

"I make my pledge to God," said Little John,
"And by my true loyalty,
You are one of the best swordsmen,
That ever yet I did see.

"Could you shoot as well with a bow,
To greenwood you should go with me,
And two times in the year your clothing
Changed it should be.

"And every year from Robin Hood
Twenty marks as your fee."
"Put up your sword," said the cook,
"And fellows we will be."

Then he fed to Little John
The sweetmeats of a doe,
Good bread and full good wine;
They ate and drank thereto.

And when they had drunk well,
Their troths together they plight
That they would be with Robin
That very same night.

They went to the treasure-house,
As fast as they might go;
The locks that were of full good steel,
They broke them every one.

>They took away the silver vessels,
>And all that they might get;
>Dishes, cups, nor spoons.
>They did not forget.

>And they took the good pence,
>Three hundred pounds and more,
>And went straight to Robin Hood
>Under the green wood hoar [ancient].

Then Little John had a bright idea (lines 721–764):

>Little John there him bethought
>On a crafty trick;
>Five miles in the forest he ran;
>All his wishes came to pass.

>Then he met the proud sheriff,
>Hunting with hounds and horn;
>Little John knew about courtesy,
>Then kneeled before him.

>"God save you, my dear master,
>And Christ watch over you."
>"Reynold Greenleaf," said the sheriff,
>"Where now have you been?"

>"I have been in this forest;
>A fair sight I did see;
>It was one of the fairest sights
>That ever yet I did see.

>"Yonder I saw a right fair hart [deer],
>His color is of green;
>Seven score deer in a herd
>Are together with him.

>"Their antlers are so sharp master,
>Of sixty, and well more,
>That I dared not shoot for dread
>Lest they would me slay."

>"I make my pledge to God," said the sheriff,
>"That sight would I gladly see."
>"Hasten thitherward, my dear master,
>At once, and go with me."

>The sheriff rode, and Little John
>On foot he was so smart [nimble],
>And when they came before Robin,
>"Lo, sir, here is the master hart!"

>Still stood the proud sheriff,
>A sorry man was he;

> "Woe to you, Reynold Greenleaf,
> You have betrayed now me."

> "I make my pledge to God," said Little John,
> "Master, you are to blame;
> I was mis-served of my dinner
> When I was with you at home."

> Soon he was to supper set,
> And served well with silver white,
> And when the sheriff saw his vessels,
> For sorrow he might not eat.

Robin finally permits the sheriff to leave, but only after he has promised to do them no harm.

In the next section of the ballad, the day has arrived on which the knight is due to repay Robin his four hundred pounds. Little John and Much went up to the Sayles and looked for a guest to dine with Robin (lines 849–864):

> But as they looked in Barnsdale,
> By the high way,
> Then they were aware of two black [Benedictine] monks,
> Each on a good palfrey.

> Then bespake Little John
> To Much he did say,
> "I dare lay my life as a pledge,
> These monks have brought our pay.

> "Make glad cheer," said Little John,
> "And make ready our bows of ewe,
> And look your hearts be sure and strong,
> Your strings trusty and true.

> "The monk has two and fifty men,
> And seven sumpters [pack horses] full strong;
> There rides no bishop in this land
> So royally, I understand."

So Little John hailed the monk (lines 873–888):

> "Abide, low-born monk," said Little John,
> "No further may you go;
> If you do, by dear worthy God,
> Your death is in my hand.

> "And evil luck on your head," said Little John,
> "Right under your hat-band;
> For you have made our master angry,
> He is fasting so long."

> "Who is your master," said the monk;
> Little John said, "Robin Hood,"

"He is a strong thief," said the monk.
"Of him never heard I good."

"You lie then," said Little John,
"And that shall make you sorry;
He is a yeoman of the forest,
To dine he has bidden thee."

So Little John and Much took the monk to dine with Robin Hood (lines 925–972):

"Eat gladly, monk," said Robin,
"Thank you, sir," said he.
"Where is your abbey, when you are at home,
And who is your patron?"

"Saint Mary's Abbey," said the monk,
"Though I be humble here."
"In what office?" said Robin,
"Sir, the high cellarer [chief steward]."

"You are the more welcome," said Robin,
"So may I always prosper;
Fill of the best wine," said Robin,
"This monk shall drink to me.

"But I greatly marvel," said Robin,
"Of all this long day;
I fear Our Lady be angry with me,
She sent me not my pay."

"Have no doubt, master," said Little John,
"You have no need, I say;
This monk has it brought, I dare well swear,
For he is of her abbey."

"And she was a guarantor," said Robin,
"Between a knight and me,
Of a little money that I him lent,
Under the greenwood tree.

"And if you have that silver brought,
I pray you let me see;
And I shall help you in return,
If you have need of me."

The monk swore a full great oath,
With a sorry cheer [miserable countenance],
"Of the security you speak to me,
I never heard before."

"I make my pledge to God," said Robin,
"Monk you are to blame;
For God is held to be a righteous man,
And so is his dame.

> "You told with your own tongue,
> You may not say nay,
> How you are her servant,
> And serve her every day.
>
> "And you are made her messenger,
> My money for to pay;
> Therefore I may thank you more
> You have come at your day.
>
> "What is in your coffers?" said Robin,
> "Truth then tell to me."
> "Sir," he said, "twenty marks,
> As I may prosper."

So Robin asked Little John to see if the monk was telling the truth (lines 985–1000):

> Little John spread his mantle down,
> As he had done before,
> And counted out from the monk's travelling chest
> Eight hundred pounds and more.
>
> Little John let it lie full still,
> And went to his master in haste;
> "Sir," he said, "the monk is true enough,
> Our Lady has doubled your cast [throw]."
>
> "I make my pledge to God," said Robin,
> "Monk, what did I tell you?
> Our Lady is the truest woman
> That ever yet I found.
>
> "By dear worthy God," said Robin,
> "To search all England through,
> Yet found I never to my pay
> A guarantor more true."

After this the monk departed and the knight arrived, explaining why he was late. The knight then offered Robin his four hundred pounds, but Robin refused, saying he had already got the money from the monk; indeed, Robin gave the knight the four hundred pounds that the monk had overpaid him.

In the next section, the sheriff of Nottingham held an archery contest in which Robin and his men took part. All Robin's men performed well, but Robin won. The sheriff tried to seize him, but he escaped. Little John was wounded, and Much had to carry him (lines 1229–1240):

> Up he took him on his back,
> And bare him well a mile;
> Many a time he laid him down,
> And shot another while.

> Then there was a fair castle,
> A little within the wood;
> Double-ditched it was about,
> And walled, by the Rood [Cross].

> And there dwelled that gentle knight,
> Sir Richard at the Lee,
> That Robin had given his property,
> Under the greenwood tree.

Lee is a village near Lancaster, so presumably Sir Richard owned a castle close to Nottingham. It is possible that this castle is linked to the Foliot family. In 1252 Jordan Foliot was licensed to fortify his manor house at Grimston in Nottinghamshire: all that remains now is a circular bank and ditch.[6] The Foliots also had a fortified manor house at Fenwick in South Yorkshire, not far from Barnsdale.[7] In the 1260s a certain outlaw called Roger Godberd terrorized the counties of Nottinghamshire, Derbyshire and Leicestershire. He was captured in 1272, and after his capture, Richard Foliot was accused of sheltering him: as a result, the sheriff of Yorkshire confiscated his manor house at Fenwick.[8] Clearly, the story of Roger Godberd and Richard Foliot could have fed into the Robin Hood story.

The sheriff then rode to Sir Richard's castle, but Sir Richard refused to surrender Robin Hood. So the sheriff went to London and saw the king, who promised he would come to Nottingham. Meanwhile, Little John recovered from his wound, and he and Robin returned to the forest. But the sheriff had not forgotten Sir Richard (lines 1321–1352):

Ever he awaited this gentle knight,
Sir Richard at the Lee,
As he went on hawking, by the river side,
And let his hawks flee.

Then he took this gentle knight,
With men of arms strong.
And led him toward Nottingham,
Bound both hand and foot.

The sheriff swore a full great oath,
By Him that died on the Rood [Cross],
He would rather than a hundred pound.
That he had Robin Hood.

This heard the knight's wife,
A fair lady and a free;
She set her on a good palfrey,
To greenwood at once rode she.

When she came in the forest,
Under the greenwood tree,
There she found Robin Hood,
And all his fair company.

"God save you, good Robin,
And all your good company,
For Our dear Lady's love,
A boon grant you to me.

"Let you never my wedded lord
Shamefully slain be;
He is fast bound toward Nottingham,
For the love of thee."

At once then said good Robin,
To that lady free,
"What man has your lord taken?"
"The proud sheriff," then said she.

So Robin and his men immediately set off for Nottingham and soon encountered the sheriff (lines 1377–1412):

"Abide, you proud sheriff," he said,
"Abide and speak with me;
Of some tidings of our king
I would gladly hear of ye.

"This seven year, by dear worthy God,
Never went I so fast on foot;
I make my pledge to God, you proud sheriff,
It is not for your good."

Robin bent a full good bow,
An arrow he drew at will;

> He hit so the proud sheriff
> Upon the ground he lay full still.
>
> And before he might up arise,
> On his feet to stand,
> He smote off the sheriff's head
> With his bright brand [sword],
>
> "Lie there, you proud sheriff,
> Badly may you end!
> There might no man trust in you,
> While you were alive."
>
> His men drew on their bright swords,
> That were so sharp and keen,
> And laid on the sheriff's men,
> And drove them down forthwith.
>
> Robin leapt to that knight,
> And cut in two his bonds,
> And took him in his hand a bow,
> And bade him by him stand.
>
> Leave your horse behind you,
> And learn for to run;
> You shall come with me to greenwood,
> Through more, moss and fen.
>
> "You shall with me to greenwood,
> Without any lying,
> Till I have got the grace
> Of Edward, our comely [handsome] king."

As in *Robin Hood and the Monk*, "our comely king" probably refers to Edward III. He is called "our comely king" by the 14th century poet Laurence Minot in *Poem IV*, which records Edward's military campaign in France with his ally the Duke of Brabant (1339–1341).[9]

In the next section of the poem the king went to Nottingham in order to capture Robin Hood and the gentle knight (lines 1421–1432):

> When they had told him the case
> Our king understood their tale;
> And seized in his hands
> The knight's lands all.
>
> Through all of Lancashire
> He went both far and near,
> Till he came to Plompton Park;
> He missed many of his deer.
>
> There our king was wont to see
> Herds many one,
> He could scarcely find one deer,
> That bore any good horn.

Plompton Park is probably Plumpton in Cumbria, which is part of Inglewood Forest, mentioned by Andrew of Wyntoun as one of the haunts of Robin Hood. Inglewood was a royal forest and all the deer belonged to the king—which explains his annoyance at finding so few deer.

The king was unable to find Robin, so after six months he went into the forest disguised as an abbot and accompanied by five knights (lines 1485–1548):

> Our king was great above his cowl,
> A broad hat on his crown [top of his head],
> Right as he were abbot-like,
> They rode up into the town.

> Stiff boots our king had on,
> Forsooth as I you say;
> He rode singing to greenwood,
> The company was clothed in gray.

> His baggage horse and his great pack horses,
> Followed our king behind,
> Till the came to the greenwood,
> A mile under the woods.

> There they met with good Robin,
> Standing on the way,
> And so many a bold archer,
> Forsooth as I you say.

> Robin took the king's horse,
> Hastily in that place,
> And said, "Sir abbot, by your leave,
> A while ye must abide.

> "We are yeomen of this forest,
> Under the greenwood tree;
> We live by our king's deer,
> Under the greenwood tree.

> "And ye have churches and rents both,
> And gold full great plenty;
> Give us some of your spending
> For holy charity."

> Then bespoke our comely king,
> At once then said he;
> "I brought no more to greenwood
> But forty pounds with me.

> "I have lain at Nottingham
> This fortnight with our king,
> And spent I have full much good,
> On many a great lordling.

> "And I have but forty pounds,
> No more then have I me;

But if I had a hundred pounds,
I promise half to thee."

Robin took the forty pounds,
And divided it in two parts;
Half he gave his merry men,
And bade them merry to be.

Full courteously Robin did say;
"Sir, have this for your spending;
We shall meet another day."
"Thank you," then said our king.

"But well Edward, our king, greets you.
And sends to you his seal,
And bids you come to Nottingham,
Both to food and meat."

He took out the broad shield,
And soon he let him see;
Robin knew his manners,
And set him on his knee.

"I love no man in all the world
So well as I do my king;
Welcome is my lord's seal;
And monk, for your tidings,

"Sir abbot, for your tidings,
Today you shall dine with me,
For the love of my king,
Under my tristel [trysting] tree."

After dinner, Robin arranged an archery contest; whoever failed to hit the target had to suffer a blow. Robin missed and asked the "abbot" to deliver the blow. The king knocked him down and revealed himself. Robin, his men, and Sir Richard all knelt in homage. After this the king asked Robin and his men to go to court with him, and Robin agreed. Robin stayed at court for over a year, but he missed his old life and returned to the forest, living there for twenty-two years. A prioress from Kirklees in West Yorkshire finally killed Robin at the instigation of her lover Roger of Doncaster, by treacherously bleeding him to death (bleeding was a recognized medical treatment in the Middle Ages).

Adam Bell, Clim of the Clough, and William of Cloudesley

The ballad called *Adam Bell, Clim of the Clough, and William of Cloudesley*, or at least the three heroes of the ballad, seems to date from the 15th century. A Parliament Roll for Wiltshire in 1432 "adds to a list of local members, presumably in a spirit of satire, a sequence of outlaw names—Robin Hood, Little John, Much, Scathelock and Reynold are there, but, remarkably in so southern an area, the list is led by 'Adam Belle, Clim O'Cluw, Willyam Cloudesle.'" However, the earliest version of the ballad dates from the mid–16th century.[10] One of the main interests of this ballad is that it is set mainly in Inglewood Forest, which Andrew of Wyntoun associates with Robin Hood and which was also a haunt of Arthur and his knights. *Adam Bell* is not a Robin Hood tale, but it has many of the features of Robin Hood tales. The poem starts as usual in the forest (lines 1–36)[11]:

> Merry it was in green forest,
> Among the leaves green,
> Where men walk both east and west,
> With bows and arrows keen,
>
> To rouse the deer out of their den;
> Such sights as have oft been seen,
> As by the yeomen of the north country,
> By them it is as I mean.
>
> One of them was called Adam Bell,
> The other Clim of the Clough,
> The third was William of Cloudesley,
> An archer good enough.
>
> They were outlawed for poaching deer,
> These three yeomen every one;
> They swore themselves brother upon a day,
> And to Inglewood Forest had gone.
>
> Now attend and listen, gentlemen,
> Who of entertainments love to hear:
> Two of them were single men,
> The third had a wedded wife.
>
> William was the wedded man,
> Much more then was his care:
> He said to his brothers upon a day,
> To Carlisle he would fare.
>
> For to speak with fair Alice his wife,
> And with his children three:
> "By my troth," said Adam Bell,
> "Not by the counsel of me.
>
> "For if you go to Carlisle, brother,
> And from this wild wood wend,
> If the justice may take you,
> Your life would be at an end."
>
> "If I come not tomorrow, brother,
> By sunrise to you again,

> Trust not else but that I am taken,
> Or else that I am slain."

So William went to Carlisle and saw his wife, but an old woman informed the sheriff, and William was eventually captured. William was to be hanged, the city gates were closed, and a gallows was set up in the marketplace (lines 169–184):

> A little boy stood among them,
> And asked what meant that gallows-tree;
> They said, "To hang a good yeoman,
> Called William of Cloudesley."
>
> The little boy was the town swineherd,
> And kept there Alice's swine;
> Full oft he had seen Cloudesley in the woods,
> And given him there to dine.
>
> He went out of a crevice in the wall,
> And lightly to the wood did go;
> There he met with these strong young men,
> Shortly and at once.
>
> "Alas!" then said the little boy,
> "You tarry here all too long;
> Cloudesley is taken and condemned to death,
> All ready for to hang."

So Adam Bell and Clim of the Clough went to Carlisle and found the gates closed, so Clim came up with a solution (lines 215–220):

> "Let us say we are messengers,
> Come straight from our king."
>
> Adam said, "I have a letter written well,
> Now let us cunningly work;
> We will say we have the king's seal,
> I think the porter no clerk [the porter can't read]."

They persuaded the porter to let them in, wrung his neck, took his keys, then proceeded to the marketplace (lines 302–337).

Then bespake good Adam Bell,
To Clim of the Clough so free;
"Brother, see you mark the justice well;
Lo yonder you may him see.

"And at the sheriff shoot I will,
Strongly with an arrow keen."
A better shot in merry Carlisle,
This seven years was not seen.

The loosed their arrows both at once,
Of no man had they dread;
One hit the justice, the other the sheriff,
And both their sides did bleed.

All men moved away that them stood near,
When the justice fell to the ground,
And the sheriff fell near him by;
Either had his death wound.

All the citizens fast did flee,
They dared no longer abide;
There quickly they freed Cloudesley,
Where he with ropes lay tied.

William rushed to an officer of the town,
His axe out of his hand he wrung [wrenched];
On each side he struck them down,
He thought he had tarried too long.

William said to his brethren two,
This day let us together live and die;
If ever you have need as I have now,
The same shall you find by me.

They shot so well at that time,
For their strings were of silk full sure,
That they held the streets on every side;
That battle did long endure.

They fought together as brethren true,
Like hardy men and bold;
Many a man to the ground they threw,
And made many a heart cold.

The three outlaws then returned to Inglewood, and William thought they
should ask the king for a pardon (lines 432–443):

And when they had supped well,
For sure without lying,
Cloudesley said, "We will to our king,
To get us a letter of pardon.

"Alice shall be at sojourning,
In a nunnery here beside;

My two sons shall with her go,
And there they shall abide.

"Mine eldest son shall go with me,
For him I have no care,
And he shall bring you word again
How it is we fare."

So they went to London and saw the King, but when he heard their names he threatened to hang them. However, the Queen asked him to pardon them, and the King granted her request. Immediately, messengers arrived from the north (lines 532–551):

And when they came before the king,
They kneeled down upon their knees,
And said, "Lord, your officers greet you well,
Of Carlisle in the north country."

"How fare my justice," said the king,
"And my sheriff also?"
"Sir, they be slain, without a lie,
And many an officer more."

"And who has them slain?" said the king,
"At once do tell me."
"Adam Bell, and Clim of the Clough,
And William of Cloudesley."

"Alas, for pity," then said our king,
"My heart is wondrous sore;
I had rather than a thousand pounds,
I had known of this before.

"For I have granted them grace,
And that grieves me;
But had I known all this before,
They had been hanged all three."

The King was very annoyed, but he had a plan (lines 572–655):

The king called his best archers,
To the target range with him to go;
"I will see these fellows shot," he said,
"That in the north have wrought this woe."

The king's bowmen prepared themselves at once,
And the queen's archers also,
So did these three strong yeomen,
With them they thought to go.

There twice or thrice they shot about,
For to assay their hand;
There was no shot these three yeomen shot
That any target might them stand.

Then spoke William of Cloudesley:
"By God that for me died,
I hold him never no good archer
That shoots at targets so wide."

"Where at?" then said our king,
"I pray thee tell me."
"At such a target, sir," he said,
"As men use in my country."

William went into a field,
And his two brethren with him;
There they set up two hazel sticks,
Twenty score paces between.

"I hold him an archer," said Cloudesley,
"That yonder wand splits in two."
"Here is none such," said the king,
"Nor none that can do so."

"I shall try, sir," said Cloudesley,
"Before I farther go."
Cloudesley with a flight arrow,
Split the wand in two.

"You are the best archer," then said the king,
"Forsooth that ever I see."
"And yet for your love," said William,
"I will show more mastery.

"I have a son who's seven years old,
He is to me full dear;
I will him tie to a stake,
All shall see that be here,

"And lay an apple upon his head,
And go six score paces from him,
And I myself with a broad arrow,
Shall split the arrow in two."

"Now hasten," then said the king,
"By Him that died on a tree,
But if you do not as you have said,
Hanged shall you be.

"If you touch his head or gown,
In sight that men may see,
By all the saints that be in heaven,
I shall hang you all three."

"That I have promised," said William,
"I will it never forsake."
And there even before the king,
In the earth he drove a stake.

And bound thereto his eldest son,
And bade him stand still thereat,
And turned the child's face from him,
Because he should not start [flinch].

An apple upon his head he set,
And then his bow he bent;
Six score paces were then measured out,
And thither Cloudesley went.

Then he drew out a fair broad arrow,
His bow was great and long;
He set that arrow in his bow,
That was both stiff and strong.

He prayed the people that were there
That they would quietly stand;
"For he that shoots for such a wager,
Requires a steady hand."

Many people prayed for Cloudesley,
That his life saved might be,
And when he made himself ready to shoot,
There was many a weeping eye.

Thus Cloudesley split the apple in two,
That many a man did see;
"May God forbid," said the king,
"That you should shoot at me!
"I give you eighteen pence a day,
And my bow should you bear,
And over all the north country,
I make you chief ranger."

This is obviously not a Robin Hood tale, but the rescue of William Cloudesley by Adam Bell and Clim of the Clough has a close resemblance to Little John and Much's rescue of Robin in *Robin Hood and the Monk*; and like Robin in the *Gest*, Adam Bell and his brother outlaws receive a pardon from the king and a place in his household.

With *Adam Bell, Clim of the Clough, and William of Cloudesley*, the cycle of Arthurian romances and Robin Hood ballads comes full circle. Starting off with a hunter/warrior god in Romano-British Cumbria and Northumberland, the two cycles end up in Inglewood Forest, Cumbria, with Arthur and Gawain improbably existing side by site with Adam Bell and his band of outlaws.

Chapter Notes

Introduction

1. O.J. Padel, "The Nature of Arthur," *Cambrian Medieval Celtic Studies* 27 (1994), 14.

2. Simon Young, *The Celtic Revolution* (London: Gibson Square Books, 2010), 208.

3. Rachel Bromwich (ed.), *Trioedd Ynys Prydein: The Triads of the Island of Britain* (Cardiff: University of Wales Press, 2014).

4. *Pa gur yv y porthaur* is usually translated as "What man is the gatekeeper/porter?," but here I have chosen the more dynamic title preferred by Craig Davis in a new translation.

Chapter 1

1. Rachel Bromwich (ed.), *Trioedd Ynys Prydein: The Triads of the Island of Britain* (Cardiff: University of Wales Press, 2014), 8955.

2. *Ibid.*, 8516.

3. Tacitus, *Annals*, trans. Alfred John Church and William Jackson Brodribb (New York: Random House, 1942), Book 12, Chapters 33–38.

4. Tacitus, *Annals*, trans. Alfred John Church and William Jackson Brodribb (New York: Random House, 1942), Book 14, Chapters 31–37.

5. Tacitus, *Annals*, trans. Alfred John Church and William Jackson Brodribb (New York: Random House, 1942), Book 14, Chapter 30.

6. Coflein, *Llyn Cerrig Bach*.

7. David J. Breeze, "Why Did the Romans Fail to Conquer Scotland?," *Proceedings of the Society of Antiquaries of Scotland* 118 (1988), 3–4.

8. Murray Cook, "Romans, Picts, and Development: Continuity and Change in Aberdeenshire's Archaeology and Informed Planning Decisions," *Stirling International Journal of Postgraduate Research* 1.1 (2012), 5–6.

9. John C. Mann and David J. Breeze, "Ptolemy, Tacitus, and the Tribes of North Britain," *Proceedings of the Society of Antiquaries of Scotland* 117 (1987), 85.

10. *Ibid.*, 89.

11. Anne Ross, *Pagan Celtic Britain* (Chicago: Academy Chicago Publishers, 1996), 158.

12. Ian Armit, "Great Sites: Traprain Law," *British Archaeology* 57 (2001).

13. Anne Ross, "The Human Head in Insular Pagan Celtic Religion," *Proceeding of the Society of Antiquaries of Scotland* 91 (1957/8), 32.

14. Anne Ross, *Pagan Celtic Britain*, 203.

15. *Ibid.*, 115–116.

16. National Museums of Scotland, *Sculptured Stone*, at the website http://nms.scran.ac.uk/database/record.php?usi=000-180-001-448-C.

17. Anne Ross, *Pagan Celtic Britain*, 209.

18. *Ibid.*, 223.

19. *Ibid.*

20. Mick Aston, "Bewcastle: A Site in Need of a Project," *British Archaeology* 106 (May/June 2009).

21. Anne Ross, *Pagan Celtic Britain*, 224.

22. Pastscape, *Robin of Risingham*.

23. "Roman Carving Discovered by a Team Looking for Prehistoric Rock Art," *Archaeo News* 19 (March 2006).

24. Pastscape, *Monument No. 1051403*.

Chapter 2

1. Gildas, *On the Ruin and Conquest of Britain*, trans. Hugh Williams (London: Cymmrodorion, 1899), Chapter 22.
2. *Ibid.*, Chapter 23.
3. *Ibid.*, Chapter 24.
4. John Koch, *Celtic Culture*: A Historical Encyclopedia (Santa Barbara, CA: ABC-CLIO, 2006), 585. The asterisk here, *Dubria, signifies a hypothetical form of the word.
5. Julius Pokorny, Indogermanisches etymologisches Wörterbuch (Bern: Francke, 1959), 261–267.
6. John Koch, *Celtic Culture*: A Historical Encyclopedia, 584.
7. Barry C. Burnham and J.S. Wacher, *The Small Towns of Roman Britain* (London: Batsford, 1990), 116.
8. *Ibid.*, 115–116.
9. Pastscape, *Monument No. 1200574*.
10. John Koch, *Celtic Culture*: A Historical Encyclopedia, 303.
11. Pastscape, *Birdoswald Roman Fort*.
12. Bede, *Ecclesiastical History of the English Nation* (London: J.M. Dent; New York: E.P. Dutton, 1910), Book 2, Chapter 1.
13. *Ibid.*, Book 1, Chapter 34.
14. John Koch, *Celtic Culture*: A Historical Encyclopedia, 303.
15. Bede, *Ecclesiastical History of the English Nation*, Book 2, Chapter 13.
16. *Ibid.*, Book 2, Chapter 14.
17. Paul Frodsham, "Forgetting *Gefrin*: Elements of the Past in the Past at Yeavering," in Paul Frodsham, Peter Topping, Dave Cowley (eds), *We Were Always Chasing Time: Papers Presented to Keith Blood* (Newcastle upon Tyne: Northern Archaeology Group, 1999), 191–207.
18. Nennius, *History of the Britons*, trans. J.A. Giles (London: Henry G. Bohn, 1848), Chapter 63.
19. *Ibid.*, Chapter 57.
20. Martin Grimmer, "The Exogamous Marriages of Oswiu of Northumbria," *Heroic Age* 9 (2006).
21. Bede, *Ecclesiastical History of the English Nation*, Book 1, Chapter 22.
22. *Ibid.*, Book 2, Chapter 20.
23. Rachel Bromwich (ed.), *Trioedd Ynys Prydein: The Triads of the Island of Britain* (Cardiff: University of Wales Press, 2014), 8801–8808.
24. *Ibid.*, 8811–8817.
25. Bede, *Ecclesiastical History of the English Nation*, Book 2, Chapter 5.
26. Rachel Bromwich (ed.), *Trioedd Ynys Prydein: The Triads of the Island of Britain*, 8821.
27. Canmore, *Edinburgh Castle*.
28. Vindolanda Charitable Trust, *Vindolanda Excavations Official Blog*, at the website http://vindolanda3.rssing.com/chan-23497899/latest.php.
29. English Heritage, *History of Housesteads Roman Fort*.
30. Rachel Bromwich (ed.), *Trioedd Ynys Prydein: The Triads of the Island of Britain*, 3019.
31. *Ibid.*, 2971.
32. *Ibid.*, 3019–3025.
33. Taliesin, *Song for Urien Rheged*, at the website http://www.maryjones.us/ctexts/t32.html.
34. Rachel Bromwich (ed.), *Trioedd Ynys Prydein: The Triads of the Island of Britain*, 14158.
35. *Ibid.*
36. *Ibid.*, 14165.
37. Mike McCarthy, "Rheged: An Early Historic Kingdom Near the Solway," *Proceedings of the Society of Antiquarians of Scotland* 132 (2002), 366.
38. Pastscape, *Castra Exploratorum Roman Fort*.
39. W.F. Skene, "The Site of the Battle of Arthuret," *Proceedings of the Society of Antiquaries of Scotland* 6 (1864), 91–98.
40. Hector Munro Chadwick, *Early Scotland* (Cambridge, UK: Cambridge University Press, 2013), 143.
41. Rachel Bromwich (ed.), *Trioedd Ynys Prydein: The Triads of the Island of Britain*, 9187.
42. Mike McCarthy, "Rheged: An Early Historic Kingdom Near the Solway," 374.
43. Jack Hunter, *The Lost Town of Innermessan*, at the website Scottish Corpus of Texts and Speech, http://www.scottishcorpus.ac.uk/document/?documentid=1371.
44. Historic Scotland, *Kirkmadrine Early Christian Stones*.
45. Canmore, *Trusty's Hill, Anwoth*.
46. GUARD Archaeology, *The Galloway Picts Project*, at the website http://www.guard-archaeology.co.uk/news12/gallowayNews.html.
47. Bede, *Ecclesiastical History of the English Nation*, Book 3, Chapter 4.
48. Canmore, *Whithorn Priory*.

49. Canmore, *Whithorn, Bruce Street, Whithorn Priory.*

50. Whithorn Priory and Museum, *The Latinus Stone.*

51. Dennis Harding, *Iron Age Hillforts in Britain and Beyond* (Oxford, UK: Oxford University Press, 2012), 167.

52. Ian Haynes and Tony Wilmott, "Maryport's Mystery Monuments," *Current Archaeology* 289, April 2014.

53. Bede, *Ecclesiastical History of the English Nation,* Book 1, Chapter 1.

54. *Ibid.,* Book 1, Chapter 12.

55. Leslie Alcock, Elizabeth A. Alcock and Stephen T. Driscoll, "Reconnaissance Excavations on Early Historic Fortifications and Other Royal Sites in Scotland, 1974–84: 4, Excavations at Alt Clut, Clyde Rock, Strathclyde, 1974–75," *Proceedings of the Society of Antiquaries of Scotland* 120 (1990), 98–99.

56. *Ibid.,* 113.

57. Headland Archaeology, *Recent Excavations on Inchmarnock and the Identification of an Early Monastic School-House.*

58. Rachel Bromwich (ed.), *Trioedd Ynys Prydein: The Triads of the Island of Britain,* 13772.

59. Bede, *Ecclesiastical History of the English Nation,* Book 4, Chapter 26.

60. Alex Woolf, "Dun Nechtain, Fortriu and the Geography of the Picts," *The Scottish Historical Review* 85 (2006), 184.

61. *Ibid.,* 187.

62. *Ibid.,* 186.

63. *Ibid.,* 188.

64. *Ibid.,* 192.

65. Anne Crone, Alex Woolf and Rod McCullagh, "The Sacking of Auldhame: Investigating a Viking Burial in a Monastic Graveyard," *Current Archaeology* (August 8, 2014).

Chapter 3

1. Rachel Bromwich, *Trioedd Ynys Prydein: The Triads of the Island of Britain* (Cardiff: University of Wales Press, 2014), 8367.

2. Michelle Ziegler, "Artur mac Aedan of Dal Riata," *The Heroic Age* Issue 1 (Spring/Summer 1999).

3. *Ibid.*

4. John Koch, *Celtic culture:* A Historical Encyclopedia, 742.

5. Barry Cunliffe, *Iron Age Communities in Britain* (Taylor & Francis e-library, 2005), 3172.

6. Peter C. Jupp and Clare Gittings, *Death in England* (Manchester: Manchester University Press, 1999), 49.

7. Martin Schönfelder, "Bear-Claws in Germanic Graves," *Oxford Journal of Archaeology* 13.2 (1994), 217–227.

8. Michael Speidel, *Ancient Germanic Warriors* (London: Taylor & Francis, 2002), 14.

9. *Ibid.,* 36.

10. P.H. Sawyer, *From Roman Britain to Norman England* (London: Routledge, 2002), 66.

11. Anne Ross, *Pagan Celtic Britain* (Chicago: Academy Chicago Publishers, 1996), 435.

12. John Morris, *Nennius: British History and the Welsh Annals* (Chichester, UK: Phillimore & Co., 1980), 35.

13. Bede, *Ecclesiastical History of the English Nation* (London: J.M. Dent; New York: E.P. Dutton, 1910), Book 1, Chapter 15.

14. *Ibid.,* Book 2, Chapter 5.

15. Bernard S. Bachrach, "The Question of King Arthur's Existence and of Romano-British Naval Operations," in Robert B. Patterson (ed.), *The Haskins Society Journal: Studies in Medieval History* Volume 2 (1990), 21.

16. Thomas Green, *Lincolnshire and the Arthurian Legend,* at the website http://www.arthuriana.co.uk/notes&queries/N&Q3_ArthLincs.pdf.

17. Thomas Green, "The British Kingdom of Lindsey," *Cambrian Medieval Celtic Studies* 54 (2008), 1–43.

18. Thomas Green, *A Bibliographic Guide to Welsh Arthurian Literature,* http://www.arthuriana.co.uk/notes&queries/N&Q1_ArthLit.pdf.

19. Patrick K. Ford, *The Mabinogi and Other Medieval Welsh Tales* (Berkeley: University of California Press, 2008), 184–5.

20. *Ibid.,* 187.

21. C.P. Lewis and A.T. Thacker (eds.), "Early Medieval Chester 400–1230," in *A History of the County of Chester: Volume 5 part 1: the City of Chester: General History and Topography,* at the website http://www.british-history.ac.uk/vch/ches/vol5/pt1/pp16–33.

22. Mike Ashley, *A Brief History of King Arthur* (London: Hachette UK, 2013).

23. Rachel Bromwich, *Trioedd Ynys Pry-*

dein: The Triads of the Island of Britain, 12239.

24. Taliesin, "Song for Urien," *Book of Taliesin XXXVI,* at the website http://www.maryjones.us/ctexts/t36.html.

25. Gildas, *On the Ruin and Conquest of Britain,* trans. Hugh Williams (London: Cymmrodorion, 1899), Chapter 26.

26. Thomas Green, *Lincolnshire and the Arthurian Legend.*

27. Nennius, *History of the Britons,* trans. J.A. Giles (London: Henry G. Bohn, 1848), at the website http://d.lib.rochester.edu/camelot/text/nennius-history-of-the-britons.

28. The Clwyd-Powy Archaeological Trust, *Historic Landscape Chracterisation: The Elan Valley,* at the website http://www.cpat.org.uk/projects/longer/histland/elan/evland.htm.

29. William W. Kibler and R. Barton Palmer, *Medieval Arthurian Epic and Romance* (Jefferson, NC: McFarland, 2014).

30. Noémie Beck, "The River Marne: Matrona," in *Goddesses in Celtic Religion* (Thesis submitted to the University of Lyon for the degree of Diplôme d'Études Anglophones, 4 December 2009).

31. Robin Melrose, *Religion in Britain from the Megaliths to Arthur* (Jefferson, NC: McFarland, 2016), 189.

32. Anna Crone, "The Clochmabenstane, Gretna," *Transactions of the Dumfriesshire and Galloway Natural History and Antiquarian Society* 58 (1983), 16–20.

33. Rachel Bromwich, *Trioedd Ynys Prydein: The Triads of the Island of Britain,* 12238.

34. *Ibid.,* 12251.

35. *Ibid.,* 12047.

36. *Ibid.,* 9022.

37. Thomas Green, *Arthuriana: Early Arthurian Tradition and the Origins of the Legend* (lulu.com, 2009), 76.

Chapter 4

1. Rachel Bromwich and Daniel Simon Evans, *Culhwch and Olwen: An Edition and Study of the Oldest Arthurian Tale* (Cardiff: University of Wales Press, 1992), 43.

2. *Ibid.,* 44.

3. "Culhwch and Olwen," in Gwyn Jones and Thomas Jones (eds.), *The Mabinogion* (London: Everyman, 1949).

4. Rachel Bromwich and Daniel Simon Evans, *Culhwch and Olwen,* xxx.

5. *Ibid.,* xxxii.

6. Robin Melrose, *Religion in Britain from the Megaliths to Arthur* (Jefferson, NC: McFarland, 2016), 157.

7. Rachel Bromwich and Daniel Simon Evans, *Culhwch and Olwen,* 142.

8. *Ibid.,* 143.

9. *Ibid.*

10. *Ibid.,* 144.

11. *Ibid.*

12. M.L. West, *Indo-European Poetry and Myth* (Oxford: Oxford University Press, 2007), 287.

13. *Ibid.,* 378.

14. *Ibid.,* 378–379.

15. Rachel Bromwich and Daniel Simon Evans, *Culhwch and Olwen,* 151.

16. *Ibid.,* 151–2.

17. Calvert Watkins, *How to Kill a Dragon: Aspects of Indo-European Poetics* (New York: Oxford University Press, 1995), 429.

18. Racel Bromwich and Daniel Simon Evans, *Cilhwch and Olwen,* 129.

19. *Ibid.,* 123.

20. *Ibid.,* lxviii.

21. Thomas Owen Clancy and Gilbert Markus, *The Triumph Tree: Scotland's Earliest Poetry, 550–1350* (Edinburgh: Canongate, 1998), 72.

22. Rachel Bromwich and Daniel Simon Evans, *Culhwch and Olwen,* lxix.

23. *Ibid.,* 2960.

24. O.J. Padel, "The Nature of Arthur," *Cambrian Medieval Celtic Studies* 27 (1994), 14.

25. Thomas Green, *The Historicity and Historicisation of Arthur,* at the website http://www.arthuriana.co.uk/historicity/arthur.htm.

26. Simon Young, *The Celtic Revolution* (London: Gibson Square Books, 2010), 208.

27. Proinsias MacCana, "Reviewed Work: *The Wisdom of the Outlaw: The Boyhood Deeds of Finn in Gaelic Narrative Tradition* by Joseph Falaky Nagy," *The Canadian Journal of Irish Studies* 14 (1988), 86.

28. John Pitcher, *Medieval and Renaissance Drama in England* (Madison, NJ: Fairleigh Dickinson University Press, 2001), 47.

29. John Koch, *Celtic Culture: A Historical Encyclopedia,* 1360.

Chapter 5

1. Alan Lane, "Citadel of the First Scots," *British Archaeology* 62 (December 2001).

2. Bede, *Ecclesiastical History of the English Nation* (London: J.M. Dent; New York: E.P. Dutton, 1910), Book 3, Chapter 4.

3. Canmore, *Iona, Early Christian Monastery*.

4. Bede, *Ecclesiastical History*, Book 3, Chapter 2.

5. William Reeves (ed.), *Life of St Columba* (Edinburgh: Edmonston and Douglas, 1874), Chapter 1.

6. Pastscape, *Lindisfarne Priory*.

7. Bede, *Ecclesiastical History*, Book 3, Chapter 12.

8. *Ibid.*, Book 3, Chapter 6.

9. Sarah Groves, "Bodies in the Bowl Hole—An Early Medieval Inhumation Cemetery at Bamburgh, Northumberland," *The School of Historical Studies Postgraduate Forum e-Journal* 2 (2003).

10. Details of both at the Bamburgh Castle website.

11. Bede, *Ecclesiastical History*, Book 3, Chapter 9.

12. *Ibid.*, Book 2, Chapter 15.

13. *Ibid.*, Book 2, Chapter 5.

14. British Museum, *The Sutton Hoo Ship Burial*.

15. British Museum, *Who Was Buried at Sutton Hoo?*.

16. Seamus Heaney, *Beowulf* (London: Faber and Faber, 2000), 3–4.

17. Wikipedia, *Vendel*.

18. Bede, *Ecclesiastical History*, Book 2, Chapter 20.

19. *Ibid.*, Book 3, Chapter 24.

20. Nennius, *History of the Britons*, trans. J.A. Giles (London: Henry G. Bohn, 1848), Chapter 65.

21. Bede, *Ecclesiastical History*, Book 3, Chapter 24.

22. "Rethinking the Staffordshire Hoard—Piecing Together the Wealth of Anglo-Saxon Kings," *Current Archaeology* 290 (March 31, 2014).

23. Michelle P. Brown, *The Manuscript Context for the Inscription*, at the website of the Portable Antiquities Scheme, https://finds.org.uk/staffshoardsymposium/papers/michellebrown.

24. Bede, *Ecclesiastical History*, Book 3, Chapter 21.

25. Charles Wycliffe Goodwin, *The Anglo-Saxon Version of the Life of St Guthlac* (London: John Russell Smith, 1848), 21.

26. *Ibid.*, 27.

27. Pastscape, *Monument No. 1408333*.

28. David Farmer, *The Oxford Dictionary of Saints* (Oxford: Oxford University Press, 2011), 202.

29. Michael Swanton, *The Anglo-Saxon Chronicle* (New York: Routledge, 1998), 62.

30. *Ibid.*, 59.

31. *Ibid.*, 60.

32. *Ibid.*, 71.

33. Antonia Gransden, *Legends, Traditions and History in Medieval England* (London: Bloomsbury, 1992), 84.

34. *Ibid.*, 85.

35. Barry M. Marsden, "The Vikings in Derbyshire," *Derbyshire Life and Countryside* (March/April 2007).

36. *Ibid.*

37. Pastscape, *Monument No. 313084*.

38. Michael Swanton, *Anglo-Saxon Chronicle*, 74.

39. *Ibid.*, 76.

40. *Ibid.*, 93.

41. *Ibid.*, 97.

42. *Ibid.*, 102–3.

43. *Ibid.*, 103.

44. *Ibid.*, 104.

45. *The Battle of Brunaburh*, at the website http://loki.stockton.edu/~kinsellt/litresources/brun/brun2.html#modtext.

46. Michael Swanton, *Anglo-Saxon Chronicle*, 110.

47. G.R. Isaac, "Armes Prydein Fawr and St David," in J. Wyn Evans and Jonathan M. Wooding, *St David of Wales: Cult, Church and Nation* (Woodbridge, UK: Boydell Press, 2007), 171.

48. *Ibid.*, 175.

49. Rachel Bromwich, *Trioedd Ynys Prydein: The Triads of the Island of Britain*, 8781.

50. G.R. Isaac, "Armes Prydein Fawr and St David," 177.

51. Douglas B. Killings, *The Battle of Maldon*, at the website www.english.ox.ac.uk.

52. James Ingram, *Anglo-Saxon Chronicle* (London: Everyman, 1912).

53. *Ibid.*

54. Richard Cavendish, "The St Brice's Day Massacre," *History Today* 52 (11 November 2002).

55. Nadia Durrani, "Vengeance on the Vikings," *Archaeology* (October 01, 2013).

56. Jan Ragnar Hagland and Bruce Watson, "Fact or Folklore: The Viking Attack on London Bridge," *London Archaeologist* (Spring 2005), 331.

57. *Ibid.*, 328.

58. A.S. Kline, *The Seafarer*, at the web-

site http://www.poetryintranslation.com/
PITBR/English/Seafarer.htm.
　59. A.S. Kline, *The Wanderer*, at the website http://www.poetryintranslation.com/
PITBR/English/Wanderer.htm.

Chapter 6

　1. Wikipedia, *Heorot*.
　2. Seamus Heaney, *Beowulf* (London:
Faber and Faber, 2000).
　3. Ruth Johnston Staver, *A Companion
to Beowulf* (Portsmouth, NH: Greenwood,
2005), 2.
　4. Wikipedia, *Othere*.
　5. Wikipedia, *Eadgils*.
　6. Andy Orchard, *Pride and Prodigies:
Studies in the Monsters of the Beowulf Manuscript* (Toronto: University of Toronto Press,
2003), 259.
　7. Michael Lapidge, "*Beowulf*, Aldhelm,
the *Liber Monstrorum* and Wessex," in *Anglo-
Latin Literature, 600–899* (London: A&C
Black, 1996), 304–5.
　8. Michael Swanton, *Beowulf: Revised
Edition* (Manchester: Manchester University Press, 1997), 3.
　9. Sam Newton, *The Origins of Beowulf
and the Pre-Viking Kingdom of East Anglia*
(Woodbridge, UK: DS Brewer, 2004), 19.
　10. Seamus Heaney, *Beowulf*.
　11. Sam Newton, *The Origins of Beowulf
and the Pre-Viking Kingdom of East Anglia*,
134–135.
　12. Peter Warner, *The Origins of Suffolk*
(Manchester: Manchester University Press,
1996), 120.
　13. Seamus Heaney, *Beowulf*.
　14. Richard Morris, *The Blickling Homilies of the Tenth Century* (London: The Early
English Text Society, 1880).
　15. Michael Lapidge, "*Beowulf*, Aldhelm,
the *Liber Monstrorum* and Wessex," in *Anglo-
Latin Literature, 600–899*, 299–300.
　16. *Ibid.*, 300.
　17. "Explanatory Notes," at the website
Beowulf on Steorarume (*Beowulf in Cyber-
space*), www.heorot.dk, edited by Dr. Ben-
jamin Slade.
　18. *Ibid.*
　19. R.W. Chambers, *Beowulf: An Introduction to the Study of the Poem with a Discussion of the Stories of Offa and Finn* (Cambridge, UK: Cambridge University Press,
1921), 366.

　20. *Ibid.*, 368–369.
　21. *Ibid.*, 55.
　22. *Ibid.*, 369.

Chapter 7

　1. John Koch, *Celtic Culture*: A Historical Encyclopedia, 1722.
　2. *Ibid.*
　3. J.A.Giles, "Geoffrey of Monmouth's
British History," in *Six Old English Chronicles* (London: Henry G. Bohn, 1848), 224.
　4. Caitlin R. Green, *A Guide to Arthurian
Archaeology*, at the website http://www.
arthuriana.co.uk/n&q/artharch.htm.
　5. Ken Dark, *Britain and the End of the
Roman Empire* (Stroud, UK: The History
Press, 2006), 153–154.
　6. Pastscape, *Monument No. 431901*.
　7. J.A.Giles, "Geoffrey of Monmouth's
British History," 225.
　8. Caitlin R. Green, *Myrddin & Merlin:
A Guide to the Early Evolution of the Merlin
Legend*, at the website http://www.arthuriana.
co.uk/n&q/myrddin.htm.
　9. Rachel Bromwich (ed.), *Trioedd Ynys
Prydein: The Triads of the Island of Britain*
(Cardiff: University of Wales Press, 2014),
12904–12910.
　10. Cynthia Whiddon Green, *Jocelyn, a
Monk of Furness: The Life of Kentigern
(Mungo)*, at the website http://legacy.
fordham.edu/halsall/basis/jocelyn-lifeof
kentigern.asp.
　11. Peter H. Goodrich and Raymond H.
Thompson, *Merlin: A Casebook* (New York
and London: Routledge, 2003), 107.
　12. Ken Dark, *Britain and the End of the
Roman Empire*, 101.
　13. Michael Fulford, Mark Handley and
Amanda Clarke, "An Early Date for Ogham:
The Silchester Ogham Stone Rehabilitated,"
Medieval Archaeology 44 (2000), 1–23.
　14. Pastscape, *Calleva Atrebatum*.
　15. Thomas Green, *A Bibliographic Guide
to Welsh Arthurian Literature*, at the website
http://www.arthuriana.co.uk/notes&queries/
N&Q1_ArthLit.pdf.
　16. William Jenkins Rees and Thomas
Wakeman, *Lives of the Cambro-British Saints*
(London: Longman & Co., 1853), 398.
　17. Pastscape, *Monument No. 188644*.
　18. "Carhampton, Religious History," in
*Victoria County History of Somerset: Work in
Progress*.

19. Rachel Bromwich (ed.), *Trioedd Ynys Prydein: The Triads of the Island of Britain*, 14193–14198.

20. Joseph L. Duggan, *The Romances of Chrétien de Troyes* (New Haven, CT: Yale University Press, 2008), 232.

21. Rachel Bromwich (ed.), *Trioedd Ynys Prydein: The Triads of the Island of Britain*, 6009.

22. Lincolnshire Museums, *Gods and Goddesses of Roman Ancaster*.

23. Anne Ross, *Pagan Celtic Britain* (Chicago: Academy Chicago Publishers, 1996), 268.

24. *Ibid.*, 285–286.

25. John O' Donovan, *Sanas Chormaic: Cormac's Glossary* (Calcutta: Irish Archaeological and Celtic Society, 1868).

26. National Museums Scotland, *Sculpture, of Goddess Brigantia*.

27. Coflein, *Isca Legionary Fortress*.

28. Caitlin R. Green, *Pre-Galfridian Arthurian Characters*, at the website http://www.arthuriana.co.uk/n&q/figures.htm .

29. Kenneth Jackson, "Once Again Arthur's Battles," *Modern Philology* 43 (1945), 56.

30. J.A.Giles, "Geoffrey of Monmouth's British History," 251–252.

31. Karl Heinz Göller, "The Dream of the Dragon and the Bear," in *The Alliterative Morte Arthure: A Reassessment of the Poem* (Woodbridge, UK: Boydell & Brewer, 1981), 135.

32. J.A.Giles, "Geoffrey of Monmouth's British History," 252.

33. *Ibid.*, 268.

34. Thomas Green, *A Bibliographic Guide to Welsh Arthurian Literature*, http://www.arthuriana.co.uk/notes&queries/N&Q1_ArthLit.pdf.

35. Caradoc of Llancarfan, *Life of Gildas*, trans. Hugh Williams (London: Cymmrodorion, 1899).

36. Geoffrey of Monmouth, *Life of Merlin*, trans. John Jay Perry (Urbana, IL: The University of Illinois, 1925).

37. John Rhys, *Studies in the Arthurian Legend* (Oxford: Clarendon Press, 1891), 348–349.

38. John Koch, *Celtic Culture: A Historical Encyclopedia*, 1456.

39. Sarah Higley, trans., "The Spoils of Annwn," The Camelot Project at the University of Rochester, http://www.lib.rochester.edu/camelot/.

40. Will Parker, *The Mabinogi of Branwen*, at the website www.mabinogi.net.

41. F.E. Romer, *Pomponius Mela's Description of the World* (Ann Arbor: University of Michigan Press, 1998), 115.

42. Plutarch, The Obsolescence of Oracles," in *Moralia* Vol. V, trans. Frank Cole Babbitt (Cambridge, MA: Harvard University Press, 1936), Chapter 18.

43. A.R. Burn, "Holy Men on Islands in Pre-Christian Britain," *Glasgow Archaeological Journal* 1 (1969), 2.

44. Polly Groome and Will Steele, *Caldey Island: Tir Gofal Farm Historic Environment Report*, at the website http://www.herwales.co.uk/her/groups/DAT/media/DAT%20Reports/39860%20TG%20Caldey.pdf.

45. Trevor D. Ford (ed.), *Limestones and Caves of Wales* (Cambridge: Cambridge University Press, 2011), 84.

46. Gerald of Wales, *On the Instruction of Princes*, trans. John William Sutton, at the website http://d.lib.rochester.edu/camelot/text/gerald-of-wales-arthurs-tomb .

47. E.K, Chambers, *Arthur of Britain* (London: Sidgwick & Jackson, 1927), 17.

48. Rachel Bromwich, *Trioedd Ynys Prydein: The Triads of the Island of Britain*, 10596.

49. Sir Thomas Malory and Helen Cooper (ed.), *Le Morte Darthur: The Winchester Manuscript* (Oxford: Oxford University Press, 1998), 10985.

50. J. Armitage Robinson, *Two Glastonbury Legends* (Cambridge: Cambridge University Press, 1926), 51–2.

51. Thomas Green, *A Gazetteer of Arthurian Onomastic and Topographic Folklore*, at the website http://www.arthuriana.co.uk/notes&queries/N&Q2_ArthFolk.pdf.

52. Thomas Green, *A Bibliographic Guide to Welsh Arthurian Literature*.

53. J.A.Giles, "Geoffrey of Monmouth's British History," 235–236.

54. *Lake Lumonoy*, at the website http://www.wondersofbritain.org/wonder1/index.html.

55. Canmore, *Luss, St Kessog's Church and Churchyard*.

Chapter 8

1. Françoise Le Saux, *Layamons's Brut: The Poem and Its Sources* (Woodbridge, UK: D.S. Brewer, 1989), 10.

2. R. Barton Palmer, "Lawman. *Brut*: A Selection," in William W. Kibler and R. Barton Palmer (eds.), *Medieval Arthurian Epic and Romance: Eight New Translations* (Jefferson, NC: McFarland, 2014).

3. Rosamund Allen, *Lawman: Brut*, quoted in N.H.G.E. Veldhoen, "Towards National Identity," in Ludo Jongen and Sjaak Onderdelinden, "*Der muoz mir süezer worte jehen*,": *Liber amicorum für Norbert Voorwinden* (Leiden, Netherlands: Brill, 1997), 21.

4. N.H.G.E. Veldhoen, "Towards National Identity," 22–23.

5. Seamus Heaney, *Beowulf* (London: Faber and Faber, 200).

6. Richard Morris, *The Blickling Homilies of the Tenth Century* (London: The Early English Text Society, 1880).

7. Rosamund Allen, *Brut: Lawman* (New York: St. Martin's Press, 1992).

8. Rosamund Allen, *Lawman: Brut*, quoted in N.H.G.E. Veldhoen, "Towards National Identity," 24–25.

9. *Ibid.*, 28–29.

10. R. Barton Palmer, "Lawman. *Brut*: A Selection.,"

11. Valerie Krishna, *The Alliterative Morte Arthure: A New Verse Translation* (Lanham, MD: University Press of America, 1983).

12. Karl Heinz Göller, "The Dream of the Dragon and the Bear," in *The Alliterative Morte Arthure: A Reassessment of the Poem* (Woodbridge, UK: Boydell & Brewer, 1981), 137.

13. Valerie Krishna, *The Alliterative Morte Arthure: A New Verse Translation*, xiii.

Chapter 9

1. J.A. Giles, "Geoffrey of Monmouth's British History," in *Six Old English Chronicles* (London: Henry G. Bohn, 1848), 255.

2. Simon Armitage, *Sir Gawain and the Green Knight* (London: Faber and Faber, 2009).

3. Nigel Bryant, *The High Book of the Grail* (Woodbridge, UK: Boydell & Brewer, 2007), 80.

4. *Ibid.*, 81.

5. *Ibid.*, 182.

6. James R. Hulbert, "The Name of the Green Knight: Bercilak or Bertilak," in *The Manly Anniversary Studies in Language and Literature* (Chicago: University of Chicago Press, 1923).

7. Leila K. Norako, *Morgan le Fay*, at the

Camelot Project website, http://d.lib.rochester.edu/camelot/theme/morgan.

8. Dominique Battles, *Cultural Differences and Material Culture in Middle English Romance: Normans and Saxons* (New York: Routledge, 2013), 45.

9. *The Wanderer*, at the website http://www.anglo-saxons.net/hwaet/?do=get&type=text&id=wdr.

10. *The Seafarer*, at the website http://www.anglo-saxons.net/hwaet/?do=get&type=text&id=Sfr.

11. Dominique Battles, *Cultural Differences and Material Culture in Middle English Romance: Normans and Saxons*, 95–96.

12. *Ibid.*, 96.

13. *Ibid.*, 76.

14. *Ibid.*, 77.

15. *Ibid.*, 100.

16. Pastscape, *Swythamley Park*.

17. Pastscape, *Dieulacres Abbey*.

18. *Lud's Church*, at the website http://www.peakdistrictinformation.com/visits/ludschurch.php .

19. Timothy Husband and Gloria Gilmore-House, *The Wild Man: Medieval Myth and Symbolism* (New York: The Metropolitan Museum of Art, 1980), 1.

20. Juanita Wood and Charles A. Curry, *Wooden Images: Misericords and Medieval England* (Madison, NJ: Fairleigh Dickinson University Press, 1999), 81.

21. Ronald L. Ecker and Eugene J. Crook, *Geoffrey Chaucer The Canterbury Tales: A Complete Translation into Modern English*, at the website http://english.fsu.edu/canterbury/friar.html.

22. Richard Hayman, "Green Men and the Way of All Flesh," *British Archaeology* 100 (May/June 2008).

Chapter 10

1. Pastscape, *Monument No. 11095*.

2. Pastscape, *Voreda Roman Fort*.

3. Pastscape, *Monument No. 11329*.

4. Oxford Archaeology, *Shadows in the Sand: Excavation of a Viking-Age Cemetery at Cumwhitton, Cumbria*, at the website http://oxfordarchaeology.com/publications/oanorth-publications/294-shadows-in-the-sand-excavation-of-a-viking-age-cemetery-at-cumwhitton-cumbria.

5. Pastscape, *The Giants Grave and the Giants Thumb*.

6. W.G. Collingwood, "The Giant's Grave, Penrith," *Transactions of the Cumberland and Westmorland Antiquarian and Archaeological Society* 23 (1923), 127.

7. Tim Clarkson, *Strathclyde and the Anglo-Saxons in the Viking Age* (Edinburgh: Birlinn, 2014).

8. *Ibid.*

9. Pastscape, *Castle Hewen.*

10. Pastscape, *Carlisle Castle.*

11. Pastscape, *Armathwaite Priory.*

12. Pastscape, *Armathwaite Castle.*

13. Valerie Krishna, "The Adventures of Arthur at Tarn Wadling," *Five Middle English Arthurian Romances* (London and New York: Routledge, 2015).

14. Giles Watson, *The Three Dead Kings,* at the website http://gileswatson.deviantart.com/art/The-Three-Dead-Kings-306948886.

15. Valerie Krishna, "The Vows of King Arthur, Sir Kay and Baldwin of Britain," *Five Middle English Arthurian Romances.*

16. Thomas Hahn (ed.), *The Avowyng of Arthur,* at the website http://d.lib.rochester.edu/teams/text/hahn-sir-gawain-avowyng-of-arthur.

17. Thomas Hahn (ed.), *The Wedding of Sir Gawain and Dame Ragnelle: Introduction,* at the website http://d.lib.rochester.edu/teams/text/hahn-sir-gawain-wedding-of-sir-gawain-and-dame-ragnelle-introduction.

18. Valerie Krishna, "The Wedding of Sir Gawain and Dame Ragnell," *Five Middle English Arthurian Romances.*

19. Peter Ackroyd, *The History of England Volume 1: Foundation* (London: Macmillan, 2011).

20. Thomas Hahn (ed.), *The Wedding of Sir Gawain and Dame Ragnelle: Introduction,* at the website http://d.lib.rochester.edu/teams/text/hahn-sir-gawain-wedding-of-sir-gawain-and-dame-ragnelle-introduction.

21. Valerie Krishna, "Introduction," *Five Middle English Arthurian Romances,* 21.

Chapter 11

1. Michael Swanton, *The Anglo-Saxon Chronicle,* at the website *Viking Sources in Translation,* https://classesv2.yale.edu/access/content/user/haw6/Vikings/AS%20Chronicle%20Peterborough%20MS.html.

2. *Ibid.*

3. Michael Swanton, Stephen Knight and Thomas H. Ohlgren, *Hereward the Wake: Introduction,* at the website http://d.lib.rochester.edu/teams/text/hereward-the-wake-introduction.

4. Peter Rex, *1066: A New History of the Norman Conquest* (Stroud, UK: Amberley, 2011), 89–90.

5. *Ibid.,* 90.

6. Michael Swanton, Stephen Knight and Thomas H. Ohlgren, *Hereward the Wake,* at the website http://d.lib.rochester.edu/teams/text/hereward-the-wake-introduction.

7. John C. Appleby and Paul Dalton, *Outlaws in Medieval and Early Modern England* (Farnham, UK: Ashgate Publishing, 2009), 12.

8. Michael Swanton, *The Anglo-Saxon Chronicle.*

9. John H. Chandler, *Robin Hood: Development of a Popular Hero,* at the website http://www.library.rochester.edu/robbins/robin-hood-chandler.

10. Thomas H. Ohlgren, *Robin Hood: The Early Poems, 1465–1560* (Newark: University of Delaware Press, 2007), 18.

11. Stephen Knight and Thomas H. Ohlgren (eds.), *Robin Hood and Other Outlaw Tales: The Chronicler's Robin Hood,* at the website http://d.lib.rochester.edu/teams/publication/knight-and-ohlgren-robin-hood-and-other-outlaw-tales.

12. *Ibid.*

13. *Ibid.*

14. J.R. Maddicott, "Birth and Setting of the Ballads," in Stephen Thomas Knight, *Robin Hood: an Anthology of Scholarship and Criticism* (Woodbridge,UK: Boydell & Brewer, 1999), 250.

15. Stephen Knight and Thomas H. Ohlgren (eds.), *Robin Hood and the Monk: Introduction,* at the website http://d.lib.rochester.edu/teams/text/robin-hood-and-the-monk-introduction .

16. *Ibid.*

17. Stephen Knight and Thomas H. Ohlgren (eds.), *Robin Hood and the Monk,* at the website http://d.lib.rochester.edu/teams/text/robin-hood-and-the-monk.

18. Pastscape, *King Johns Palace.*

19. *Robin Hood's Prison? Sheriff's Dungeon Found at Nottingham Gaol,* at the website *Culture 24,* http://www.culture24.org.uk/history-and-heritage/art51465.

20. Stephen Knight and Thomas H. Ohlgren, *Robin Hood and Guy of Gisborne: Introduction,* at the website http://d.lib.rochester.edu/teams/text/robin-hood-and-guy-of-gisborne-introduction.

21. Stephen Knight and Thomas H. Ohlgren (eds.), *Robin Hood and Guy of Gisborne*, at the website http://d.lib.rochester.edu/teams/text/robin-hood-and-guy-of-gisborne.

22. *Northern Lancashire and Bowland*, at the website http://www.robinhoodlegend.com/northern-lancashire-bowland/.

23. Stuart Kane, "Horseplay: Robin Hood, Guy of Gisborne, and the Neg(oti)ation of the Bestial," in Thomas Hahn (ed.), *Robin Hood in Popular Culture* (Woodbridge, UK: Boydell & Brewer, 2000), 106.

24. Antha Cotton-Spreckelmeyer, "Robin Hood: Outlaw or Exile?," in Alexander L. Kaufman (ed.), *British Outlaws of Literature and History* (Jefferson, NC: McFarland & Company Inc., 2011), 140.

25. *Ibid.*, 141.

Chapter 12

1. Stephen Knight and Thomas H. Ohlgren (eds.), *A Geste of Robyn Hode: Introduction*, at the website http://d.lib.rochester.edu/teams/text/gest-of-robyn-hode-introduction.

2. Stephen Knight and Thomas H. Ohlgren, *A Gest of Robyn Hode*, at the website http://d.lib.rochester.edu/teams/text/gest-of-robyn-hode.

3. *Yorkshire Guide: Wentbridge*, at the website http://www.yorkshireguides.com/wentbridge.html.

4. Pastscape, *St Marys Abbey*.

5. J.R. Maddicott,"Birth and Setting of the Ballads," in Stephen Thomas Knight, *Robin Hood: An Anthology of Scholarship and Criticism* (Woodbridge,UK: Boydell & Brewer, 1999), 239–240.

6. Pastscape, *Jordans Castle*.

7. ,"The Inheritance of Richard Foliot of Grimston, Nottinghamshire, 1236," at the website *Henry III Fine Rolls Project*, http://www.finerollshenry3.org.uk/content/month/fm-02–2009.html.

8. ,"The Many Robin Hoods," at the website *Robin Hood: The Facts and Fiction*, http://www.robinhoodlegend.com/the-many-robin-hoods-7/.

9. Richard H. Osberg (ed.), *The Poems of Laurence Minot 1333–1352*, at the website http://d.lib.rochester.edu/teams/text/osberg-poems-of-laurence-minot-1333–1352 .

10. Stephen Knight and Thomas H. Ohlgren (eds.), *Adam Bell, Clim of the Clough, and William of Cloudesley: Introduction*, at the website http://d.lib.rochester.edu/teams/text/adam-bell-clim-of-the-clough-william-of-cloudesley-introduction.

11. Stephen Knight and Thomas H. Ohlgren, *Adam Bell, Clim of the Clough and William of Cloudesley*, at the website http://d.lib.rochester.edu/teams/text/adam-bell-clim-of-the-clough-william-of-cloudesley.

Bibliography

Ackroyd, Peter. *The History of England Volume I: Foundation.* London: Macmillan, 2011.

Alcock, Leslie, Alcock, Elizabeth A., and Driscoll, Stephen T. "Reconnaissance Excavations on Early Historic Fortifications and Other Royal Sites in Scotland, 1974–84: 4, Excavations at Alt Clut, Clyde Rock, Strathclyde, 1974–75," *Proceedings of the Society of Antiquaries of Scotland* 120 (1990): 95–149.

Allen, Rosamund. *Brut: Lawman.* New York: St. Martin's Press, 1992.

Appleby, John C., and Dalton, Paul. *Outlaws in Medieval and Early Modern England.* Farnham, UK: Ashgate Publishing, 2009.

Armit, Ian. "Great Sites: Traprain Law," *British Archaeology* 57 (2001).

Armitage, Simon. *Sir Gawain and the Green Knight.* London: Faber and Faber, 2009.

Ashley, Mike. *A Brief History of King Arthur.* London: Hachette UK, 2013.

Aston, Mick. "Bewcastle: A Site in Need of a Project," *British Archaeology* 106 (May/June 2009).

Bachrach, Bernard S. "The Question of King Arthur's Existence and of Romano-British Naval Operations," *The Haskins Society Journal: Studies in Medieval History* Volume 2 (1990): 13–28.

Battles, Dominique. *Cultural Differences and Material Culture in Middle English Romance: Normans and Saxons.* New York: Routledge, 2013.

Beck, Noémie. *Goddesses in Celtic Religion.* Ph.D. diss., University of Lyon, 4 December 2009.

Bede. *Ecclesiastical History of the English Nation.* London: J.M. Dent; New York: E.P. Dutton, 1910.

Breeze, David J. "Why Did the Romans Fail to Conquer Scotland?" *Proceedings of the Society of Antiquaries of Scotland* 118 (1988): 3–22.

Bromwich, Rachel. *Trioedd Ynys Prydein: The Triads of the Island of Britain.* Cardiff: University of Wales Press, 2014.

Bromwich Rachel, and Evans, Daniel Simon. *Culhwch and Olwen: An Edition and Study of the Oldest Arthurian Tale.* Cardiff: University of Wales Press, 1992.

Brown, Michelle P. "The Manuscript Context for the Inscription." *Staffordshire Hoard Symposium,* British Museum, March 2010. https://finds.org.uk/staffordshiresymposium/papers/michellebrown.

Bryant, Nigel. *The High Book of the Grail.* Woodbridge, UK: Boydell & Brewer, 2007.

Burn, A.R. "Holy Men on Islands in Pre–Christian Britain." *Glasgow Archaeological Journal* 1 (1969): 2–6.

Burnham, Barry C., and Wacher, J.S. *The Small Towns of Roman Britain*. London: Batsford, 1990.

Caradoc of Llancarfan. *Life of Gildas*. Translated by Hugh Williams. London: Cymmrodorion, 1899.

Cavendish, Richard. "The St. Brice's Day Massacre," *History Today* 52 (11 November 2002).

Chadwick, Hector Munro. *Early Scotland*. Cambridge, UK: Cambridge University Press, 2013.

Chambers, E.K. *Arthur of Britain*. London: Sidgwick & Jackson, 1927.

Chambers, R.W. *Beowulf: An Introduction to the Study of the Poem with a Discussion of the Stories of Offa and Finn*. Cambridge, UK: Cambridge University Press, 1921.

Chandler, John H. *Robin Hood: Development of a Popular Hero*. http://www.library.rochester.edu/robbins/robin-hood-chandler.

Clancy, Thomas Owen, and Markus, Gilbert. *The Triumph Tree: Scotland's Earliest Poetry, 550–1350*. Edinburgh: Canongate, 1998.

Clarkson, Tim. *Strathclyde and the Anglo-Saxons in the Viking Age*. Edinburgh: Birlinn, 2014.

Collingwood, W.G. "The Giant's Grave, Penrith." *Transactions of the Cumberland and Westmoreland Antiquarian and Archaeological Society* 23 (1923): 115–128.

Cook, Murray. "Romans, Picts and Development: Continuity and Change in Aberdeenshire's Archaeology and Informed Planning Decisions," *International Journal of Postgraduate Research* 1.1 (2012): 1–13.

Cooper, Helen. *Sir Thomas Malory Le Morte Darthur: The Winchester Manuscript*. Oxford, UK: Oxford University Press, 1998.

Cotton-Spreckelmyer, Antha. "Robin Hood: Outlaw or Exile?" In *British Outlaws of Literature and History*. Edited by Alexander L. Kaufman. Jefferson, NC: McFarland, 2011.

Crone, Anne, "The Lochmabenstane, Gretna," *Transactions of the Dumfriesshire and Galloway Natural History and Antiquarian Society* 58 (1983): 16–20.

Crone, Anne, Woolf, Alex, and McCullagh, Rod. "The Sacking of Auldhame: Investigating a Viking Burial in a Monastic Graveyard," *Current Archaeology* (Aug. 8, 2014).

Cunliffe, Barry. *Iron Age Communities in Britain*. Taylor & Francis e-library, 2005.

Dark, Ken. *Britain and the End of the Roman Empire*. Stroud, UK: The History Press, 2006.

Duggan, Joseph L. *The Romances of Chretien De Troyes*. New Haven, CT: Yale University Press, 2008.

Durrani, Nadia. "The Vengeance of the Vikings," *Archaeology* (October 01, 2013).

Eadgils. Wikipedia. https://en.wikipedia.org/wiki/Eadgils#Gesta_Danorum.

Ecker, Ronald L., and Crook, Eugene J. *Geoffrey Chaucer the Canterbury Tales: A Complete Translation into Modern English*. http://english.fsu.edu/canterbury/.

Farmer, David. *The Oxford Dictionary of Saints*. Oxford, UK: Oxford University Press, 2011.

Ford, Patrick K. *The Mabinogi and Other Welsh Medieval Tales*. Berkeley: University of California Press, 2008.

Ford, Trevor D. *Limestones and Caves of Wales*. Cambridge, UK: Cambridge University Press, 2011.

Frodsham, Paul. "Forgetting *Gefrin*: Elements of the Past in the Past at Yeavering." In *We Were Always Chasing Time. Papers Presented to Keith Blood*. Edited by Paul Frodsham, Peter Topping, Dave Cowley. Newcastle upon Tyne: Northern Archaeology Group, 1999.

Fulford, Michael, Handley, Mark, and Clarke, Amanda. "An Early Date for Ogham: The Silchester Ogham Stone Rehabilitated," *Medieval Archaeology* 44 (2000): 1–23.

Geoffrey of Monmouth. *Life of Merlin.* Translated by John Jay Perry. Urbana: The University of Illinois, 1925.

Gerald of Wales. *On the Instruction of Princes.* Translated by John William Sutton. http://d.lib.rochester.edu/camelot/text/gerald-of-wales-arthurs-tomb.

Gildas. *On the Ruin and Conquest of Britain.* Translated by Hugh Williams. London: Cymmrodorion, 1899.

Giles, J.A. *Six Old English Chronicles.* London:Henry G. Bohn, 1848.

Göller, Karl Heinz. *The Alliterative Morte Arthure: A Reassessment of the Poem.* Woodbridge, UK: Boydell & Brewer, 1981.

Goodrich, Peter H., and Thompson, Raymond H. *Merlin: A Casebook.* New York: Routledge, 2003.

Goodwin, Charles Wycliffe. *The Anglo-Saxon Version of the Life of St. Guthlac.* London: John Russell Smith, 1848.

Gransden, Antonia. *Legends, Traditions and History in Medieval England.* London: Bloomsbury, 1992.

Green, Caitlin R. *A Guide to Arthurian Archaeology.* http://www.arthuriana.co.uk/n&q/artharch.htm.

Green, Caitlin R. *The Historicity and Historicisation of Arthur.* http://www.arthuriana.co.uk/historicity/arthur.htm.

Green, Caitlin R. *Myrddin & Merlin: A Guide to the Early Evolution of the Merlin Legend.* http://www.arthuriana.co.uk/n&q/myrddin.htm.

Green, Caitlin R. *Pre-Galfridian Arthurian Characters.* http://www.arthuriana.co.uk/n&q/figures.htm.

Green, Cynthia Whiddon. *Jocelyn, a Monk of Furness: The Life of Kentigern (Mungo).* http://legacy.fordham.edu/halsall/basis/jocelyn-lifeofkentigern.asp.

Green, Thomas. *Arthuriana: Early Arthurian Tradition and the Origins of the Legend.* lulu.com, 2009.

Green, Thomas. *A Bibliographic Guide to Welsh Arthurian Literature.* http://www.arthuriana.co.uk/notes&queries/N&Q1_ArthLit.pdf.

Green, Thomas. "The British Kingdom of Lindsey," *Cambrian Medieval Celtic Studies* 54 (2008): 1–43.

Green, Thomas. *A Gazetteer of Arthurian Onomastic and Topographic Folklore.* http://www.arthuriana.co.uk/notes&queries/N&Q2_ArthFolk.pdf.

Green, Thomas. *Lincolnshire and the Arthurian Legend.* http://www.arthuriana.co.uk/notes&queries/N&Q3_ArthLincs.pdf.

Grimmer, Martin. "The Exogamous Marriages of Oswiu of Northumbria," *Heroic Age* 9 (2006).

Groome, Polly, and Steele, Will. *Caldey Island: Tir Gofal Farm Historic Environment Report.* http://www.herwales.co.uk/her/groups/DAT/media/DAT%20Reports/39860%20TG%20Caldey.pdf.

Groves, Sarah. "Bodies in the Bowl Hole—An Early Medieval Inhumation Cemetery at Bamburgh, Northumberland," *The School of Historical Studies Postgraduate Forum E-Journal* 2 (2003).

GUARD Archaeology. *The Galloway Picts Project.* At the website http://www.guard-archaeology.co.uk/news12/gallowayNews.html.

Hagland, Jan Ragnar, and Watson, Bruce. "Fact or Folklore: The Viking Attack on London Bridge," *London Archaeologist* (Spring 2005): 328–332.

Hahn, Thomas. *The Avowyng of Arthur.* http://d.lib.rochester.edu/teams/text/hahn-sir-gawain-avowyng-of-arthur.

Hahn, Thomas. *The Wedding of Sir Gawain and Dame Ragnelle: Introduction.* http://d. lib.rochester.edu/teams/text/hahn-sir-gawain-wedding-of-sir-gawain-and-dame-ragnelle-introduction.

Harding, Dennis. *Iron Age Hillforts in Britain and Beyond.* Oxford, UK: Oxford University Press, 2012.

Hayman, Richard, "Green Men & the Way of All Flesh," *British Archaeology* 100 (May/ June 2008).

Haynes, Ian, and Wilmott, Tony. "Maryport's Mystery Monuments," *Current Archaeology* 289 (April 2014).

Headland Aarchaeology. *Recent Excavations on Inchmarnock & the Identification of an Early Monastic School-House.* http://www.headlandarchaeology.com/Images/news/downloads/IMK99-Webnews.pdf.

Heaney, Seamus. *Beowulf.* London: Faber and Faber, 2000.

Heorot. Wikipedia. https://en.wikipedia.org/wiki/Heorot.

Higley, Sarah, trans. "The Spoils of Annwn." The Camelot Project at the University of Rochester. http://www.lib.rochester.edu/camelot/.

Hulbert, James R. "The Name of the Green Knight: Bercilak or Bertilak." In *The Manly Anniverary Studies in Language and Literature.* Chicago: University of Chicago Press, 1923.

Hunter, Jack. *The Lost Town of Innermessan.* At the website Scottish Corpus of Texts and Speech http://www.scottishcorpus.ac.uk/documents/documentid=1371.

Husband, Timothy, and Gilmore-House, Gloria. *The Wild Man: Medieval Myth and Symbolism.* New York: The Metropolitan Museum of Art, 1980.

Ingram, James. *Anglo-Saxon Chronicle.* London: Everyman, 1912.

Isaac, G.R. "Armes Prydein Fawr and St David." In *St David of Wales: Cult Church and Nation.* Edited by J. Wyn Evans and Jonathan M. Wooding. Woodbridge, UK: The Boydell Press, 2007.

Jackson, Kenneth. "Once Again Arthur's Battles," *Modern Philology* 43 (1945): 44–57.

Jones, Gwyn, and Jones, Thomas. *The Mabinogion.* London: Everyman, 1949.

Jongen, Ludo, and Onderdelinden, Sjaak. *"Der Muoz Mir Süezer Worte Jehen": Liber Amicorum Für Norbert Voorwinden.* Leiden, Netherlands: Brill, 1997.

Jupp, Peter C., and Gittings, Clare. *Death in England.* Manchester, UK: Manchester University Press, 1999.

Kane, Stuart. "Horseplay: Robin Hood, Guy of Gisborne and the Neg(Oti)Ation of the Bestial." In *Robin Hood in Popular Culture.* Edited by Thomas Hahn. Woodbridge, UK: Boydell & Brewer, 2000.

Kibler, William W., and Palmer, R. Barton. *Medieval Arthurian Epic and Romance: Eight New Translations.* Jefferson, NC: McFarland, 2014.

Killings, Douglas B. *The Battle of Maldon.* http://www.english.ox.ac.uk/oecoursepack/maldon_resources/Translations/Killingsfull.htm.

Kline, A.S. *The Seafarer.* http://www.poetryintranslation.com/PITBR/English/Seafarer.htm.

Kline, A.S. *The Wanderer.* http://www.poetryintranslation.com/PITBR/English/Wanderer.htm.

Knight, Stephen, and Ohlgren, Thomas H. *Adam Bell, Clim of the Clough, and William of Cloudesley.* http://d.lib.rochester.edu/teams/text/adam-bell-clim-of-the-clough-william-of-cloudesley.

Knight, Stephen, and Ohlgren, Thomas H. *Adam Bell, Clim of the Clough, and William of Cloudesley: Introduction.* http://d.lib.rochester.edu/teams/text/adam-bell-clim-of-the-clough-william-of-cloudesley-introduction.

Knight, Stephen, and Ohlgren, Thomas H. *A Gest of Robyn Hode.* http://d.lib.rochester.edu/teams/text/gest-of-robyn-hode.

Knight, Stephen, and Ohlgren, Thomas H. *A Gest of Robyn Hode: Introduction.* http://d.lib.rochester.edu/teams/text/gest-of-robyn-hode-introduction.

Knight, Stephen, and Ohlgren, Thomas H. *Robin Hood and Guy of Gisborne.* http://d.lib.rochester.edu/teams/text/robin-hood-and-guy-of-gisborne.

Knight, Stephen, and Ohlgren, Thomas H. *Robin Hood and Guy of Gisborne: Introduction.* http://d.lib.rochester.edu/teams/text/robin-hood-and-guy-of-gisborne-introduction.

Knight, Stephen, and Ohlgren, Thomas H. *Robin Hood and Other Outlaw Tales: The Chronicler's Robin Hood.* http://d.lib.rochester.edu/teams/publication/knight-and-ohlgren-robin-hood-and-other-outlaw-tales.

Knight, Stephen, and Ohlgren, Thomas H. *Robin Hood and the Monk.* http://d.lib.rochester.edu/teams/text/robin-hood-and-the-monk.

Knight, Stephen, and Ohlgren, Thomas H. *Robin Hood and the Monk: Introduction.* http://d.lib.rochester.edu/teams/text/robin-hood-and-the-monk-introduction.

Koch, John. *Celtic Culture: A Historical Encyclopedia.* Santa Barbara, CA: ABC-CLIO, 2006.

Krishna, Valerie. *The Alliterative Morte Arthure: A New Verse Translation.* Lanham, MD: University Press of America, 1983.

Krishna, Valerie. *Five Middle English Arthurian Romances.* London: Routledge, 2015.

Lane, Alan. "Citadel of the First Scots," *British Archaeology* 62 (December 2001).

Lapidge, Michael. "*Beowulf,* Aldhelm, the *Liber Monstrorum* and Wessex." In *Anglo-Saxon Literature 600–899.* London: A&C Black, 1996.

Le Saux, Françoise. *Layamon's Brut: The Poem and Its Sources.* Woodbridge, UK: DS Brewer, 1989.

Lewis, C.P., and Thacker, A.T. *A History of the County of Chester: Volume 5 Part 1, the City of Chester: General History and Topography.* http://www.british-history.ac.uk/vch/ches/vol5/pt1.

MacCana, Proinsas. "Reviewed Work: The *Wisdom of the Outlaw: The Boyhood Deeds of Finn in Gaelic Narrative Tradition* by Joseph Falaky Nagy," *The Canadian Journal of Irish Studies* 14 (1988): 86–88.

Maddicott, J.R. "Birth and Setting of the Ballads." In *Robin Hood: An Anthology of Scholarship and Criticism.* Edited by Stephen Thomas Knight.Woodbridge, UK: Boydell & Brewer, 1999.

Mann, John C., and Breeze, David J. "Ptolemy, Tacitus, and the Tribes of North Britain," *Proceedings of the Society of Antiquaries of Scotland* 117 (1987): 85–91.

Marsden, Barry M. "The Vikings in Derbyshire," *Derbyshire Life and Countryside* (March & April 2007).

McCarthy, Mike. "Rheged: An Early Historic Kingdom Neat the Solway," *Proceedings of the Society of Antiquaries of Scotland* 132 (2002): 357–381.

Melrose, Robin. *Religion in Britain from the Megaliths to Arthur.* Jefferson, NC: McFarland, 2016.

Morris, John. *Nennius: British History and the Welsh Annals.* Chichester, UK: Phillimore & Co. Ltd.,1980.

Morris, Richard. *The Blickling Homilies of the Tenth Century.* London: The Early English Text Society, 1880.

Nennius. *History of the Britons.* Translated by J.A. Giles. London: Henry G. Bohn, 1848.

Newton, Sam. *The Origins of Beowulf and the Pre-Viking Kingdom of East Anglia.* Woodbridge, UK: DS Brewer, 2004.

Norako, Leila K. *Morgan Le Fay.* http://d.lib.rochester.edu/camelot/theme/morgan.

O'Donovan, John. *Sanas Cormaic. Cormac's Glossary.* Calcutta: Irish Archaeological and Celtic Society, 1868.

Ohlgren, Thomas H. *Ronin Hood: The Early Poems 1465–1560*. Newark: University of Delaware Press, 2007.

Ohthere. Wikipedia. https://en.wikipedia.org/wiki/Ohthere.

Orchard, Andy. *Pride and Prodigies: Studies in the Monsters of the Beowulf Manuscript*. Toronto: University of Toronto Press, 2003.

Osberg, Richard H. *The Poems of Laurence Minot 1333–1352*. http://d.lib.rochester.edu/teams/text/osberg-poems-of-laurence-minot-1333–1352.

Padel, O.J. "The Nature of Arthur," *Cambrian Medieval Celtic Studies* 27 (1994): 1–31.

Parker, Will. *The Mabinogi of Branwen*. http://www.mabinogi.net/branwen.htm.

Pitcher, John. *Medieval and Renaissance Drama in England*. Madison, NJ: Fairleigh Dickinson University Press, 2001.

Plutarch. "The Obsolescence of Oracles." In *Moralia* Vol. V. Translated by Frank Cole Babbitt. Cambridge, MA: Harvard University Press, 1936.

Pokorny, Julius. Indogermanisches etymologisches Wörterbuch. Bern, Switzerland: Francke, 1959. http://www.indoeuropean.nl.

Rees, William Jenkins, and Wakeman, Thomas. *Lives of the Cambro-British Saints*. London: Longman & Co., 1853.

Reeves, William. *Life of St Columba*. Edinburgh: Edmonston and Douglas, 1874.

Rex, Peter. *1066: A New History of the Norman Conquest*. Stroud, UK: Amberley, 2011.

Rhys, John. *Studies in the Arthurian Legend*. Oxford, UK: The Clarendon Press, 1891.

Robinson, J. Armitage. *Two Glastonbury Legends*. Cambridge, UK: Cambridge University Press, 1926.

Romer, F.E. *Pomponius Mela's Description of the World*. Ann Arbor: University of Michigan Press, 1998.

Ross, Anne. "The Human Head in Insular Pagan Celtic Religion," *Proceedings of the Society of Antiquaries of Scotland* 91 (1957/8): 10–43.

Ross, Anne. *Pagan Celtic Britain*. Chicago: Academy Chicago Publishers, 1996.

Sawyer, P.H. *From Roman Britain to Norman England*. London: Routledge, 2002.

Schönfelder, Martin. "Bear-Claws in Germanic Graves." *Oxford Journal of Archaeology* 13.2 (1994): 217–227.

Skene, W.F. "The Site of the Battle of Arthuret," *Proceedings of the Society of Antiquaries of Scotland* 6 (1864): 91–98.

Speidel, Michael. *Ancient Germanic Warriors*. London: Taylor & Francis, 2002.

Staver, Ruth Johnston. *A Companion to Beowulf*. Portsmouth, NH: Greenwood Publising Group, 2005.

Swanton, Michael. *The Anglo-SaxonChronicle*. New York: Routledge, 1998.

Swanton, Michael. *Beowulf: Revised Edition*. Manchester, UK: Manchester University Press, 1997.

Swanton, Michael, Knight, Stephen, and Ohlgren, Thomas H. *Hereward the Wake: Introduction*. http://d.lib.rochester.edu/teams/text/hereward-the-wake-introduction.

Tacitus. Annals. Translated by Alfred John Church and William Jackson Brodribb. New York: Random House, 1942. http://www.perseus.tufts.edu.

Taliesin, "The Book of Taliesin." In W.F. Skene, *The Four Ancient Books of Wales*. Edinburgh: Edmonston and Douglas, 1868.

Vendel. Wikipedia. https://en.wikipedia.org/wiki/Vendel.

Warner, Peter. *The Origins of Suffolk*. Manchester, UK: Manchester University Press, 1996.

Watkins, Calvert. *How to Kill a Dragon: Aspects of Indo-European Poetics*. Oxford, UK: Oxford University Press, 1995.

Watson, Giles. *The Three Dead Kings*. http://gileswatson.deviantart.com/art/The-Three-Dead-Kings-306948886.

West, M.L. *Indo-European Poetry and Myth*. Oxford, UK: Oxford University Press, 2007.

Wood, Juanita, and Curry, Charles, A. *Wooden Images: Misericords and Medieval England*. Madison, NJ: Fairleigh Dickinson University Press, 1999.

Woolf, Alex. "Dun Nechtain, Fortriu and the Geography of the Picts," *The Scottish Historical Review* 85 (2006): 182–201.

Young, Simon. *The Celtic Revolution*. London: Gibson Square Books, 2010.

Ziegler, Michelle. "Artur Mac Aidan of Dal Riata," *Heroic Age* 1 (Spring/Summer 1999).

Index